THE DUCHESS OF MALFI

A Critical Guide

Edited by Christina Luckyj

Continuum International Publishing Group

The Tower Building
11 York Road
London SE1 7NX

80 Maiden Lane, Suite 704
New York
NY 10038

www.continuumbooks.com

British Library Cataloguing-in-Publication Data
A catalogue record for this book is available from the British Library.

ISBN: 978–08264-4327–4 (Hardback)
978–08264-4124–9 (Paperback)

Library of Congress Cataloguing-in-Publication Data
A catalog record for this book is available from the Library of Congress.

Typeset by Newgen Imaging Systems Pvt Ltd, Chennai, India
Printed and bound in India

Contents

	Acknowledgements	vii
	Series Introduction	viii
	Timeline	ix
	Introduction *Christina Luckyj*	1
Chapter 1	The Critical Backstory *David Gunby*	14
Chapter 2	The Duchess High and Low: A Performance History of *The Duchess of Malfi* *Roberta Barker*	42
Chapter 3	The State of the Art: Critical Approaches 2000–08 *Dympna Callaghan*	66
Chapter 4	Staging Secret Interiors: *The Duchess of Malfi* as Inns of Court and Anticourt Drama *Curtis Perry and Melissa Walter*	87
Chapter 5	The Duchess's Marriage in Contemporary Contexts *Leah S. Marcus*	106
Chapter 6	'Can this be certain?': The Duchess of Malfi's Secrets *Frances E. Dolan*	119

Chapter 7 'Greek is Turned Turk': Catholic Nostalgia in *The Duchess of Malfi* 136
Todd Borlik

Chapter 8 A Survey of Resources 153
Christy Desmet

Bibliography 175
Notes on Contributors 193
Index 196

Acknowledgements

I am grateful to Lisa Hopkins and Andrew Hiscock, general editors of this series, for giving me the opportunity to edit this volume on a play I wrote about many years ago – a play that continues to 'haunt' me as much as the Duchess does Bosola. I also thank the staff at Continuum for their patience with and understanding of my obligations as department Chair, which invariably led to delays in the publication schedule. Most of all, I want to express my gratitude to all the contributors to this volume. Scattered across the globe, busy with their own commitments, they nonetheless responded promptly and graciously to my requests and suggestions. I can only conclude that they too are lovers of this extraordinary, enigmatic and endlessly fascinating play. In particular, Leah Marcus generously provided us with the proofs of her Arden edition of *The Duchess of Malfi*, published by the Arden Shakespeare, an imprint of A&C Black Publishers Ltd. We all benefited from her work on the text and from her Introduction, which overlaps slightly with her contribution to this volume.

As always, my deepest thanks to Keith, Julia and Stefan Lawson: 'All discord without this circumference / Is only to be pitied and not feared'.

Series Introduction

The drama of Shakespeare and his contemporaries has remained at the very heart of English curricula internationally and the pedagogic needs surrounding this body of literature have grown increasingly complex as more sophisticated resources become available to scholars, tutors and students. This series aims to offer a clear picture of the critical and performative contexts of a range of chosen texts. In addition, each volume furnishes readers with invaluable insights into the landscape of current scholarly research as well as including new pieces of research by leading critics.

This series is designed to respond to the clearly identified needs of scholars, tutors and students for volumes which will bridge the gap between accounts of previous critical developments and performance history and an acquaintance with new research initiatives related to the chosen plays. Thus, our ambition is to offer innovative and challenging Guides which will provide practical, accessible and thought-provoking analyses of Renaissance drama. Each volume is organized according to a progressive reading strategy involving introductory discussion, critical review and cutting-edge scholarly debate. It has been an enormous pleasure to work with so many dedicated scholars of Renaissance drama and we are sure that this series will encourage you to read 400-year-old playtexts with fresh eyes.

Andrew Hiscock and Lisa Hopkins

Timeline

1478: Birth of Giovanna d'Aragona.

1498: Giovanna rules as regent in the Duchy of Amalfi after her husband's death.

1510: Giovanna's clandestine marriage to Antonio Bologna revealed.

1511: Giovanna and her two younger children imprisoned and presumably killed.

1513: Antonio Bologna murdered by Daniele da Bozzolo.

1554–1573: The four volumes of Matteo Bandello's *Novelle* published ('Il signor Antonio Bologna sposa la duchesse d'Amalfi' being the twenty-sixth in Part One).

1565: Belleforest, *Histoires tragiques* published (including 'The Unfortunate marriage of Seigneur Antonio Bologna with the Duchess of Malfi, and the piteous death of both').

1567: William Painter, *Palace of Pleasure* published ('The Infortunate Mariage of a Gentleman, called Antonio Bologna, with the Duchesse of Malfi, and the pitifull death of them bothe', being the twenty-third novel).

1578/79: John Webster born to John Webster Sr. a wealthy London coachmaker.

1598: John Webster (possibly the dramatist) admitted to the Middle Temple, Inns of Court.

1602: Payment to Webster (with a team of collaborators including Dekker, Heywood, Chettle, Munday, Middleton and Drayton) recorded in Henslowe's *Diary* for plays now lost.

1604: Webster provides the Induction for the third edition of *The Malcontent* by John Marston, performed by the King's Men at the Globe.

1604: Webster collaborates with Thomas Dekker on *Westward Ho*, a popular citizen comedy for the Children of Paul's.

1605: Webster collaborates again with Thomas Dekker on *Northward Ho*.

1606: Webster marries Sara Peniall, who at age 17 is pregnant with their first child.

1612: Webster's first independent play, *The White Devil*, performed by Queen Anne's Men, not well received at the Red Bull.

1612: *The White Devil* published by Thomas Archer containing Webster's angry and defensive Address to the Reader in which he lambasts audiences as 'ignorant asses'.

1612: Publication of *A Monumentall Column*, Webster's elegiac tribute to Prince Henry, eldest son of King James and popular Protestant champion, who dies at the age of 18.

1613/14: Webster's second independent play *The Duchess of Malfi* performed by the King's Men at the Globe and Blackfriars Theatres.

1615: Webster contributes thirty-two Characters (including 'An Excellent Actor' and 'A Virtuous Widow') to the sixth edition of Sir Thomas Overbury's *The Wife*, a bestseller memorializing Overbury's scandalous death by poison at the hands of the King's favourite Robert Carr and his new wife Frances Howard.

1617/18: Revival of *The Duchess of Malfi* attended by the chaplain to the Venetian ambassador Orazio Busino, who records his repugnance for what he perceives as the play's virulent anti-Catholicism.

1618: Webster's third independent play *The Devil's Law-Case* performed by the Queens' Men.

1621: Webster collaborates with Middleton on *Anything for a Quiet Life*, a city comedy.

1623: First Quarto of *The Duchess of Malfi* published by John Waterson, containing a list of actors' names and commendatory verses by Middleton, Ford and Rowley.

1623: *The Devil's Law-Case* published.

1624: Webster collaborates with Dekker, Ford and Rowley on *A Late Murder of the Son upon the Mother, or Keep the Widow Waking* (now lost).

1625: Webster collaborates with Rowley on *A Cure for a Cuckold.*

1626: Webster collaborates with Ford and Massinger to complete Fletcher's *The Fair Maid of the Inn.*

1627?: Webster collaborates with Heywood on *Appius and Virginia*, a tragedy.

1630: *The Duchess of Malfi* revived by the King's Men for public and court performances.

1640: Second quarto of *The Duchess of Malfi* published.

1662: *The Duchess of Malfi* performed with Thomas Betterton as Bosola and Mary Betterton as the Duchess.

1678: Third quarto of *The Duchess of Malfi* published.

1708: Fourth quarto of *The Duchess of Malfi* published as *The Unfortunate Duchess of Malfy or the Unnatural Brothers* with new cast list, added stage directions and substantial cuts.

1733: *The Duchess of Malfi*, heavily revised by Lewis Theobald and retitled *The Fatal Secret*, plays at Covent Garden for only two nights.

1808: Excerpts of *The Duchess of Malfi* published in Charles Lamb's *Specimens of the English Dramatick Poets.*

1830: Publication of Alexander Dyce's edition of *The Works of John Webster.*

1850: *The Duchess of Malfi*, radically revised and adapted by R. H. Horne, produced for Sadler's Wells by Samuel Phelps, stars Isabella Glyn as the Duchess.

1892: *The Duchess of Malfi* staged by William Poel for the Independent Theatre Society with the aim of restoring the original text and historicizing the play. The production included costumes influenced by Holbein and a Renaissance Dance of Death for the madmen.

1893: William Archer's virulent attack on the sensationalism of *The Duchess of Malfi* published, followed by Poel's defence.

1905: Elmer E. Stoll's *John Webster: The periods of his work as determined by his relationship to the drama of the day* published, the first book of criticism devoted exclusively to Webster.

1919: *The Duchess of Malfi* staged by the Phoenix Society at the Lyric Theatre.

1927: F. L. Lucas's four-volume edition of *The Complete Works of John Webster* published.

1945: *The Duchess of Malfi* staged at the Haymarket Theatre in an acclaimed landmark production directed by George Rylands and starring Peggy Ashcroft as a touchingly human Duchess and John Gielgud as an incestuously driven Ferdinand; the play's horrors are now seen to mirror the horrors of the World War Two death camps.

1946: Bertolt Brecht and W. H. Auden collaborate on an adaptation of *The Duchess of Malfi* for a widely panned New York production directed by Rylands starring Elisabeth Bergner as the Duchess and the African-American actor Canada Lee as Bosola.

1960: *The Duchess of Malfi* staged by the Royal Shakespeare Company, with Donald McWhinnie directing and Ashcroft again in the title role.

1971: The Stratford Festival in Ontario stages *The Duchess of Malfi* with Pat Galloway's Duchess as a haughty, wilful aristocrat with a sense of humour; in the same year the Royal Shakespeare Company features Judi Dench as a passionate and direct Duchess.

1971: Peter Gill directs *The Duchess of Malfi* at the Royal Court in an experimental production that abandoned psychological realism for abstract minimalism.

1980: *The Duchess of Malfi* at the Royal Exchange, Manchester, stars Helen Mirren as a sensual heroine who discovers dignity in the death scenes.

1985: *The Duchess of Malfi* directed by Philip Prowse for the Royal National Theatre plays up the play's 'baroque' horrors; a scythe-bearing figure representing Death is on stage throughout.

1989: Bill Alexander directs *The Duchess of Malfi* for the Royal Shakespeare Company in Stratford-upon-Avon, with Bob Hoskins as Bosola and Harriett Walter as the Duchess in a production that emphasizes the ordinary humanity of the loving couple.

1995: Juliet Stevenson stars as the Duchess for the Royal Shakespeare Company.

1995: Publication of Volume I of the Cambridge old spelling edition of *The Works of John Webster*, ed. by David Gunby, David Carnegie and Antony Hammond, containing *The White Devil* and *The Duchess of Malfi*.

2006: Peter Hinton directs *The Duchess of Malfi* for Ontario's Stratford Festival in a punk / goth interpretation.

Introduction

Christina Luckyj

In the 1998 film *Shakespeare in Love*, John Webster makes a brief appearance as a dirty street urchin with a Cockney accent and a puerile taste for mutilation, torture and gore. 'Lots of blood', says the aspiring playwright admiringly of Shakespeare's *Titus Andronicus*. 'That's the only writing'.[1] The film gets one thing right: Webster was indeed about 15 years Shakespeare's junior and, unlike him, a native of London. About everything else it is mostly wrong. Born about 1580 to a wealthy coachmaker (a 'Renaissance Henry Ford'[2]), Webster was probably educated at the famous Merchant Taylors' School before proceeding to the Inns of Court to study law and cultivate prestigious social connections. His prefaces reveal him as a careful playwright with an awareness of the conventions of classical tragedy and a command of Latin.[3] After a shaky beginning to his independent playwriting career – his first solo effort, *The White Devil*, was a flop in the theatre – his *Duchess of Malfi* was picked up by the prestigious King's Men (Shakespeare's company), and was apparently considered a 'masterpiece' by his fellow dramatists.[4] In our own time, *The Duchess of Malfi* is respectably ensconced in the canon of English literature, appearing as the paradigmatic non-Shakespearean Renaissance play in the *Norton Anthology of English Literature*, where it is paired up with *King Lear* and *Twelfth Night*. It is the lead title in the launch of the Arden Early Modern Drama Series (still listed under The Arden Shakespeare), and its performance history is probably longer than any Renaissance play apart from Shakespeare's. Yet the film's notion of Webster as a low-born sensationalist indulging in excess dates back to his own time: his contemporary Henry Fitzjeffrey offers a satiric portrait of Webster, 'playwright-cartwright', labouring to give birth to 'Some centaur strange: some huge Bucephalus, / Or Pallas (sure) engendered in his brain'.[5] This view is picked up again in William Archer's Victorian attack on Webster's 'drenching the stage with blood even beyond the wont of his contemporaries and searching out every possible circumstance of horror',[6] and continues in some recent avant-garde productions of the play, as Roberta Barker points out in her chapter on the play's theatre history. Webster's 'edginess' continues to be advertised in the Cambridge *Selected Plays*, which calls him 'the most controversial of all Jacobean dramatists', while the Oxford edition heralds him as 'radically and creatively experimental'.[7] In the market, as in the popular film, Webster is both Shakespeare's 'brother', legitimized by association, and Shakespeare's 'other', marginalized by difference.

If Webster has been seen as both strange and familiar, both grotesque and recognizably mainstream (i.e. Shakespearean), this may be due in part to the conspicuously mixed style of *The Duchess of Malfi* itself. Frequently juxtaposing highly stylized elements with more naturalistic action and dialogue, the play showcases a hybridity that becomes especially challenging for actors; as Peter Thomson observes, 'we must expect the "impure" confusion of realism and convention [...] to reach the point of crisis for anyone who tries to act in his plays'.[8] On one hand, the delicate naturalism of the wooing scene between the Duchess and Antonio with the rapid give-and-take of their flirtatious banter may remind us of similar scenes in *The Taming of the Shrew* or *Much Ado About Nothing*. On the other hand, the bizarre masque of madmen or the stagey verbal set pieces (such as Ferdinand's tale of Love, Death and Reputation) suggest a far more overtly stylized and formal approach. At first glance Webster's mixture of stylistic registers may seem appropriate to the play's primary conflict: after all, it is Ferdinand who uses horror-mongering forms such as the 'spectacle' of the wax corpses and the severed hand; the Duchess, by contrast, often reaches for analogies from the natural world, likening herself to the 'robin redbreast and the nightingale' (4.2.13). Yet, like other characters, the Duchess also frequently turns to artifice. Told that she looks like 'some reverend monument / Whose ruins are even pitied', the Duchess embraces the formal pose quite deliberately: 'Very proper', she responds, 'And Fortune seems only to have her eyesight / To behold my tragedy' (4.2.32–5). Sometimes the pose is assumed only to be abruptly abandoned, as when the Duchess's quietly self-assured Senecan set piece on Death's multiple exits is punctuated by her desperate cry: 'Any way, for heaven sake, / So I were out of your whispering' (4.2.214–15). At other times, rhetorical set piece offers various characters the opportunity to hold and dominate the stage while attempting to impose order on the chaotic experiences they undergo, mapping by contrast the unassimilable, unspeakable nature of much of the play's action. We can see this, for example, when the

Duchess delivers the tale of the Salmon and the Dogfish just before she is hauled off to prison (3.5.121–42). Formal artifice can also offer an alternative perspective on the action, especially in the Duchess's death scene, where Ferdinand is absent and Bosola, disguised as an old man, reminds the Duchess of her physical mortality. Here, the action suddenly seems transformed into an allegorical tableau: even as Bosola is the Duchess's hired assassin in the plot, his disguise suggests Time or Death confronting Youth and Beauty, bringing her 'By degrees to mortification' (4.2.170). In a famous essay, Inga-Stina Ekeblad observes that, consistent with what T. S. Eliot first termed the 'impure art' of the Elizabethans, the scene imitates and inverts the structure of the traditional wedding masque.[9] It also offers a double vision of the Duchess's fate: seen naturalistically, she is a helpless individual victim of her brothers' revenge; seen allegorically, she is an Everywoman who faces, and finally accepts, the inevitable triumph of Death. Webster's artifice in designing the emblematic death scene thus allows the Duchess an agency and dignity the realism of the action denies her. If such textural variations and stylistic hybridity mark Webster out as fundamentally different from Shakespeare, who generally represents his characters without recourse to highly 'artificial' set pieces or sententiae, they nonetheless contribute to Webster's richly multi-layered effect.

Comparisons with Shakespeare may be invidious but they are inevitable. Webster himself invites them in his preface to *The White Devil*, where he aligns himself with Chapman, Jonson, Beaumont and Fletcher, as well as with 'the right happy and copious industry' of Shakespeare, Dekker and Heywood. Coming from a playwright who 'was a long time in finishing this tragedy', the allusion to Shakespeare's popularity may be both genuinely envious as well as a little contemptuous of his fellow dramatist's prolific output, especially as it is implicitly contrasted with both 'the full and heightened style of Master Chapman' and 'the labored and understanding works of Master Jonson'.[10] Yet Webster's compliment to Shakespeare, however ambivalent, may help us to see fundamental parallels and differences between them. Both of them owe a debt to Thomas Kyd, whose *Spanish Tragedy* inaugurated the vogue for revenge plays – though where Shakespeare develops Kyd's anguished Hieronimo into the conflicted figure of the revenger Hamlet, Webster expands the story of Bel-Imperia, a strong and sexually vital woman imprisoned by her brother for seducing a social inferior, into a full-blown portrait of the Duchess's marriage to Antonio with its challenge to existing social structures. Indeed, *The Duchess of Malfi* inverts the usual structure of revenge tragedy: insofar as the Arragonian brothers seek to exact revenge for the Duchess's breach of social order, they are the villains of the piece; as in *The White Devil*, Webster arouses sympathy for the objects of revenge rather than the revenger.[11] In the final act, it is Bosola who finally adopts the revenger's conventional pose: fatally compromised by having committed the very act for which he seeks revenge, he finally succeeds, like Hieronimo, in destroying the corrupt nobles who have attempted to eradicate the Duchess's radical challenge to the class system.

Among Shakespeare's works *The Duchess of Malfi* is frequently compared to *Othello* (as Christy Desmet observes), but its nearer contemporary *The Winter's Tale* may offer an equally illuminating parallel. Where Shakespeare toys with the fantasy of a match between apparent social unequals Perdita and Florizel, his heroine is always actually a lost princess – as her horror of the notion of grafting (a metaphor for cross-class marriage) makes clear.[12] The Duchess of Malfi, by contrast, approves of grafting as 'a bettering of nature' (2.1.151) – a view that her own mixed marriage literalizes. Thus Webster presents the emergent notion of 'meritocracy' positively, whereas Shakespeare mocks attempts at upward class mobility, as in the figure of Malvolio in *Twelfth Night*. Hermione, a ruler and a mother like the Duchess, also appears pregnant onstage and suffers false accusations regarding her sexual promiscuity with heroic dignity. Indeed, the final scene in which Hermione's statue turns to warm life may be echoed in the Duchess's early insistence to Antonio that she is 'flesh and blood' not a 'figure cut in alabaster' (1.2.364–5). If so, the parallels between the women highlight essential differences between them: unlike Hermione's, the Duchess's death is irredeemable, her flesh and blood are perishable (as Bosola reminds her) and her intense sufferings, the result of her own social choices, stand at the luminous centre of the play. This tragic isolation singles the Duchess out among female characters in Renaissance drama: while Shakespeare also gives dramatic prominence to a number of complex tragic women such as Juliet and Cleopatra, they remain defined by and dedicated to their lovers in death as in life. By contrast, the Duchess of Malfi is, Frank Whigham points out, 'the first fully tragic female figure in Renaissance drama'.[13] Webster eschews the simple kind of heroic martyrdom that Hermione represents by suggesting that the Duchess's solitary and heroic death, however undeserved, is crucially the outcome of her own desire. Though she is no revenger, the Duchess, like Hamlet, acts on human impulses in the name of virtue only to discover that she cannot control the consequences of her choices.

Thus, unlike Shakespeare, whose tragic female characters such as Desdemona, Hermione and Cordelia represent virtue victimized, Webster chooses instead to offer a far more nuanced portrait of a woman whose chosen departure from 'the path / Of simple virtue' (1.2.357–8) leaves her exposed to the mercies of others – and to the judgements of early modern audiences. Webster's main source for the plot of *The*

Duchess of Malfi was William Painter's *Palace of Pleasure* (1567), a translation of Belleforest's *Histoires tragiques* (1565), itself an adaptation of Matteo Bandello's original Italian novella fictionalizing historical events that had occurred more than a century earlier. In Painter's version, neither the Arragonian brothers nor Bosola make an appearance until well after the birth of the Duchess's second child, whereas in the play they cast a shadow over the Duchess from the beginning, heightening her ambiguity. For if Ferdinand in Act I clearly confirms Antonio's 'character' of him as a 'most perverse and turbulent nature' (1.2.88) and a living embodiment of tyranny, Ferdinand's caricature of his sister as a 'lusty widow' (1.2.256) who intends to violate her vow never to remarry is also confirmed by the action that follows. Certainly, Antonio's initial idealization of the Duchess's 'divine [...] continence' (1.2.118), framed in the outdated Petrarchan language of Elizabethan love sonnets, is startlingly undone by her sexually forward wooing of him with 'but half a blush' (1.2.370). And the scene in which Ferdinand suborns Bosola to do his bidding by offering him gold and a promotion precedes and inevitably colours the scene in which the Duchess offers a ring and a 'wealthy mine' (1.2.341) to help her servant Antonio 'raise' himself (1.2.330). In Act II, we see her gobbling up 'apri*cocks*' (2.1.137; pun intended)[14] in a suggestive evocation of her sexual appetite, and she becomes the victim and satiric butt of Bosola, a character whose role Webster greatly expands from the source. These elements have led to some critics claiming that she should be perceived as flawed and guilty,[15] while others insist that she must be seen as heroic and virtuous.[16] Such a divided response to the Duchess is anticipated in Painter, who declares, given that 'M. Bologna was one of the wisest & most perfect gentlemen that the land of *Naples* that tyme brought forth, & for his beautie, proportion, galantnesse, valiance, & good grace, without comparison [...] Who then could blame this faire Princesse, if [...] she did set her minde on him, or fantasie to marrie him?' (353).[17] At the same time, Painter *does* blame her: 'you see this great and mightie Duchesse trot & run after the male, like a female Wolfe or Lionesse (when they goe to sault,) and forget the Noble bloud of *Aragon* whereof she was descended' (372). His curious ambivalence reaches its peak when his severe judgement on the Arragonian brothers as 'more butcherly' (383) than some legendary tyrants of history is matched by his moral disapprobation for the lovers: 'We ought never to clime higher than our force permitteth, ne yet surmount the bounds of duety, and lesse suffer our selves to be haled fondly forth with desire of brutal sensualitie' (388). Although Webster never endorses Painter's severe censure of the lovers, he does not shy away from showing the Duchess in potentially compromising situations, thus challenging conventional moral judgements.

What kinds of 'conventional' seventeenth-century judgements were brought to bear on a figure like the Duchess? Until recently, most early modern males, like Hamlet, were thought to have regarded the remarrying 'lusty' widow with the same loathing and contempt expressed by their Roman Catholic forbears. 'For what body would not abhorre her, that after her first husbands death, sheweth her selfe to long after another & casteth away her spouse Christ?' asks Vives in his *Instruction of a Christen Woman*.[18] Barbara Todd explains that 'the remarriage of any widow confronted every man with the threatening prospect of his own death and the entry of another into his place' (55).[19] More recently, however, Jennifer Panek has suggested that early modern widows, far from being discouraged from remarriage, were in fact frequently coerced into it by a society that depended on the recirculation of their assets; the 'lusty widow' stereotype, she argues, functioned as an enabler rather than a preventer of remarriage, representing men as providers of pleasure in exchange for goods.[20] Thus, the Duchess may not be quite as transgressive as she may first appear. Although she represents herself as a pioneer 'going into a wilderness' (1.2.275), the marriage she seeks in wooing Antonio is in some ways quite conventional, as she later points out to Ferdinand: 'Why might not I marry? / I have not gone about, in this, to create / Any new world, or custom' (3.2.108–10). If she begins the play advertising her legal independence as a widow by making her 'will' (1.2.292) – a right to which only widows were entitled – she does so in order to give up authority to her husband and become a *feme covert*. 'If I had a husband now, this care were quit' (1.2.298), she declares. After handing her wedding ring to Antonio, she announces, 'You may discover what a wealthy mine / I make you lord of' (341–42), immediately declaring her subordination as a wife whose property becomes her husband's upon marriage. Yet even here the Duchess remains unconventional: partly because her marriage remains secret, she retains her 'masculine' authority as widow and ruler and continues both to issue commands and to generate the action; Antonio aptly remarks, 'My rule is only in the night' (3.2.8). Indeed, the Duchess is far more active in Webster's play than in Painter's narrative; whereas her counterpart in the source has to be reminded by her maid of her aristocratic privilege and admonished for her dependence on Antonio,[21] Webster's Duchess famously announces 'I am Duchess of Malfi still' (4.2.137). In Painter, the maid and Antonio generate the plans to fly to Ancona and then Milan that in Webster come from the Duchess herself. Rather than advancing an oversimplified view of the Duchess as right or wrong, good or evil, Webster suggests that she occupies a complex position at the contested site of conflicting contemporary attitudes to marriage, women and authority, as Frances Dolan argues in her essay in this volume.

How would the Duchess of Malfi have been received by early modern audiences? That would no doubt have depended not only on their individual views about gender and class, but also on their particular religio-political allegiances, as Leah Marcus observes in her chapter; like modern audiences, Renaissance audiences did not share a single uniform response. Evidence suggests that powerful and unconventional women who lived in early modern London aroused both positive and negative reactions in their contemporaries. One such woman who may have been in Webster's mind while writing *The Duchess of Malfi* was King James's cousin Arbella Stuart, whose marriage to William Seymour was forbidden by the King and punished by imprisonment in the Tower, where she eventually starved to death. Belinda Peters notes that while some of James's subjects saw his actions as a justifiable response to Arbella's rebellious marriage, for others 'usurpation of the rights associated with marriage, even by an anointed king, was understood by more than just playwrights, clerics and political theorists as an act of tyranny'.[22] Sara Jayne Steen has also argued convincingly from primary sources that, while some of Stuart's contemporaries censured her actions, many were deeply sympathetic to what they saw as a love match in the face of royal disapprobation.[23] Another contemporary woman who elicited a mixed response was Lady Anne Clifford, who waged a protracted battle with King James for the estates she believed were her rightful inheritance, despite the fact that her father had entailed them to her uncle in default of male heirs. In a June 1617 entry in her *Diary*, Clifford records that 'many did Condemn me for standing out so in this business, so on the other side many did Commend me in regard that I have done that which is both just and honourable'.[24] *The Duchess of Malfi* itself represents public opinion about its heroine as ambivalent: if the pilgrims refer to her 'mean' marriage and her 'looseness' (3.4.25, 30), they also comment on the cruel and violent injustice of the Arragonian brothers' proceedings against her as a 'free prince' (3.4.26–37). Often derided as unruly and disobedient, strong and independent-minded women who pursued marital or dynastic goals to which they appeared to be entitled could clearly also be admired.

Like Arbella Stuart and Anne Clifford, the Duchess of Malfi can challenge the traditional restrictions associated with her gender largely because of her rank – her 'greatness' trumps her role as 'woman' (1.2.410). Yet paradoxically, rank is also precisely what she seeks to cast aside by marrying Antonio; the play supports Bosola's contention that 'Some would think the souls of princes were brought forth by some more weighty cause than those of meaner persons; they are deceived [...] the like passions sway them' (2.1.106–10). His view, that the high-born can be as sensual as their social inferiors, is the corollary of the Duchess's insistence that the low-born can outrank their superiors in virtue (3.5.117–19). The Duchess, however, is no ordinary woman: rather, she clings to her identity as 'Duchess of Malfi still' (4.2.137) and, while kneeling submissively to face death, *commands* her executioners to 'pull down heaven' upon her (4.2.223). Like Webster himself, who appeals to his 'eminent' patron George Harding, Baron Berkeley while insisting that 'the ancientest nobility [is] but a relic of time past' (121), the Duchess both embraces and renounces traditional hierarchies of class and gender. Indeed, Mary Beth Rose has argued that the play collapses under the burden of its own contradictions, as 'the relation between past and future emerges [...] as one of conflicting loyalties between two worthwhile modes of thought and being'.[25] The play thus straddles past and present, the old and the new, as Antonio himself suggests of the Duchess: 'She stains the time past, lights the time to come' (1.2.127).

Dominant and submissive, aristocratic and humble, driven both to 'pray' and to 'curse' (4.1.92–3), the Duchess is a figure whose paradoxical and fluid nature is shared by other major characters – especially by Bosola who, as Ferdinand's servant and critic, is impelled first by a perverse sense of loyalty to commit murderous acts and later by a complex mixture of penitence and bitterness to avenge the very acts he committed. Both the Duchess and Bosola are distinguished by their strangely metatheatrical awareness: subjected to Ferdinand's theatrical torments, the Duchess cries: 'I account this world a tedious theatre, / For I do play a part in't 'gainst my will' (4.1.81–2); having murdered Antonio in error, Bosola laments 'Such a mistake as I have often seen / In a play' (5.5.93–4). If the other characters appear to be mired in the fictional world, Bosola and the Duchess appear to have independent lives outside the fiction that allow them to comment on it, thus heightening our sense of their richness and depth. Yet even Ferdinand and the Cardinal are far from cardboard villains. Both experience arresting moments of insight: gazing on his sister's dead body, Ferdinand's eyes 'dazzle' (4.2.254) in a startling realignment of his vision; looking into a pond, the Cardinal sees 'a thing armed with a rake / That seems to strike' at him (5.5.6–7). Their recognitions usher in the sprawling – and, for readers and audiences, often frustrating – final act from which the Duchess has been withdrawn. Transformed into a magical talisman of 'sacred innocence' (4.2.355) rather than worldly desire, associated with the 'ruins of an ancient abbey [...] Piece of a cloister' (5.3.2–5), the Duchess has on one hand become a living 'relic' whose godliness continues to function for others even after her death.[26] On the other hand, the Duchess is vividly reanimated – both analogically, in Julia, another 'great wom[a]n of pleasure' (5.2.179) whose spirited wooing ends in brutal murder,[27] and literally, as echo or even as spectral character.[28]

Her liminal presence with its potential to arouse 'a guilty conscience' (5.5.4) may place her on a continuum of Catholic and Protestant beliefs, as Todd Borlik argues in his chapter.

The Duchess's central role as a catalyst for social transformation and tragic recognition may also have had political significance for Webster's audiences and readers; as John Russell Brown observes, 'The story of the tragedy was a syndrome for contemporary issues' (p. xxxix). *The Duchess of Malfi* was first performed in 1613, a year marked by two prominent marriages: the auspicious political marriage of King James's daughter Princess Elizabeth to the Protestant Prince Frederick, and the scandalous second marriage of Frances Howard to the King's Scottish favourite Robert Carr, a couple whose association with court corruption was later spectacularly confirmed by their arrest for the murder of Sir Thomas Overbury.[29] Certainly, when Bosola compares the Arragonian brothers to 'plum trees, that grow crooked over standing pools; they are rich and o'erladen with fruit, but none but crows, pies and caterpillars feed on them' (1.1.49–52), it is hard to resist seeing this as a slur on James, who showered gifts (including this lavish wedding) on favourites such as Carr. The relationship between Antonio and the Duchess offers a utopian alternative, as Bosola describes it: 'For know, an honest statesman to a prince / Is like a cedar, planted by a spring: / The spring bathes the tree's root; the grateful tree / Rewards it with his shadow' (3.2.265–8). However disingenuously, Bosola here wistfully gives voice to the imagined possibility of a creative and complementary relationship between ruler and virtuous advisor. James himself appropriated the emergent ideal of companionate marriage to reassure those members of the 1610 Parliament who feared his contempt for the common law, declaring that 'The marriage between law and prerogative is inseparable and like twins they must joy and mourn together, live and die together, the separation of the one is the ruin of the other'.[30] Despite the failure of the Great Contract, a proposal for the surrender of some of James's monarchical rights in exchange for funds approved by Parliament, members of Parliament continued to use the marriage metaphor to describe the ideal relation between themselves and the king: 'Look to nourish the love between the king and the Parliament, for that is the bed out of which issue may be raised, if not at this time yet at another', declared the Solicitor in November 1610.[31] Can we see in the close and intimate marriage between the Duchess and Antonio not merely a private relationship but also an idealized political symbiosis between 'judicious' ruler and 'most provident council', as Antonio puts it in his opening speech (1.1.6–18)?

Containing 'diverse things printed that the length of the play would not bear in the presentment', the quarto of *The Duchess of Malfi* was published in 1623, a decade after the first performance. Extant in two different states (Q1a and Q1b), it may well have been corrected in mid-run by Webster himself.[32] Carefully prepared for readers, the play may have been printed to capitalize on recent political events.[33] When James's son-in-law Frederick accepted the crown of Bohemia in 1618 after a successful Protestant uprising against the unpopular Catholic Hapsburgs, the absolutist James disapproved. But when Spanish troops under the Holy Roman Emperor Ferdinand II of Austria drove Frederick into exile with Princess Elizabeth and their children, James's Protestant subjects expected their King to intervene. James not only refused to defend international Protestantism, but continued to pursue alliances with Spain, seeking a Spanish match for his son Charles.[34] His subjects' outrage cut across class lines to unite Protestants: the London mob staged hysterical anti-Spanish demonstrations while key court figures pressed for military involvement. In 1623 *The Duchess of Malfi* may have called to mind this contemporary crisis – the flight, banishment and separation of Antonio and the Duchess reflecting the recent humiliating exile of Princess Elizabeth, who in 1620 fled Prague, heavily pregnant, with her servants and children, persecuted by the Catholic Emperor Ferdinand and actively rejected by her family of origin.[35]

If *The Duchess of Malfi* may have evoked topical events for early modern readers and audiences, it has continued to serve as a mirror for contemporary experiences. Not until the two world wars were critics inclined to accept Webster's dark and violent world as anything more than egregious horror, observes David Gunby in his historical survey of Webster criticism; such collective traumas may explain the twentieth-century focus on Webster's 'moral vision' as either anarchic or moralistic. More recently, as Dympna Callaghan observes in her account of twenty-first-century criticism, our interest in gender and sexuality, death and horror – reflected in a contemporary taste for the gothic – has driven interpretations of *The Duchess of Malfi*. And, as Roberta Barker argues in her chapter on performance history, the play's dialogue between 'high' and 'low' has allowed both 'elite' and 'popular' interpretations to hold the stage. The new historicism is an important influence on the four chapters that devote fresh attention to Webster's place in the complex landscape of seventeenth-century religion and politics. In their essay, 'Staging Secret Interiors: *The Duchess of Malfi* as Inns of Court and Anticourt Drama', Curtis Perry and Melissa Walter read the 'proto-Gothic' spaces of Webster's play as allegories for the secret operations of tyranny. Locating *The Duchess of Malfi* in a politicized Senecan-Boccaccian tradition filtered through the admonitory Elizabethan Inns of Court drama *Gismond of Salerne*, they argue that in Webster's play the Arragonian brothers impose their own corrupt interiority on the

Duchess via the play's imaginary architecture. In their view, the play reworks established literary tropes to register immediate fears about corruption and favouritism in the court of King James. In her essay 'The Duchess's Marriage in Contemporary Contexts', Leah S. Marcus also situates the play in its contemporary political context, arguing that it represents the Duchess's clandestine marriage as a form of Protestant – even Puritan – resistance to James's attempt to regulate marriage practices through his 'popish' ecclesiastical courts. Webster's religio-political allegiances become especially clear, she claims, when his play is compared to Shakespeare's more orthodox *Measure for Measure*. Frances E. Dolan's 'Can This be Certain?': The Duchess of Malfi's Secrets' takes up the secrecy of the Duchess's marriage, here to consider it as a source of both vulnerability and power. Importantly, she reminds us of how little we and the play's characters can know, really, about the intimate relation between Antonio and the Duchess – a relation that both entices and eludes us. Even the turn to social history, as it offers evidence of a complex and contradictory culture in flux, does not help us pluck out the heart of their mystery. For Todd Borlik, in his essay, '"Greek is Turned Turk": Catholic Nostalgia in *The Duchess of Malfi*', the power of this play resides in its position between two competing faiths; thus he reads three key episodes (the visit to the shrine of Our Lady of Loreto, Antonio's meditation among the ruins and the Duchess's death scene) to argue that the play excoriates corrupt Catholicism while mourning its salvific potential. Arguing from sometimes divergent positions, these essays attest to the play's enduring and mysterious power to stimulate and elude interpretation. Finally, Christy Desmet's essay on teaching resources surveys print and online editions, discusses a range of possible pedagogical approaches to the play and offers an annotated bibliography of criticism.

All citations to Webster's play in this volume, unless otherwise noted, refer to the 2009 edition of *The Duchess of Malfi*, edited by Leah Marcus, and published by the Arden Shakespeare, an imprint of A&C Black Publishers Ltd.

Notes

1. *Shakespeare in Love*, dir. by John Madden, perf. by Joseph Fiennes, Gwyneth Paltrow, Judi Dench (Universal, 1998).
2. Charles Forker, *The Skull Beneath the Skin: The Achievement of John Webster* (Carbondale: Southern Illinois University Press, 1986), p. 4.
3. See Webster's Preface to *The White Devil*, in which he answers imagined objections that 'this is no true dramatic poem' by showing his knowledge of 'all the critical laws, as height of style, and gravity of person', and subsequently reveals that he 'was a long-time in finishing this tragedy' (*The White Devil*, ed. by Christina Luckyj [London: A&C Black, 2008], pp. 5–6).

4. Both Thomas Middleton and John Ford use the term 'masterpiece' in the commendatory verses attached to *The Duchess of Malfi*; indeed, Ford writes: 'Crown him a poet, whom nor Rome, nor Greece, / Transcend in all theirs, for a masterpiece' (p. 126).
5. In Don D. Moore, ed. *Webster: The Critical Heritage* (London: Routledge, 1981), p. 33.
6. In Moore, p. 139.
7. *The Selected Plays of John Webster*, ed. by Jonathan Dollimore and Alan Sinfield (Cambridge: Cambridge University Press, 1983), back cover of paperback ed.; *The Duchess of_Malfi and Other Plays*, ed. by Rene Weis (Oxford, 2009 reissue), online catalogue (http://ukcatalogue.oup.com/product/9780199539284.do?keyword=john+webster&sortby=bestMatches)
8. 'Webster and the Actor', in *John Webster*, ed. by Brian Morris (London: Ernest Benn, 1970), p. 32.
9. 'The "Impure Art" of John Webster', *Review of English Studies* n.s 9 (1958), 253–67. See David Gunby's discussion of this essay in this volume.
10. 'To the Reader', *The White Devil*, ed. by Christina Luckyj (London: Methuen, 2008), pp. 5–6.
11. See Harold Jenkins, 'The Tragedy of Revenge in Shakespeare and Webster', *Shakespeare Survey* 14 (1961), 45–55.
12. See *The Winter's Tale* 4.4.82–100.
13. Frank Whigham, 'Sexual and Social Mobility in *The Duchess of Malfi*', *PMLA* 100 (1985), 174.
14. See Dale B. J. Randall, 'The Rank and Earthy Background of Certain Physical Symbols in *The Duchess of Malfi*', in *Critical Essays on The Duchess of Malfi*, ed. by Dympna Callaghan. Randall concludes that apricocks were commonly perceived both as aphrodisiacs and as a bawdy euphemism for the penis.
15. See Joyce E. Peterson, *Curs'd Example: The Duchess of Malfi and Commonweal Tragedy* (Columbia: University of Missouri Press, 1978), and Lisa Jardine, *Still Harping on Daughters: Women and Drama in the Age of Shakespeare* (Sussex: Harvester, 1983).
16. For an example of what has become the prevailing view of *The Duchess of Malfi*, see Linda Woodbridge, 'Queen of Apricots: The Duchess of Malfi, Hero of Desire', in *The Female Tragic Hero in English Renaissance Drama*, ed. by Naomi Conn Liebler (New York: Palgrave, 2002), pp. 161–84.
17. Leah Marcus, ed. *The Duchess of Malfi* (London: Arden, 2009), p. 353.
18. Joannes Ludovicus Vives, *A Very Fruteful and Pleasant Boke Called the Instruction of a Christian Woman*, trans. by R. Hyrde (London, 1529), sig. Cc5r.
19. 'The Remarrying Widow: A Stereotype Reconsidered', in *Women in English Society 1500–1800*, ed. by Mary Prior (London: Methuen, 1985), pp. 54–92; see also Linda Woodbridge, *Women and the English Renaissance* (Urbana: University of Illinois Press, 1984), p. 178; Sara Mendelson and Patricia Crawford, *Women in Early Modern England 1550–1720* (Oxford: Oxford University Press, 1998), p. 69.
20. Jennifer Panek, *Widows and Suitors in Early Modern English Comedy* (Cambridge: Cambridge University Press, 2004), pp. 10–25 passim.
21. The maid chides the Duchess: 'Did hys only presence assure you against the waits of fortune?', and also reminds her, 'I have heard you many times speak of the constancie & force of minde, which ought to shine in the dedes of Princesses, more clerely than amongs those dames of baser house & which ought to make them appere like the sunne amid the litle starres' (in *The Duchess of Malfi*, ed. by Leah Marcus [London: A&C Black, 2009], p. 369).
22. Belinda Roberts Peters, *Marriage in Seventeenth-Century English Political Thought* (Houndmills: Palgrave Macmillan, 2004), p. 160.

23. 'The Crime of Marriage: Arbella Stuart and the Duchess of Malfi', *Sixteenth-Century Journal* 22.1 (1991), 61–76.
24. *The Diary of Anne Clifford 1616–1619: A Critical Edition*, ed. by Katherine O. Acheson (New York and London: Garland, 1995), pp. 84–5.
25. *The Expense of Spirit: Love and Sexuality in English Renaissance Drama* (Ithaca: Cornell University Press, 1988), p. 166.
26. Peter Lake observes that 'It is sometimes remarked that protestantism [...] by rejecting the sacramental world view of traditional catholicism, effectively destroyed any concept of the holy, that is, of a divine presence immanent in the material world. However, it could be argued that this view of the growth in grace of elect individuals reproduced just such a notion of the holy, located in the lives and qualities of the godly, who became, as repositories of the Holy Spirit, active in the world, almost holy objects in themselves' ('Feminine Piety and Personal Potency: The "Emancipation" of Mrs. Jane Ratcliffe', *The Seventeenth Century* 2 [1987], 145).
27. See my essay, '"Great women of pleasure": Main Plot and Subplot in *The Duchess of Malfi*', *Studies in English Literature*, 27 (1987), 267–83.
28. Antonio claims that 'on the sudden, a clear light / Presented me a face folded in sorrow' (5.3.43–4). In her edition, Marcus notes that 'Q1 lists Echo among the characters in the massed entrance for the scene [...] suggesting that the Duchess may play the part of Echo' (p. 131).
29. For a full account of the Carr-Howard marriage and its social implications, see Alastair Bellany, *The Politics of Court Scandal in Early Modern England: News Culture and the Overbury Affair, 1603–1660* (Cambridge: Cambridge University Press, 2002).
30. *Proceedings in Parliament 1610*, ed. by Elizabeth Read Foster (New Haven and London: Yale University Press, 1966), II, 50.
31. *Proceedings in Parliament* 1610, II, 312.
32. See Marcus, pp. 63–67.
33. The *Duchess* quarto shares many of the characteristics Zachary Lesser identifies with 'literary' plays printed to appeal to 'select' readers of the middling sort such as 'students at the Inns of Court, the younger sons of gentry, lacking the wealth of inheritance': the title page with its Latin motto and emphasis on the Blackfriars performance, the commendatory verses and the presence of continuous printing in the text (*Renaissance Drama and the Politics of Publication: Readings in the English Book Trade* [Cambridge: Cambridge University Press, 2004], p. 74).
34. For an account of the crisis see Derek Hirst, *England in Conflict 1603–1660: Kingdom, Community, Commonwealth* (London, 1999), pp. 103–9.
35. For an example of another historical drama that probably reflected the contemporary concern with the Princess's plight, see Jerzy Limon's *Dangerous Matter: English Drama and_Politics in 1623/24* (Cambridge: Cambridge University Press, 1986), especially chapter 2, 'The matter of the King and Queen of Bohemia'.

CHAPTER ONE

The Critical Backstory

David Gunby

The critical history of *The Duchess of Malfi* evidently began well, for the title page of the 1623 quarto tells us that it was performed by the King's Men both '*privately, at the Blackfriars, and publicly at the Globe*', while the cast list shows that it was revived at least once prior to its publication in 1623. These markers of success are echoed in the dedicatory poems by Webster's fellow dramatists Thomas Middleton, William Rowley and John Ford. Middleton and Ford particularly heap praise on Webster, Middleton regarding *The Duchess of Malfi* as 'Thy monument [...] raised in thy lifetime' (9) and declaring:

> Thy epitaph only the title be:
> Write, 'Duchess', that will fetch a tear for thee.
> For who e'er saw this Duchess live, and die
> That could get off under a bleeding eye? (15–18)

Ford goes even further, urging the reader to 'Crown [Webster] a poet whom nor Rome nor Greece/Transcend in all theirs for a masterpiece' (1–2). Save by Samuel Sheppard, however, who in 1651 makes a like claim for *The White Devil* as surpassing the plays of Euripides and Sophocles, such high praise of Webster's tragedies would not be forthcoming again until the rediscovery of the Elizabethan dramatists by Lamb and Hazlitt in the early nineteenth century.

What critical comment there is on *The Duchess of Malfi* in the intervening period is sparse and occasional. In about 1650, the clergyman Abraham Wright commented in his commonplace book on three of

Webster's plays, describing *The Duchess of Malfi* as 'A good play, especially for the plot at the latter end, otherwise plain' but adding:

> And which is against the laws of the scene, the business was two years a-doing, as may be perceived by the beginning of the third Act, where Antonio has three children by the Duchess, when in the first Act he had but one [*sic*].[1]

For Wright, the point at issue is primarily the length of time covered by the first half of the play, but later critics, relaxed about breaches of the unity of time, would offer stringent criticism of 'the latter end' of *The Duchess of Malfi*, and particularly of what came to be regarded as the inexcusably premature death of the play's heroine.

With the Restoration of Charles II in 1660, *The Duchess of Malfi* returned to the stage with a performance on 30 September 1661. John Downes writes:

> This play was so exceedingly excellently acted in all parts, chiefly Duke Ferdinand and Bosola, it filled the house eight days successively, it proving one of the best of stock tragedies. (37)

Pepys refers to the play four times in his diary, two entries, in November 1666, recording his positive response to reading the play, the others his reaction to performances of *The Duchess of Malfi*. On the first occasion, 30 September 1662, he notes that 'after dinner we took coach and to the Duke's playhouse, where we saw *The Duchess of Malfi* well performed, but Betterton and Ianthe to perfection' (37). On 25 November 1668, however, he was less impressed, noting: 'my wife and I to the Duke of York's house to see *The Duchess of Malfi*, a sorry play; and sat with little pleasure for fear of my wife's seeing me look about' (37).

The eighteenth century was a barren period, so far as *The Duchess of Malfi* was concerned. In the early 1730s Lewis Theobald rewrote the play as *The Fatal Secret*, but it secured only two stage performances. His preface makes clear his aim, which was to tame 'a strong and impetuous genius but withal a most wild and undigested one' (45). The unity of time is restored (the Duchess and Antonio are prevented even from consummating their love), the Cardinal and Ferdinand kill each other, Bosola deceives Ferdinand into thinking he has killed the Duchess, and she and Antonio, who emerges from hiding, live happily ever after. Webster, clearly, was not 'tamed' but eradicated.

A reprinting of *The Duchess of Malfi* came only in 1810, but Charles Lamb had, in his *Specimens of the English Dramatic Poets* (1808), excerpted the wooing of Antonio by the Duchess and her torture and death, as well as the fables of the Salmon and the Dogfish (3.5) and Reputation, Love and Death (3.2). Lamb's mode of criticism was impressionistic and metaphoric, his concern not with analysis, but rather with reader reaction. Sublimity, the product of a brief inspired outburst, was for him the highest literary attainment, and Webster was lauded by Lamb as achieving just such moments of sublimity. This assessment was to remain standard throughout the nineteenth century, but what was almost always added was that Webster was incapable of maintaining such greatness. H. M.'s summation in an article on *The Duchess of Malfi* in *Blackwood's Magazine* (March 1818) is representative: 'Some single scenes are to be found in [Webster's] works inferior in power of passion to nothing in the whole range of the drama [...] But our sympathies suddenly awakened, are allowed to subside' (56).

Like Lamb, William Hazlitt greatly admired Webster, believing 'his *White Devil* and *Duchess of Malfi*, upon the whole, perhaps come nearest to Shakespeare of anything we have on record'. The phrases 'upon the whole' and 'perhaps' point, however, to reservations, and the principal one is, for Hazlitt, that Webster's tragedies 'are too like Shakespeare, and often direct imitations of him, both in general conception and individual expression' (60). Hazlitt places *The White Devil* ahead of *The Duchess of Malfi*, which he finds more profound, but 'more laboured, [with] the horror [...] accumulated to an overpowering and insupportable height' (61).

Hazlitt's lectures brought a renewed interest in Webster. The publication, in 1830, of Alexander Dyce's *The Works of John Webster*, destined to remain for nearly a century the standard edition, strengthened that process. Reviews of the edition were favourable, reviewers, following Hazlitt, placing much emphasis on the dramatist's handling of horror. Thus, the anonymous reviewer in the *Gentleman's Magazine* (June 1833) concludes that Webster 'far, very far, surpasses [Jonson, Fletcher and Massinger] in the depth of his pathos, his tragic powers, and his command over the sublime, terrible and the affecting', describing *The Duchess* as 'the play in which Webster's tragic powers expand to their full height' (71–2).

Dyce's edition enabled *The Duchess of Malfi* to be better considered as literature. Samuel Phelps's 1850 production ought to have enabled Webster's tragedy to be better considered as drama. What was performed was, however, a radical revision of what Webster wrote. For though the adapter, Richard Hengist Horne, was an ardent admirer of *The Duchess of Malfi*, he nonetheless felt 'that the only way to render it available to the stage must be that of reconstructing the whole, cutting away all that could not be used, and filling up the gaps and chasms' (76).

The production was a success, and Horne's reworking of *The Duchess* held the stage for some 50 years, but reviewers were doubtful that he had succeeded in restoring or rehabilitating Webster. The anonymous reviewer in *The Times* (21 November) felt, for instance, that Horne had 'accomplished very skillfully the task of rendering the sanguinary work of John Webster tolerable on a modern stage', but that nonetheless 'the revolting nature of the story, and the anti-climax of the fifth act, in which the several villains kill one another, are beyond the reach of the reformer's skill' (81).

Of the reviews of Phelps's production the most interesting, in what it prefigures, is that of G. H. Lewes in *The Leader* (30 November). '"The Duchess of Malfi" is a feeble and a foolish work', he comments, 'I say this fully aware of the authorities against me – fully aware of the "passages" which may be quoted as specimen-bricks'. 'Other critics have declaimed against its accumulation of horrors', he continues, but

> to my mind that is not the greatest defect. Instead of 'holding the mirror up to nature', this drama holds the mirror up to Madame Tussaud's and emulates her 'chamber of horrors' but the 'worst remains behind', and that is the motiveless and false exhibition of human nature. (86)

'"The Duchess of Malfi" is a nightmare,' he concludes, 'not a tragedy', though he has to admit that 'As a terrific melodrame, it delights the pit' (87).

Lewes's comments prefigure one major strand of critical debate about Webster, led by Lewes's later editor, William Archer. Another is seen first in the strictures of Charles Kingsley, who attacks Webster's moral viewpoint and his capacity – or incapacity – for character-building. 'There is no trace', Kingsley writes of both *The White Devil* and *The Duchess of Malfi*, 'of that development of human souls for good or evil which is Shakespeare's especial power'. 'The highest aim of dramatic art', he continues, 'is to exhibit the development of the human soul, to construct dramas in which the conclusion shall depend, not on the events, but on the characters'. While acknowledging that *The Duchess of Malfi* is 'in a purer and loftier strain' than *The White Devil*, he doubts 'whether the poor Duchess is a "person" at all' (98).

Webster, however, had his defenders, and the most ardent was Algernon Swinburne, driven by his conviction that 'it is only with Shakespeare that Webster can ever be compared to his disadvantage as a tragic poet' and that, save Shakespeare, 'above all others of his country he stands indisputably supreme' (116). But Swinburne also defends Webster against the charge that he lacks a moral viewpoint. Acknowledging the latter's 'command of terror', he asserts that 'Neither Marlowe nor Shakespeare had so fine, so accurate, so infallible a sense of the delicate line of demarcation which divides the impressive and the terrible from the horrible and the loathsome' (112).

Since 1850 Horne's adaptation of *The Duchess of Malfi* had held the stage. In October 1892, however, the Independent Theatre Society presented William Poel's version of *The Duchess of Malfi*, closer to Webster's original, though still with some scene rearrangements. Reviewers praised the attempt, but were generally unimpressed. 'Webster's tragedy has fallen upon evil days', proclaimed *The Times* reviewer (22 October), while the reviewer in *The Nation* (10 November) voiced the familiar complaint about the inadequate motivation of characters and pointless intrigue: 'The intrigue of the Cardinal with Julia apparently had no other use in the tragedy save to add one more corpse to the many strewing the stage in that indescribable fifth act, which even Webster's most ardent admirers think superfluous' (128).

Of the responses to Poel's production, however, none was more vitriolic – or influential – than that of William Archer. An ardent advocate of the 'new' drama of Ibsen and Shaw, he approached Webster's plays entirely in terms of the 'well-made play'. Published in *The New Review* (January 1893), Archer's review finds little to praise in *The Duchess of Malfi*. Webster, he agrees, is a poet of great moments, but dramaturgically a failure. *The White Devil* and *The Duchess of Malfi*, he declares, are 'not constructed plays, but loose-strung, go-as-you-please romances in dialogue'. 'It is more than doubtful', he writes, 'whether Webster himself was at all clear as to his characters' motives', finding some credibility only in the portrayal of Bosola, in whom 'Webster came very near to creating [...] one of the most complex and most human villains in drama'. But even with Bosola Archer finds 'a fatal lack of clearness ruins everything' (141–2).

And then there is the horror. 'When we find a playwright', Archer writes,

> drenching the stage with blood even beyond the wont of his contemporaries and searching out every possible circumstance of horror [...] may we not reasonably, or rather must we not inevitably, conclude that he either revelled in 'violent delights' for their own sake, or wantonly pandered to the poplar craving for them? (139)

'The gist of my argument', concludes Archer,

> So far as it can be summed up in a phrase, is this: that Webster was not, in the special sense of the word, a great dramatist, but

> was a great poet who wrote haphazard dramatic or melodramatic romances for an eagerly receptive but semi-barbaric public. (143)

Archer's attack on Webster as dramatist was the most vitriolic of the nineteenth century, but not the one that skewered Webster in a phrase. That came from George Bernard Shaw, who wrote, *en passant*, of 'the opacity that prevented Webster, the Tussaud laureate, from appreciating his own stupidity'.[2] The phrase 'Tussaud laureate', for which Shaw was indebted to G. H. Lewes, stuck, and can still be found cropping up in theatre programme notes, despite having been long rejected critically.

Nineteenth-century critics tended to separate Webster the poet from Webster the dramatist, and to applaud the former even when damning the latter. In the twentieth century this tendency would continue alongside a growing move towards understanding the dramatist in Elizabethan (and later, Jacobean) terms, and reintegrating the poet and dramatist, something first argued by William Poel, in a response to William Archer's review of his production of *The Duchess*. Taking issue with the familiar judgement that 'Webster's verse to be admired must be dissociated from the play for which it was written', Poel argues that 'Webster's most celebrated passages are not great simply because they are pre-eminent in beauty of idea and felicity of expression, but because they carry with them dramatic force by being appropriate to character and situation'.[3] Little regarded at the time, Poel's defence of Webster, concluding as it does with the statement that 'To see dramatic propriety and dramatic power in *The Duchess of Malfi* there may be needed both critical and historical imagination' (145), contains within it the seeds of much that was to come to fruition in the twentieth century.

1905 saw the appearance of the first book devoted exclusively to the dramatist, Elmer E. Stoll's *John Webster: The periods of his work as determined by his relationship to the drama of the day.* Stoll's subtitle points to his thesis, which is that Webster's career falls into three periods, during which he fell successively under the influence of Dekker, Marston and Fletcher. His somewhat astonishing conclusion is that Webster 'had no spring of invention welling within him',[4] but the book is important as marking the beginning of the academic study of the dramatist. A further advance came when, in 1914, C. V. Boyer's *The Villain as Hero in Elizabethan Tragedy* argued in detail for the first time the existence in *The Duchess of Malfi* of a clear moral vision. 'The innocent', Boyer maintains 'may suffer from the heartlessness and ambition of the wicked, but they can die heroically, and keep alive the good in others, while sure retribution awaits the violator of moral law'.[5] Boyer, interested primarily in Bosola as villain-hero, finds the Duchess pathetic rather than tragic, and admits that, though Bosola is a tragically conflicted figure, his death fails to move us as it might, because 'his previous conduct has been too wicked for us to lament his fall as that of a morally good man' (164). Act V, therefore, is ultimately a failure.

In its emphasis on Bosola, Boyer's study looks forward to critical studies in the 1940s and 1950s. Rupert Brooke's *John Webster and the Elizabethan Drama* looks back to Lamb, Hazlitt and Swinburne. His critical method is traditional; he tells the story of a play and then comments on it, and some of his observations echo earlier asseverations. Thus 'Webster's supreme gift is the blinding revelation of some intense state of mind at a crisis, by some God-given phrase. All the last half of *The Duchess of Malfi* is full of them'.[6] But he is also shrewd in his delineation of other Websterian features, such as a strong satiric element, and rejects the labelling of *The Duchess of Malfi* as a revenge play as 'simply ridiculous'. 'If it is raked in', he comments, 'you must include *Othello* and a dozen more as well' (88).

With an eye to Webster's Ibsenist detractors, Brooke also comments on characterization. 'Characters in a play gain in realism', he remarks, 'if they act unexplainedly on instinct, like people in real life, and not on rational and publicly-stated grounds, like men in some modern plays' (99). William Archer would not have agreed. Indeed, he continued his onslaught on Webster in a January 1920 review of a recent Phoenix Society production of *The Duchess of Malfi*. The production proved yet again, in Archer's opinion, that *The Duchess of Malfi* was 'three hours of coarse and sanguinary melodrama', relieved only by 'occasional beauties of diction'.[7] Many of his earlier philippics are recycled, but Archer's fiercest criticism is of the fifth act:

> With the death of the Duchess, the interest of the play is over; for Antonio is admittedly a shadowy figure as to whose fate we are very indifferent; and though we are willing to see Ferdinand, the Cardinal, and Bosola punished, we could quite well dispense with that gratification. Webster, however, is not the man to leave any of his dramatis personae alive if he can help it.

'There is scarcely any room on the stage for all the corpses', Archer adds acerbically, 'which is perhaps the reason why, in the Phoenix revival, Ferdinand stands on his head to die, and waves his legs in the air' (131).

Archer had expressed the hope that criticism of the Elizabethans would be taken out of the hands of scholars without 'the elementary power of distinguishing between poetic and specifically dramatic merit' (91). In his four-volume edition of *The Complete Works of John Webster*, which appeared in 1927, F. L. Lucas worked hard to present the plays as plays, and described Archer's criticism of Elizabethan dramaturgy as 'valuable not so much for the truth which underlies some of its exaggerations, as because it provides a clear object-lesson of the way not to approach the Elizabethans'.[8] What Elizabethan audiences wanted, Lucas avers, 'was a succession of great moments [...] on the stage, not a well-made play' (17). Hence all the playwrights of the period, Shakespeare included, worked primarily in scenes.

In linking Shakespeare with his fellows, Lucas was striking a shrewd blow against the common tendency to exclude the Bard from criticism levelled at his fellow dramatists. He employs the same tactic when he tackles the charge of inconsistency in plotting – what about the confusion over whether Macbeth and his wife had children? – and that of the gratuitous resort to horror – is anything in Webster as horrible as the putting out, on stage, of Gloucester's eyes? Interestingly, however, Lucas adds a new dimension to discussion of the dead man's hand in *The Duchess of Malfi* when he writes: 'Too many of the present generation have stumbled about in the darkness among month-old corpses on the battle-fields of France to be much impressed by the falsetto uproar which this piece of "Business" occasioned in nineteenth-century minds'. 'And as for dances of madmen', Lucas continues, 'to the ordinary Elizabethan such things were a familiar piece of entertainment for a comedy or a wedding' (33–4). Here, Lucas came, without realizing it, close to the understanding of Act IV Scene Two which Inga-Stina Ekeblad was to provide three decades later.

On the whole, Lucas finds *The Duchess of Malfi* 'weaker' than *The White Devil*: in mood sadder, darker and less vigorous. His summation is brief and to the point: 'The creation of this atmosphere, its poetry and two or three supreme scenes – these are the greatness of *The Duchess of Malfi*. The characters are less outstanding: and the plot has obvious weaknesses'.[9] Besides the Duchess, Lucas feels, only the anguished Bosola holds our attention. Interestingly, however, he raises for the first time the possibility that Ferdinand is in love with his sister. At first he dismisses the idea, commenting, 'The analysis Ferdinand gives of his own motives at the end of Act IV, though muddled, is clearly intended to be accepted as true' (23). But then he has second thoughts:

> And yet, when one reads *The Fair Maid of the Inn*, with its brother confessedly half-enamoured of his sister and passionately jealous of her lover, and then turns back to the frenzies with which Ferdinand (unlike the Cardinal) hears of his sister's seduction, the agonized remorse with which he sees her dead, it is hard to be positive that some such motive had never crossed Webster's mind. (24)

'It is merely a suggestion', Lucas concludes, 'and an inessential one'. The critical history of the play since 1927 proves that it was far from that. In the last analysis, however, it is not in matters of characterization or motivation that Lucas finds the weakness of *The Duchess of Malfi*: that 'lies clearly in its plot. It lives too long, when it outlives the heroine'. 'Though there is less sub-plot', he writes, 'less irrelevant complication than in *The White Devil*, the plot of *The Duchess of Malfi* has the far worse defect of reaching its natural end before the play' (24).

Lucas was the last of a breed, more closely analytic of *The Duchess of Malfi* than Swinburne or Brooke, but employing the appreciative mode deriving originally from Lamb. T. S. Eliot was the first of a new breed, making a concerted effort to determine why a literary work succeeds or fails, supplying specific reasons for this, and rejecting what he calls 'opinion or fancy'. It should be noted, however, that Eliot actually wrote very little about Webster. His comment, in 1924, that Webster provides 'an interesting example of a very great literary and dramatic genius directed towards chaos',[10] has achieved the same status as Shaw's 'Tussaud laureate', but it was made *en passant* in his essay 'Four Elizabethan Dramatists', in which he is primarily concerned to demonstrate both that there were definite dramatic conventions that Webster and his fellow-dramatists observed, and that 'the aim of the Elizabethans was to attain complete realism without surrendering any of the advantages which as artists they observed in unrealistic conventions'. In sum, Eliot says, in a phrase which has achieved iconic status, 'the art of the Elizabethans is an impure art' (96).

F. R. Leavis's magazine, *Scrutiny*, first appeared in 1932. Intended to combine 'criticism of literature with criticism of extra-literary standards' and to exhibit 'purity of approach and rigour of critical method', *Scrutiny* rejected utterly the appreciative approach to literature. 'The Scrutiny critics' Leavis wrote, 'believe that the way to forward true appreciation of literature is to examine and discuss it, and that what the belletrist's fear of intelligence and analysis protects is not taste or sensibility'.[11] Leavis himself never wrote about Webster, but two highly influential articles were written by Leavisites: W. A. Edwards and Ian Jack. Edwards's article begins by declaring William Archer wrong in condemning Webster for inconsistencies in plotting. Webster's plays, Edwards says, should be considered as dramatic poems: inconsistencies of plotting do not, therefore, matter. On the other hand, 'incompetent plotting' does, and Webster is incompetent. Echoing Archer, Edwards is clear that 'Webster wrote melodrama because he had a taste for it, and [...] in writing his tragedies was concerned as a popular play-wright to turn out plays which would please every kind of play-goer'.[12] Webster, Edwards concludes, had no comprehensive vision of life; rather his taste for melodrama makes him seek to shock. Moreover (shades of Charles Kingsley) in Webster there is no development of character, but rather a set of static figures that are simply creatures of the moment.

Two further *Scrutiny*-type philippics against Webster were to come, in 1949 and 1956, and it is worth noting them here, since they mark the end of a strand in the critical history of *The Duchess of Malfi*. Ian Jack's 'The Case of John Webster' argues that there is in Webster no steady moral vision. 'Great tragedy' Jack writes, 'can be written only by a man who has achieved – at least for the period of composition – a profound and balanced insight into life. Webster – and his plays are our evidence – did not achieve such an insight'.[13] Aphoristically, 'integrity of life' may be proclaimed 'man's best friend', but 'there is no correspondence between the axioms and the life represented in the drama'. 'This dissociation', Jack avers, 'is the fundamental flaw in Webster' (39). Moreover, *pace* Edwards, 'there are too many inconsistencies in Webster's plays; and whereas inconsistencies are readily passed over when – as in Shakespeare – they are subservient to some important dramatic purpose, in Webster there is no deeper purpose than to make our flesh creep, and we feel an inevitable resentment'. Webster, Jack concludes 'is a decadent' (43). Clearly, neither he nor *The Duchess of Malfi* is worth further consideration.

In 'Tourneur and the Tragedy of Revenge' L. G. Salingar echoes Jack. 'Webster is sophisticated', he writes, 'but his sophistication belongs to decadence. The poet's solemnity and his groping for a new basis for tragedy only serve to expose his inner bewilderment and his lack of any deep sense of communion with his public'.[14] Of *The White Devil* and *The Duchess of Malfi* Salingar writes: 'The emotions in these two plays are chaotic[...] And every sensation is inflamed, every emotion becomes an orgy' (350). And while he acknowledges the power of the Duchess's suffering and death, he sees the remainder of the action as consisting of 'tedious moralizing, posturing and blood and thunder' (352).

While *Scrutiny* critics excoriated Webster, others were developing an understanding of what Webster was trying to do. In this regard, pioneering work was done by M. C. Bradbrook, whose *Themes and Conventions of Elizabethan Tragedy* (1935) examines the conventions that largely governed the writing and playing of plays in the period then still referred to as Elizabethan. Aiming to 'discover how an Elizabethan would approach a tragedy by Chapman, Tourneur or Middleton',[15] Bradbrook argues that the essential structure of Elizabethan drama 'lies not in the narrative or the characters but in the words' (5). Complaints about inconsistencies in plotting are thus misplaced, since the 'last thing which occurred to the Elizabethan was to put two and two together' (31).

Of Webster, however, Bradbrook is at times sharply critical. He is, she declares, too literary, and 'concerned with perfection of detail rather than general design'. He is 'capable of extraordinary power over the single phrase, yet again and again he produces one which is irrelevant to the feelings of the scene as a whole, or to the character, or to the reader's feelings towards the characters' (210). Even so, Bradbrook offers what is undoubtedly the most sympathetic and understanding account of the character of the Duchess yet, one which, in showing how the Duchess comes to an acceptance of responsibility for her actions in marrying Antonio and deceiving her brothers, argues that the prison scenes are symbolic of the Duchess's purgatory, which brings her from the pride of 'I am Duchess of Malfi still' (4.2.137) to 'I have so much obedience in my blood, / I wish it in their veins to do them good' (162–3). 'In law', Bradbrook says,

> the Duchess was innocent; by social standards she was at first reckless and intemperate; by ethical and religious standards she was an instinctive creature awakened by suffering to maturity. (209)

Una Ellis-Fermor's governing thesis in *The Jacobean Drama* (1936) is that the Jacobean dramatists are shaped by, and reflect, a general questioning and pessimism, born of the political uncertainties of the age, of which she finds in Webster the clearest perception and most profound expression. Webster, she writes, 'brings his people, by the most careful preparation, to the position in which, if ever, a man should see absolute reality – and before them is only a mist'.[16] Only the Duchess 'sees, or thinks she sees' beyond this mist, this world without hope. This vision of a world without meaning or hope, reflecting the dark and uncertain days in which Ellis-Fermor wrote, is one found also in a succession of critics after the Second World War. But so too is another vision of Webster's world, one which for the first time asserts the existence of a rigorous moral vision in the play. These two run side-by-side in the first three post-war decades.

Clifford Leech wrote twice at length on *The Duchess of Malfi*. In *John Webster* (1951), his approach echoes that of Eliot and Ellis-Fermor. Webster, Leech says, 'has excelled in the moving exploration of the human mind, yet his play is blurred in its total meaning. It is a collection of brilliant scenes, whose statements do not ultimately cohere'.[17] This being so, it is not surprising that Leech, like Ellis-Fermor, finds fault with Webster's use of *sententiae*, concluding that 'When he deliberately aimed at the impressive, he achieved only the ponderous' (116), or that he says that we find ourselves unsure whether the Duchess is guilty or innocent because Webster himself seems torn between condemnation and sympathy. There is a major difficulty, too, over the portrayal of Ferdinand. For despite providing the first psychological working-out and endorsement of Lucas's suggestion that Ferdinand has an incestuous passion for his sister, Leech nonetheless feels Webster himself may not have realized this. Ferdinand's character, Leech says, is 'amorphous [and] insufficiently thought-out' (106), and this is part of the reason why Act V is a failure. With the Duchess dead, Ferdinand must sustain interest throughout the final act. Because he cannot, 'Webster's play ends in tedium' (103). 'We can, I think, assume that Webster did not fully realize the significance of his plays' (33), Leech concludes.

In his 1963 return to *The Duchess of Malfi*, Leech modifies his views. Act V, though not wholly successful, is now seen as serving 'to suggest the presence of the dead Duchess haunting those who have lived along with her. She is mentioned in every scene; her murder is the immediate cause of every detail of the action here; Ferdinand dies invoking her'.[18] This suggests, perhaps, that Leech now feels that Webster did 'realize the significance of his play', though he never admits this. Nor does he alter his view of the characters. Bosola is 'pitifully imperfect' as a moral force, since he kills Ferdinand and the Cardinal 'for revenge at least much as for justice' (27), while Ferdinand is motivated by his incestuous passion for his sister, though unaware of what is driving him.

The presence in Webster's tragedies of a satiric element had been noted both by Brooke and by Stoll. In *The Tragic Satire of John Webster* Travis Bogard's thesis is that in his tragedies Webster deploys the techniques of satire to provide a double perspective on the characters and the action, infusing everything with satiric irony. The first critic to find Webster's *sententiae* effective, Bogard feels that in Bosola they serve to define a figure who knows what he should do but fails to do so. Interestingly, Bogard takes the view that Websterian characters do not develop, though unlike Kingsley he sees this as a strength rather than a weakness. 'Not development but stubborn consistency to self is the distinguishing element of Webster's tragic action', says Bogard. Integrity of life is the only virtue, and it is the 'entire struggle' of the central figures 'to keep themselves as they are, essentially'.[19] 'Inner struggle and development have no place in the Websterian view of life', Bogard concludes, and hence 'no regeneration through suffering is possible' (43).

The early 1960s saw the publication of two important studies of Webster's source material. One was R. W. Dent's *John Webster's Borrowing*, a monumental study of the dramatist's verbal borrowings, showing the unique density of his quarrying, with some passages composed almost entirely of borrowed material. Dent's conclusion is that Webster's borrowing is so constant and habitual that almost everything in his two great tragedies might be traceable, were the source material available. Dent notes how Webster characteristically constructs his verse in small units, how he displays a 'dominant attraction to imagery', and how he constantly develops the element of sententiousness. The result, Dent feels, is often no better than serviceable as dialogue. Of Julia's wooing of Bosola, for instance, he comments: 'The result is fairly effective and plausible dialogue, although of course too compressed and too conceited to be "realistic"'. 'Element after element might be cut', Dent concludes, 'without loss of meaning, continuity, or completeness'.[20]

The other source study, Gunnar Boklund's *The Duchess of Malfi: Sources, Themes, Characters* (1962), is the first sustained attempt precisely to determine not only Webster's sources, but also to what extent the characters in Webster differ from those in his primary source. Boklund notes, for instance, that the extreme villainy of the Arragonian brothers is largely Webster's invention, and is sceptical of an incestuous passion as Ferdinand's motivation because 'the tenor of the supposedly decisive passages is almost the same as in Painter'.[21] The Duchess Boklund finds headstrong, with Webster emphasizing her womanhood rather than her rank, but Antonio a weak man helpless in the face of forces beyond his control. Bosola, meanwhile, is enigmatic, a rationalizer, brought to face reality by the Duchess, the one character with whom he shares an ability to see through appearances, 'the sham and pretense of social life' (108). Boklund defends the horrors of Act IV, including the madmen, whom he sees as symbolizing the disorder to which Ferdinand seeks to reduce his sister. He is less certain about Act V, wishing Webster had been less prodigal with his horrors, but clear about the note on which he feels the play ends. Evil, he contends,

> may occasionally be defeated through self-destruction, as indicated by Ferdinand's madness, but otherwise only through the workings of chance, which rather than any force that might be called divine seems to govern the world of the play. (169)

Hence, while concluding that integrity of life is 'the true guiding principle of man's life', Boklund still finds Webster's vision bleak and unrelieved. 'Plot and theme combine and cooperate to produce a final effect of unrelieved futility', Boklund writes. Moreover,

> Not only does providence lack a tool in *The Duchess of Malfi*, it does not operate, even in the form of nemesis. What governs events is nothing but chance. (129–30)

Alongside this familiar strand in Webster criticism, however, a new one was being developed out of critical studies, such as Willard

Farnham's *The Medieval Heritage of Elizabethan Tragedy* (1936), of the medieval ancestry of the drama known loosely as 'Elizabethan'. E. M. W. Tillyard's *The Elizabethan World Picture* (1943) reinforced the Christian underpinning of Elizabethan drama by demonstrating the belief in a divinely ordered universe which underlay the thinking of the age, and F. P. Wilson's *Elizabethan and Jacobean* (1945) provided the first application of this new view to, *inter alia*, Webster. Wilson's thesis is simply put: 'The dramatists, alike with the poets and prose writers, assumed a Christian universe. Their plays are worked out for the most part in terms of this world, but the beliefs and moral values of the Christian religion are not challenged'.[22] In their depiction of tragic events the dramatists investigate the problem of evil and suffering, but do so within an orthodox Christian framework.

In a chapter on 'John Webster' in his *Poets and Storytellers* (1949), Lord David Cecil argues that Webster views the world from a Calvinist perspective. 'The world as seen by [Webster] is of its nature incurably corrupt', Cecil states, and 'to be involved in it is to be inescapably involved in evil'.[23] Within this world there are the good and the evil, the latter active and dynamic, the former passive. Inevitably, the good are 'swept into the turmoil set up by the furious energy of the wicked' and eventually destroyed, but they are not broken, for 'morally they triumph' (32). 'Furthermore', Cecil writes,

> though they may be destroyed, so also – and far more dreadfully – are their enemies. God is not mocked, the evil doer is caught in the net he has woven for others. And he realizes why [...] Before they die the villains are always forced to recognize the supremacy of that Divine Law, against which they have offended. (33–4)

Reading *The Duchess of Malfi* thus, Cecil finds Act V successful in embodying Webster's governing theme, the act of sin and its consequences. For in it we see not only Ferdinand and the Cardinal destroyed, but Bosola, 'the man who has elected, against the promptings of his better self, to be the devil's agent in the drama' (39) brought to repentance.

Traditionally, Webster's language had been discussed in terms of its quality. In Hereward T. Price's 'The Function of Imagery in Webster', however, the issue is functionality, the uses to which Webster puts his considerable poetic gift. What Webster does, Price argues, and what distinguishes him from other Elizabethans, is give us 'figure in action and figure in language. These he fuses so intimately as to make the play one entire figure'.[24] 'The verbal images', he adds, 'dovetail into one another exactly as they closely parallel the figure in action, rising and falling with it, inseparable from it' (719). Price's approach to Webster's language, so far removed from the traditional nineteenth- and early-twentieth-century view of the dramatist of 'great flashes' was to prove fruitful as part of a growing assertion of the dramatist's architectonic skills.

Equally fruitful has been Inga-Stina Ekeblad's 'The "Impure Art" of John Webster'. Taking as her starting point T. S. Eliot's 'The art of the Elizabethans was an impure art', combining conventions and realism, she challenges the view that 'Webster's method of mixing unrealistic conventions with psychological-realistic representation leads to lack of structure in his plays as wholes'.[25] While conceding that Webster 'often leaves us in confusion' (254), Ekeblad argues that 'at his most intense', as in Act IV Scene Two of *The Duchess of Malfi*, Webster achieves a fusion of realism and conventions, rather than confusion. On the one hand, she says, we have a penetrating and realistic portrayal of the Duchess facing torment and death, but on the other, a scene constructed in the form of a masque, within which there is an antimasque, that of the madmen. Ekeblad writes:

> In fact, if we pursue the question why Webster inserted a masque of madmen in a would-be realistic representation of how the Duchess faces death, we shall find that the madmen's masque is part of a larger structural unit – a more extensive masque. With the scene, this larger masque is being developed on a framework of 'realistic' dramatic representation – the framework itself bearing an analogous relationship to the masque structure.

'It is this structural counterpointing of "convention" and "realism"', Ekeblad continues, 'this concentrated "impurity" of art, that gives the scene its peculiar nature; indeed it contains the meaning of the scene' (255). Asserting that 'it is the Duchess's love and death, her marriage and murder, which are the focal points of the dramatic action' (255), Ekeblad demonstrates that in 4.2 Webster juxtaposes and counterpoints the two by drawing on masque conventions. The madmen, for Ekeblad, constitute an antimasque, such as was commonly substituted at the time when Webster was writing *The Duchess of Malfi*. The crucial part of the masque, however, follows – the taking out and presentation of gifts – and here Bosola, in his disguise, presenting himself as a tomb maker, offers the gift of death. Initially unwilling, the Duchess eventually comes to acceptance, and when she does, Bosola assumes his final role, that of Bellman, to sing the song with which a masque traditionally closed, his call to her to 'Strew [her] hair, with powders sweet' (183) in preparation for death, echoing the preparation of the bride for the marriage bed.

The validity or otherwise of the Duchess's marriage to Antonio continues in the 1950s to be debated. In 'Webster's *Duchess of Malfi* in the Light of Some Contemporary Ideas on Marriage and Remarriage', Frank W. Wadsworth takes up the issue first discussed with any subtlety by Muriel Bradbrook: namely that of how Webster's contemporaries would have regarded the Duchess's wooing of and marriage to Antonio. Clifford Leech had argued that Webster's audience would have condemned the Duchess. Wadsworth demonstrates, however, that there were influential defenders of remarriage in Webster's day, and concludes that as Webster portrays her, the Duchess is less lustful than in Painter, his source. He makes the same point about Antonio, showing that Webster modifies Painter's portrait of a calculating major-domo, and argues also that Webster seeks to diminish the audience's sense of a violation of 'degree' by making Antonio 'a man of worth', an ideal figure.[26]

1964 saw the appearance of two editions of *The Duchess of Malfi*, by John Russell Brown in the Revels Plays Series and by Elizabeth Brennan in the New Mermaids Series. Both are meticulously edited and annotated, and both supplied extensive introductions that repay attention as summations of the divergent critical assessments of *The Duchess of Malfi*. For Brown's reading of the play is broadly in line of descent from Ellis-Fermor via Leech, Bogard and Boklund, while Brennan's traces its ancestry back to David Cecil and F. P. Wilson.

Brown's introduction deals first with the structure of the play, noting Webster's widespread use of pairs of characters and situations, serving to reflect upon each other. Then, considering Webster's 'viewpoint', he notes radical critical disagreements, such as that Antonio's death is either a testament to 'the nobility of his endurance' or 'contemptible', while the Cardinal either 'redeems himself at the last' or is condemned as a 'coward'. Likewise 'Bosola is said to be more a chorus than a character' or 'to show a development from illusion to self-knowledge', while Ferdinand's madness is 'convincing' or 'unconvincing'. 'This disagreement should be expected', Brown concludes, since 'The main source offers conflicting judgements. The action is subtly planned. The dialogue is delicate and vexed. The play was intended for skilled performance in an intimate theatre, before a sophisticated audience'.[27] But this being so, Brown asks 'What "principle of unity" is there in this view of men and actions?' His answer is an 'atmosphere' of 'dark sensationalism and menace, contrasted with softness, intrigue, madness, moral sayings'. He goes on:

> critics have searched rigorously for a unified 'moral vision', and have divided opinion; and this division points to the play's other unity. So does the play's style and structure. It is a unity of

> empirical, responsible, sceptical, unsurprised, and deeply perceptive concern for the characters and society portrayed.

'This view sounds like a product of the 1960s', Brown goes on, and so it does, grounded in audience (or reader) perception, despite his assertion that 'it was also Jacobean' (xlix).

To turn from Brown's introduction to the Revels edition of *The Duchess of Malfi* to Elizabeth Brennan's in the New Mermaids is in some respects to read of two different plays. There are points of congruence, as when Brennan, like Brown, notes how 'the imagery of *The Duchess of Malfi* constantly suggests a series of contrasts and parallels: between light and darkness; health and sickness; sanity and insanity; life and death'.[28] But in most respects Brennan reads the play in markedly different terms. Brown finds in it no definable moral vision. Brennan, by contrast, finds a traditional Christian view of the world, with Webster's characters facing in death salvation or damnation. Not engaging at any length with the debate over the morality or otherwise of the Duchess's marriage to Antonio, Brennan stresses the Duchess's 'purity and integrity' and dismisses 'the evil with which the Duchess is supposed to be possessed' as 'a projection of the evil in the minds of her brothers' (xii). In this regard she is particularly interested in Ferdinand, subscribing to the view that he has an incestuous passion for his sister, but adding a telling dimension when she makes the point that lycanthropy, to which Ferdinand succumbs in Act V, was 'a recognized symptom of love-melancholy' (xiv).

It is in respect of Bosola's behaviour towards the Duchess after this, however, that Brennan contributes most to a developing understanding of his role in the play, pointing out his tutelary role in saving the Duchess from damnation. 'Bosola', she writes,

> has no physical comfort to offer her but, when she has lost all that means most to her in this world, Bosola prevents her from losing eternity. Mental affliction brings her to despair; to die in despair is to die denying the grace of God. Bosola's appearances in a variety of disguises are not further acts of torment; they are sympathetic attempts to make the Duchess rise from despair. (xvii)

Ironically, of course, having helped the Duchess avoid damnation, Bosola is unable to do so himself, but rather pursues a course of action which is part revenge and part justice, killing Ferdinand and the Cardinal, but also the innocent Antonio.

Following Price, Brennan discusses Webster's characteristic interlocking of language and action, but brings a new dimension to it when she relates it to one of the much-criticized 'tales' which Webster inserted in his tragedies: that of the Salmon and the Dogfish. Quoting the final six lines (3.5.133–8), and noting the capitalization of the first Quarto, Brennan comments:

> the Fisher is God; the gathering in of the fishes is a harvest at which not wheat and tares, but good and bad fish are to be judged; the Market is the Judgement; the Cook is another symbol for God; the fire represents hell fire: at the Judgement one is as close to hell as to the joys of heaven.

As Brennan notes, in this passage Webster coalesces 'comment on the difference between divine and human estimation of worth, and thus it is related to the theme of reward and desert; the attitude of the Dogfish to rank is related to the play's comments on princes and their courts' (xxi).

Brown and Brennan's editions make a useful point at which to assess how criticism of *The Duchess of Malfi* had progressed since the end of the nineteenth century. Appreciation had, of course, long given way to analysis, though in Brown's reading of the play, reader response to 'atmosphere' still figured largely, and there would be further attempts to pin down the elusive tone of the play. Charges of 'decadence' had been dropped, complaints about gratuitous 'horrors' in Act IV had given way to an understanding of their nature and purpose, and there was a developing recognition of the way Webster employed imagery and action in constructing his plays. There was also a growing understanding of the nature and function of Act V. Concerning the latter, Clive Hart's would thereafter be the only dissenting voice, his introduction to the 1972 Fountainwell edition of the play arguing that the structure of *The Duchess of Malfi*, 'excellent to start with', 'falls away at the end'. 'In Act V', he writes, 'Webster finds himself with too many major characters to dispose of, and too many minor characters involved in the plot'.[29]

Another issue which had been resolved concerned the viability of *The Duchess of Malfi* in the theatre, largely as a result of the 1945 production starring Peggy Ashcroft and John Gielgud. This and subsequent productions featuring a succession of fine Duchesses, including Ashcroft (again), Judi Dench, Helen Mirren and Harriet Walter, have rendered earlier doubts about its stage viability, such as Una Ellis-Fermor's judgement that the play is 'utterly alien to any plausible stage representation' nugatory.[30] They have also encouraged the study of *The Duchess of Malfi* in the theatre, as is evidenced by Roger Warren's paper given at the first-ever Webster conference, at Langwith College, University of York, in 1969. Entitled '*The Duchess of Malfi* on the Stage', it takes the 1960 production starring Peggy Ashcroft and Eric Porter as a point of departure for an analysis of what characterizes a successful stage representation of the play. Warren's conclusion is that *The Duchess of Malfi* shows a dramatist in total control of his medium.

Two book-length studies of *The Duchess of Malfi* in performance concur. Richard Allen Cave's *The White Devil and The Duchess of Malfi* in the Text and Performance series, and Kathleen McLuskie and Jennifer Uglow's *The Duchess of Malfi* in the Plays in Performance series, both attest to the power of the play, though also to how it can fail, when comprehensively mishandled by Philip Prowse at the National Theatre in 1985. Their assessments of this sadly misconceived production, however, also show how valuable negative examples can be. Cave's comment that 'The problems with this production were all ultimately the result of Prowse's refusal to let Webster's verse inhabit the foreground of the actors' and the audiences' imaginations',[31] and McLuskie and Uglow's that 'even such experienced actors as McKellen, Eleanor Bron and Jonathan Hyde could get no grip on a play which had been managed and manipulated beyond their recovery',[32] both point to a fundamental truth: that productions of *The Duchess of Malfi* succeed best when actors and directors alike trust the dramatist.

But though some issues had been resolved, others remained. The most fundamental difference of opinion, highlighted by the Brown and Brennan introductions, was over whether *The Duchess of Malfi* should be read in orthodox Christian terms or not and how the Duchess's suffering and death should be interpreted. In this regard, Bosola's character also becomes problematic. Is he in some sense acting in a tutelary role to the Duchess in Act IV, or simply reflecting a conflict between his duty to Ferdinand and his sympathy and admiration for her? With Ferdinand and the Cardinal the issues are clearer, there being close to a consensus that an unacknowledged incestuous passion for his sister is a driving force in Ferdinand's persecution of her.

Brennan's Christian reading of *The Duchess* received its first major support in Peter B. Murray's *A Study of John Webster* (1969). For Murray, Webster's account of the suffering of the Duchess has much in common with the biblical story of Job, though the Duchess 'is no mere allegorical figure, a fleshless counterpart to Job', but rather 'deeply and pitiably human in her anguish' as she passes through despair to hope, and dies kneeling in Christian humility.[33] In Bosola and his demonic employers, by contrast, we have analogues for Satan, Job's tormenter. Murray also argues that Bosola and Ferdinand should be read in terms of the legend of Tantalus. He bases this on the amazing assertion that 'the person who suffers the most is, amazingly, not the Duchess, but her brother Ferdinand', coupling this with the less startling claim that 'the suffering of the Duchess is also nearly matched by Bosola' (154). Like Wadsworth,

Murray sees Antonio as an ideal husband and model courtier, and defends him against the frequently levelled charge of weakness and vacillation in dealing with the Duchess's brothers. Antonio adopts 'a passive Christian-Stoic acceptance of events as the will of God', he writes, and 'this is the view that is to govern Antonio's actions through the rest of the play' (150). For Boklund, Antonio's final speech is indicative of a kind of despair, an assertion that all life is futile. Murray reads it as rather a statement that 'our *worldly* life is futile' (152).

Murray's comment about a 'Christian-Stoic acceptance of events as the will of God' finds resonances in Dominic Baker-Smith's paper, 'Religion and John Webster', read at the Langwith symposium. For Baker-Smith places Webster within a severely Calvinist world which saw 'a climax in the growth of religious pessimism and in stress on the arbitrary will of God'.[34] Predestination and the threat of eternal reprobation brought alienation in its wake, Baker-Smith argues, and in his two tragedies he finds Webster portraying a dark world in which 'human activity is either guilty or fateful, only passive acceptance escapes divine retribution' (216). In such a world, Baker-Smith finds Webster stressing 'security', that which is 'created by those defences which the ego constructs around itself; with the mental props of wealth, influence, and power man can blind himself to the nature of reality' (217). Despair and damnation follow, the only exceptions being Antonio and the Duchess, who take the path of obedient suffering. 'Webster's God', Baker-Smith concludes, 'unlike his devil, is a hidden one. This does not mean that He is not there, but we are offered "nor path nor friendly clew" to find him' (228).

A second Langwith paper, by D. C. Gunby, claims, by contrast, that Webster is working not in terms of Calvinist predestination, but rather of that other wing of Anglican theology which allows the operation of free will, contingent on the working out of divine providence. Like Baker-Smith, Gunby sees 'security' as a crucial issue, but interprets it as a state of spiritual lethargy that endangers the soul.[35] In his reading, *The Duchess of Malfi* shows the ultimate triumph of the Duchess, and the values, moral and spiritual, which she represents, over the forces of evil in Ferdinand and the Cardinal. Finding the four main characters conceived in terms of the four humours – the Cardinal phlegmatic, Ferdinand choleric, Bosola melancholic and the Duchess sanguine – Gunby argues that, through imagery as well as action, the demonic motives of Ferdinand and the Cardinal are revealed, with, in the case of Ferdinand, a three-layered set of motives, with images of fire and storm signifying anger, lust, and (with the addition of references to devils and witchcraft) the demonic. Like Brennan, Gunby sees the Duchess undergoing a spiritual pilgrimage from pride through suffering to humility, and finally to an acceptance of death as a 'gift', kneeling to enter Heaven. Bosola is seen as both minister (to the Duchess) and scourge (of Ferdinand and the Cardinal), achieving more than he knows in rousing the Duchess from despair and bringing her to an acceptance of her fate, yet dying 'confused and lost', without understanding what he has achieved (204). The end of *The Duchess of Malfi*, however, is optimistic, with Pescara's final statement containing the only sun image in a dark play, supporting the symbolic figure of the surviving son of the Duchess and Antonio.

A further contribution to a Christian interpretation of *The Duchess of Malfi* is provided by Bettie-Anne Doebler, who argues that 'Webster uses elements from the old *ars moriendi* tradition to structure the death scenes in Act IV'.[36] In the late sixteenth century, Doebler argues, the art of dying well developed an emphasis on the danger of despair, and in the torment and death of the Duchess Webster provides an exemplar of this new emphasis, with Bosola serving paradoxically to bring comfort to the woman he must torment and at the last kill. In 4.1, thus, we have an 'enactment of the temptation to despair performed by the demonic and melancholy Bosola on behalf of the satanic Ferdinand' (208), but with the Duchess rescued from the ultimate spiritual peril by Bosola, who in 4.2 becomes her comforter. When the Duchess kneels in humble acceptance of death, Doebler argues, 'the audience of the time might well have imagined the presence of an angel taking her soul up into heaven' (212). Even so, Doebler is unsure about the play's final message. The Duchess's 'Christian dying provides the predominantly conventional hope for a future justice', but 'in spite of Bosola's conversion to a minister of revenge, we are left doubting that the world can change' (213).

Non-Christian readings of *The Duchess of Malfi* are often focused upon how to read what appears a resistant or enigmatic text, to define or explain what is characteristically Websterian, and to explain, like Brown, the tone and mood of the play. Some critics have, with Bogard, found the key in the play's generic complexity. Thus J. R. Mulryne argues that the peculiar difficulty of defining in critical terms 'John Webster's "case", his "impure art"', derives from his 'conflation of tragic and comic genres', his 'experiments with the uses of tragicomedy'.[37] By 'tragicomedy' Mulryne does not, however, mean, as for Renaissance writers and critics, death threatened but finally avoided, but rather a kind of black comedy, 'a form in which comedy and tragedy, the laughable and the appalling, are so composed that neither is predominant' (135).

Jacqueline Pearson's starting point in *Tragedy and Tragicomedy in the Plays of John Webster* (1980) is, by contrast, the Renaissance concept of tragicomedy. But she has much in common with Mulryne, since she is aiming to demonstrate that 'Webster's dramatic interests are in the incoherences of real life, the mixture of modes and the collision of different images and different interpretations of action'.[38] Finding significant tragicomic elements in *The White Devil* and *The Duchess of Malfi*, as well as his later tragicomedies, she feels *The Duchess of Malfi* 'begins as a tragedy and only in the fifth act confronts tragedy with satire, tragicomedy, and a distorted view of the tragic absolutes' (84). The Duchess is truly a tragic figure, Pearson argues, but even at the play's 'tragic centre', in Act IV, Webster surrounds the tragic with what Pearson terms 'Anti-tragedy'. Examples are 'Bosola's disguises, Ferdinand's equivocating vow, his sinister joke with the dead man's hand, the Masque of Madmen [and] Cariola's desperate attempt to escape death by improvising fictions' (85). We thus have, in *The Duchess of Malfi* a 'tragedy in which a good woman achieves a tragic self-assertion' (88), but once she is gone, 'tragedy falls apart into satire, self-deception, despair and madness' (89).

Pearson finds in *The Duchess of Malfi* tragedy surrounded by anti-tragedy. In *The World's Perspective: John Webster and the Jacobean Drama* (1983), Lee Bliss argues the opposite, finding Webster 'enclosing comedy with tragedy', surrounding the world of the Duchess, domestic, harmonious, loving, a world with much in common with 'romantic comedy',[39] with that of Ferdinand, the Cardinal, and the Court, political, cynical, amoral and destructive, its values inimical to those of the Duchess. 'Webster', she writes, 'can use his generic contrasts to dramatize the desirability of the Duchess's choice as well as the impossibility of its attainment, both her culpability in political and social terms and the unimportance of any terms that inhibit re-establishing fundamentally valuable human relationships' (146). A key element in achieving this, Bliss argues, is Webster's employment of distancing techniques in order to develop and alter perspectives.

Another approach to Webster's dramaturgy is provided by Catherine Belsey's 'Emblem and Antithesis in *The Duchess of Malfi*', which argues that *The Duchess of Malfi* 'is a play poised, formally as well as historically, between the emblematic tradition of the medieval stage and the increasing commitment to realism of the post-Restoration theater'.[40] 'Contradictory structural elements in *The Duchess of Malfi*', Belsey writes,

> generate a tension between its realist features – psychological plausibility and narrative sequence – and the formality of its design. Close analysis of the text reveals that the audience is repeatedly invited by the realist surface to expect the unfolding of a situation or the interplay of specific characters, only to find that

> the actual constantly resolves into abstraction, the characters into figures in a pattern. (117)

Webster's techniques, says Belsey, result in a play in which 'the quasi-realistic surface repeatedly dissolves into *sententiae*, meditations, and fables' (123).

Belsey's concern is to expose the limitations of the liberal-humanist concept of 'character' in English Renaissance drama. In the first New Historicist reading of the play, 'Sexual and Social Mobility in *The Duchess of Malfi*', Frank Whigham also seeks to renew the way in which *The Duchess of Malfi* is read by treating familiar issues such as the Duchess's remarriage and Ferdinand's possibly incestuous passion for his sister 'in light of class strata and anthropological notions of incest'.[41] At a time of accelerating social change, and with his sister a 'cultural voyager', expressing her self-determination through marriage to a social inferior, Ferdinand is, for Whigham, 'a threatened aristocrat, frightened by the contamination of his ascriptive social rank and obsessively preoccupied with its defence', and his 'incestuous inclination toward his sister [is] a *social posture*, of hysterical compensation – a desperate expression of the desire to evade degrading association with inferiors' (169).

Revisionary approaches such as Belsey's and Whigham's have no place in Charles Forker's *Skull Beneath the Skin: The Achievement of John Webster* (1986), a traditional 'Life and Works'. For Forker's views tend to be middle of the road and eclectic, as in his handling of the Arragonian brethren. Thus, while the Cardinal is seen as 'a purposely distanced figure',[42] Ferdinand is read psychoanalytically. 'Obsession with one's twin or shadow [is] a well-known form of narcissistic self-projection', Forker notes, and Ferdinand is 'an impressively sophisticated study in the psychology of a sadist, repressed by guilt and horrified to the point of self-delusion by the nature of his own erotic urges' (308). Bosola is also read psychologically as 'a man in quest of psychological and moral authenticity', 'a moralist deeply corrupted by vice and a criminal whose conscience no dedication to depravity can wholly anesthetize' (334), but the Duchess is read more traditionally. In her, Forker argues, Webster has to balance the public and private, helplessness and strength, wilfulness and acceptance. 'One of the ways in which Webster successfully conveys the impression of dual role in his title figure', Forker writes, 'insisting equally on her public image as regnant princess and on her private personality as wife and mother, is to define her internal struggle in terms of a dialectic between heroic self-assertion and religious humility' (323).

McLuskie and Uglow refer in passing to *The Duchess of Malfi* as a 'structurally flawed text'.[43] Christina Luckyj's *A Winter's Snake: Dramatic*

Form in the Tragedies of John Webster is concerned to demonstrate that, on the contrary, Webster's two great tragedies are consummately crafted, and crafted in such a way that makes the scenes of high intensity so admired by critics from Lamb onwards structurally as well as emotionally crucial. 'Critics both recognized and admired Webster's episodic intensification as the source of his dramatic power, but were unwilling to concede that it could be a principle of construction', writes Luckyj, adding that 'The intense tragic vision they praised depended on a dramatic organization they recognized only as a failure'.[44] For Webster's dramaturgy is, Luckyj argues, 'founded on juxtapositions, parallels and repetitions which resist reduction to a single moral belief, yet need not lead to a chaotic vision of human experience' (xx).

'Like Shakespeare', Luckyj writes,

> Webster uses repetitive form, de-emphasizing the play's linear progression for the advantage of re-working and expanding his basic material. In the central acts of both his major tragedies, Webster repeats and modulates large dramatic sequences of events to clarify and intensify the direction of his play. (1)

Thus Acts I and II begin alike, with Antonio and Delio greeting each other, and the opening of Act III is clearly designed to alert us to that fact, with Delio, welcomed back as Antonio was in Act I, commenting:

> Methinks 'twas yesterday. Let me but wink,
> And not behold your face, which to mine eye
> Is somewhat leaner, verily I should dream
> It were within this half-hour. (3.1.8–11)

As Luckyj comments, 'dramatic convention is thus exposed', and in being thus exposed emphasizes the fact that dramatically we are 'back at the beginning – this second cycle repeats the substance of the first in order to illuminate the progress of the tragedy' (19). One of the effects of repetitive form of this kind, Luckyj points out, is that it de-emphasizes causation in drama. 'Because there is no single, direct linear narrative proceeding from the Duchess's wooing of Antonio to her death', she writes, 'it is dramatically impossible to see the latter as a result of the former – though some commentators have tried to force the play into this pattern' (23).

What of Act V, most egregious of the structural deficiencies traditionally attributed to Webster? Luckyj's reading is intriguing, depending as it does on an Act IV in which the death of the Duchess is not (then) seen as tragic. The Duchess, Luckyj argues, 'dies a martyr', a victim of 'either a relentless fate or overpowering human evil' (101), and the play veers accordingly towards melodrama. But in the fifth act Webster applies the necessary correction when on the one hand he reanimates the Duchess, through the Julia sub-plot, 'as an unconventional, wilful and sexually vital woman', and on the other 'casts a new light retrospectively on the forces that led the Duchess to death, and reveals them to be human, frail, and error-prone' (100). 'When the Duchess's death can be seen as the result of errors that might have been corrected, yet were not', Luckyj concludes, 'then the play approaches tragedy' (101). What we experience in the last act, thereby is 'collective tragedy', where 'the Duchess's courageous virtue and her enemies' struggles of conscience are set against [a] nihilistic vision of life made meaningless by death' (143).

What, since the Brown and Brennan editions, of the Duchess herself? Alexander Allison commented, in 1964, on 'a general disposition [...] either wholly to moralize the duchess or wholly to sentimentalize her'.[45] A year earlier, P. F. Vernon, discussing 'The Duchess of Malfi's Guilt', had moralized, stating that the Duchess's wooing of Antonio is 'couched in hints and equivocations which resemble the lascivious language of Julia and Bosola in the last act'.[46] Two decades later we find Lee Bliss describing her (without moralizing) as 'earthy' and 'wilful', but concluding that the Duchess 'seeks private happiness at the expense of public stability' and hence is 'a "bad" ruler, certainly a poor example of Antonio's ideal'.[47] Luckyj agrees that she is wilful, as well as 'unconventional' and 'sexually vital', but finds no difficulty in linking her with Julia, either sexually or in the manner of her death, commenting that the latter's 'startlingly casual murder casts new light retrospectively on the psychotic forces behind the murder of the Duchess, showing them to be merely exaggerations of forces that regularly destroy women in the real world'.[48]

Luckyj's critical approach is traditional, but her comment about 'forces that regularly destroy women in the real world' hints, in passing, at what in the 1980s was emerging as the dominant element in the critical history of *The Duchess of Malfi*: feminist criticism. An early example of this was Charlotte Spivack's '*The Duchess of Malfi*: A Fearful Madness', which appeared in 1979, in the second issue of the *Journal of Women's Studies in Literature*. Spivack's approach is essentialist; she sees the Duchess represented as a 'complete woman, with both integrity of self-hood and the power to transform others'.[49] As such, Spivack argues, she 'fulfils both the elementary and the transformative nature of the feminine archetype' (124), the first, the matriarchal, over which the unconscious is dominant, and the second the transformative, the dynamic element of the psyche. Taking Cariola's comment at the end of Act I –'Whether the spirit of greatness or of woman / Reign most in her, I know not; but it shows / A fearful madness' (410–12) – as a crucial articulation of the Duchess's dilemma, Spivack argues that the Duchess achieves wholeness through incorporating the spirits both of greatness and of woman. 'She clings to her ducal role and authoritative position', Spivack writes, 'asserting its authenticity at several points in the play' (124), and she maintains it until death. Her greatness is thus not superficial or a matter of rank, but 'an inward quality outwardly demonstrated [...] in terms of supreme rational and conscious control' (125). But equally, Spivack maintains, through the 'deep resources of primordial womanhood', the Duchess achieves a tranquillity of spirit, unshaken in the face of death, achieving thereby 'a totality of selfhood', 'a woman embodying both the elementary and the transformative functions of the feminine principle' (128).

'In the beginnings of feminist criticism', writes Theodora Jankowski, 'the lack of a well-defined theoretical position had the positive effect of allowing for [...] often contradictory viewpoints which shared an overall commitment to a feminist problematic'.[50] This can be seen in the distance between Spivack's Duchess and Lisa Jardine's. For in *Still Harping on Daughters: Women and Drama in the Age of Shakespeare* (1983) Jardine undertakes a New Historicist reading of Webster's Duchess. 'Lower in her sexual drive than "a beast that wants discourse of reason"', Jardine writes, 'the Duchess of Malfi, like Hamlet's mother, steps out of the path of duty and marries for lust'.[51] 'In so doing', she argues,

> she is metamorphosed from ideal mirror of virtue [...] into lascivious whore. It is not merely that her brothers see her as such; the dominant strain in the subsequent representation of her is such. [...] From the moment of her assertion of sexual independence, the Duchess moves with dignity but inexorably towards a ritual chastisement worthy of a flagrant breach of public order. (77)

Jardine sees the Duchess as losing her status as duchess and despite her protests, ceasing to be 'Duchess of Malfi still'. Thus, she argues,

> the Duchess is reduced to the safe composite stereotype of penitent whore, Virgin majestic in grief, serving mother, and patient and true turtle-dove mourning her one true love. Strength of purpose is eroded into strength of character in adversity. (91)

Archetype or 'safe composite stereotype', the Duchess, in the hands of a succession of feminist critics, was to be re-envisioned, and *The Duchess of Malfi* likewise.

Notes

1. Quoted in Don D. Moore, *Webster: The Critical Heritage* (London: Routledge & Kegan Paul, 1981), 35.
2. George Bernard Shaw, *Our Theatre in the Nineties* 3 vols (London: Constable, 1932), III, 317.
3. Moore, *Critical Heritage*, 143–4.
4. Elmer E. Stoll, *John Webster: The Periods of His Work as Determined by His Relationship to the Drama of the Day* (Boston: 1905), 209.
5. C. V. Boyer, *The Villain as Hero in Elizabethan Tragedy* (London: 1914), 153.
6. Rupert Brooke, *John Webster and the Elizabethan Drama* (London: Sidgwick & Jackson, 1916), 107.
7. Repr. in *The Old Drama and the New* (London: 1923), 126.
8. *The Complete Works of John Webster*, ed. by F. L. Lucas, 4 vols (London: Sidgwick & Jackson, 1927), I, 16–7.
9. *The Complete Works of John Webster*, ed. by F. L. Lucas, 4 vols (London: Sidgwick & Jackson, 1927), II. 21.
10. T. S. Eliot, 'Four Elizabethan Dramatists', reprinted in T. S. Eliot, *Selected Essays* (London: Faber and Faber, 1932), 98.
11. F. R Leavis, *Determinations* (London: Chatto and Windus 1934), 44.
12. W. A. Edwards, 'John Webster', *Scrutiny*, 2 (1933), 19.
13. Ian Jack, 'The Case of John Webster', *Scrutiny*, 16 (1949), 38.
14. L. G. Salingar, 'Tourneur and the Tragedy of Revenge', in *The Age of Shakespeare*, ed. by Boris Ford (Harmondsworth: Penguin, 1955), 349.
15. M. C. Bradbrook, *Themes and Conventions of Elizabethan Tragedy* (Cambridge: Cambridge University Press, 1935), 1.
16. Una Ellis-Fermor, *The Jacobean Drama: An Interpretation* (London: Methuen, 1936), 172.
17. Clifford Leech, *John Webster* (London: Hogarth Press, 1961), 65.
18. Clifford Leech, *Webster: The Duchess of Malfi*. Studies in English Literature, 8 (London: Edward Arnold, 1963), 39.
19. Travis Bogard, *The Tragic Satire of John Webster* (Berkeley: University of California Press, 1955), 55.
20. Robert W. Dent, *John Webster's Borrowing* (Berkeley: University of California Press, 1960), 14.
21. Gunnar Boklund, *The Duchess of Malfi: Sources, Themes, Characters* (Cambridge, Mass: Harvard University Press, 1962), 99.
22. F. P. Wilson, *Elizabethan and* Jacobean (Oxford: Oxford University Press), 1947), 7.
23. David Cecil, 'John Webster', in *Poets and Story-Tellers* (London: Constable, 1949), 29–30.
24. Hereward T. Price, 'The Function of Imagery in Webster', *PMLA*, 70 (1955), 717–39, (p. 719).
25. Inga-Stina Ekeblad, 'The Impure Art of John Webster', *Review of English Studies*, n.s. 9 (1958), 253–67, (p. 253).
26. Frank W. Wadsworth, 'Webster's *Duchess of Malfi* in the Light of Some Contemporary Ideas on Marriage and Remarriage', *Philological Quarterly*, 35 (1957), 394–407, (p. 403).
27. John Webster, *The Duchess of Malfi*, ed. by John Russell Brown (London: Methuen, 1964), xlviii.
28. John Webster, *The Duchess of Malfi*, ed. by Elizabeth Brennan (London: Ernest Benn, 1964), xxiii.

29. *John Webster: The Duchess of Malfi*, ed. by Clive Hart (Edinburgh: Oliver & Boyd, 1972), 8.
30. Una Ellis-Fermor, *The Jacobean Drama: An Interpretation* (London: Methuen, 1936), 43–4.
31. Richard Allen Cave, *The White Devil and The Duchess of Malfi* (Basingstoke: Macmillan, 1988), 69.
32. *The Duchess of Malfi by John Webster*, ed. by Kathleen McLuskie and Jennifer Uglow (Bristol: Bristol Classical Press, 1989), 62.
33. Peter B. Murray, *A Study of John Webster* (The Hague: Mouton, 1969), 132.
34. Dominic Baker-Smith, 'Religion and John Webster", in *John Webster*, ed. by Brian Morris (London: Ernest Benn, 1970), 211.
35. D. C. Gunby, '*The Duchess of Malfi*: A Theological Approach', in *John Webster*, ed. by Brian Morris (London: Ernest Benn, 1970), 193–4.
36. Bettie Anne Doebler, 'Continuity in the Art of Dying: *The Duchess of Malfi*', *Comparative Drama*, 14 (1980), 203–15, (p. 203).
37. J. R. Mulryne, 'Webster and the Uses of Tragicomedy', in *John Webster*, ed. by Brian Morris (London: Ernest Benn, 1970), 133.
38. Jacqueline Pearson, *Tragedy and Tragicomedy in the Plays of John Webster* (Manchester: Manchester University Press, 1980), 1.
39. Lee Bliss, *The World's Perspective: John Webster and the Jacobean Drama* (Brighton: The Harvester Press, 1983), 151.
40. Catherine Belsey, 'Emblem and Antithesis in *The Duchess of Malfi*', *Renaissance Drama*, n.s. 11 (1980), 115–34 (p. 115).
41. Frank Whigham, 'Sexual and Social Mobility in *The Duchess of Malfi*', *PMLA* 100 (1985), 167-86, (p. 167)
42. Charles R. Forker, *Skull Beneath the Skin: The Achievement of John Webster* (Carbondale: Southern Illinois University Press, 1986), 313.
43. *The Duchess of Malfi* by *John Webster*, ed. by Kathleen McLuskie and Jennifer Uglow (Bristol: Bristol Classical Press, 1989), 1.
44. Christina Luckyj, *A Winter's Snake: Dramatic Form in the Tragedies of John Webster* (Athens: University of Georgia Press, 1989), xviii.
45. Alexander Allison, 'Ethical Themes in *The Duchess of Malfi*', *Studies in English Literature*, 4 (1964), 263–73, (p. 263).
46. P. F. Vernon, 'The Duchess of Malfi's Guilt', *Notes and Queries*, n.s. 10 (1963), 335–8, (p. 337).
47. Lee Bliss, *The World's Perspective: John Webster and the Jacobean Drama* (Brighton: The Harvester Press, 1983), 145.
48. Christina Luckyj, *A Winter's Snake: Dramatic Form in the Tragedies of John Webster* (Athens: University of Georgia Press, 1989), 91.
49. Charlotte Spivack, '*The Duchess of Malfi*: A Fearful Madness', *Journal of Women's Studies in Literature*, 2 (1979), 122–32, (122).
50. Jankowski, Theodora Jankowski, *Women in Power in the Early Modern Drama* (Urbana: University of Illinois Press, 1992), 1.
51. Lisa Jardine, *Still Harping on Daughters* (Brighton: The Harvester Press, 1983), 71.

CHAPTER TWO

The Duchess High and Low: A Performance History of *The Duchess of Malfi*

Roberta Barker

The Double Life of the Duchess of Malfi

The title page of the first quarto edition of John Webster's *The Duchess of Malfi* boasts that the play was 'Presented privately, at the Black- / Friers; and publiquely at the Globe, By the / Kings Majesties Servants' (A2r). This advertisement has fostered debate about the varying ways in which Webster's tragedy might originally have been staged at the outdoor Globe Theatre and at the indoor Blackfriars,[1] but it also sparks discussion about early modern marketing practices. It foregrounds the crossover appeal of *The Duchess of Malfi*: its ability to please a range of audience members. Buy this volume, the title page bids its readers; both the high-paying 'private' habitués at the Blackfriars and the more varied 'public' of the Globe have enjoyed *The Duchess of Malfi*, and so will you.

From this first inscription onwards, the theatrical life of *The Duchess of Malfi* has hinged on the relationship between high and low. An intense negotiation between elements generally perceived as characteristic of elite culture and those widely seen as typical of popular forms took root in the themes and the original performance conditions of Webster's tragedy and has recurred throughout its performance history. Fêted in its own time, *The Duchess of Malfi* was rejected in the eighteenth century by critics who viewed it as too crass for neo-classical canons. After a century-long drought in performances, *The Duchess of Malfi* returned to the stage in the nineteenth century through the offices of theatre artists who sought to educate their audiences in the mysteries of early English theatre by using the populist performance vocabulary of melodrama. For much of the twentieth century, the dominant theatrical interpretation of *The Duchess of Malfi* strove to eliminate such melodrama and to mitigate the play's reputation for vulgar sensationalism, relying upon a combination of Renaissance design elements and Stanislavskian acting techniques to provide the signifiers of high cultural respectability. From 1995 onwards, an overwhelming number of major productions of *The Duchess of Malfi* have instead featured modern dress and have linked the play to mainstream contemporary cinematic tropes. Where the twentieth century struggled to foreground the play's elite credentials, the twenty-first has so far tended to emphasize its popular appeal. Yet the continuing stage vitality of *The Duchess of Malfi* may finally reside, not in one or the other of these alternatives, but in the possibilities created by their encounter.

The Duchess Lively Body'd

Binary oppositions between 'high' and 'low', 'elite' and 'popular' culture are notoriously unstable, and the terms themselves open to endless contestation.[2] Their use always necessitates simplification; for example, I imply above that Blackfriars was associated with elite and the Globe with popular audiences, but the clientele of both theatres probably represented a range of social positions.[3] This discussion will use 'high' and 'low', 'elite' and 'popular' not as absolute categories but as historically contingent signifiers for ways of constructing performances and their spectators across a variety of times and places. I employ two basic premises: first, that high culture is often associated with groups who enjoy power or prestige within a given society and may thus prove difficult for others to access, while low culture is associated with a broader audience and is more easily accessible;[4] and second, that high culture is often defined as ennobling or improving its consumers (or as pretentiously claiming to do so), while popular culture entertains them (or plays to their baser instincts).[5]

A negotiation between high and popular culture so defined has marked the performance history of *The Duchess of Malfi* from its première onwards. Webster's tragedy is ideally situated to engage my first definition of these two terms, dominated as it is by a narrative and thematic negotiation between high and low positions on the social hierarchy. Its aristocratic heroine is doomed when her choice of a lower-born husband enrages her princely brothers; her killer, the spy Bosola, ascribes his sins to the underling's need to 'thrive somehow' in a corrupt hierarchical society.[6] One of the few early modern spectators to have left a record of his experience of Webster's tragedy places the relationship between high and low at the very heart of *The Duchess of Malfi*. In his dedicatory poem to the first quarto edition of the play, William Rowley contemplates the figure of Webster's heroine:

> I never saw thy Dutchesse, till the day,
> That she was lively body'd in thy Play;
> How'ere she answer'd her low-rated Love,
> Her brothers anger, did so fatall proove,
> Yet my opinion is, she might speake more,
> But (never in her life) so well before.[7]

Rowley stresses as praiseworthy the rhetoric Webster places in the noble Duchess's mouth to defend her choice of 'low-rated' partner. The conflict between her 'low-rated Love' and the fury of her high-born brothers, and her eloquent struggle to bridge this gap, emerges as *the* aspect of the play worthy of memorialization in print.

Rowley recalls a Duchess characterized not just by her words but by her gestures: a Duchess 'lively body'd' onstage. The acting skills of the King's Men who originally performed *The Duchess of Malfi* must have struck others as worthy of record, for it is the first extant English play to be published with a list of 'The Actors Names' who played in it.[8] The list seems to note both the players who appeared in the première of the play and those who appeared in a revival, likely sometime in the early 1620s.[9] John Lowin, one of the earliest actors to play Falstaff and Sir Epicure Mammon, is cited first in the list as the Bosola of both casts.[10] Richard Burbage, the creator of so many Shakespearean tragic heroes, played Ferdinand in the play's first incarnation. Richard Robinson, whose skills as a boy actress Ben Jonson himself had praised, played the Cardinal in its second cast once he had graduated to adult male roles.[11] Richard Sharp is the sole listed Duchess, but some scholars have argued plausibly that Robinson may have created the role and bequeathed it to Sharp in the later revival.[12] Whoever he may have been, the actor who played the Duchess is singled out by Rowley from this exalted theatrical company for his 'lively' skills of personation. In the third dedicatory poem appended to the first quarto, Thomas Middleton too stresses the impact of the Duchess's role in performance: 'For who e're saw this Dutchesse live, and dye', he demands, 'That could get off under a Bleeding Eye[?]'.[13]

Such praise is remarkable not least because one might have expected the two most celebrated members of the cast, Lowin and Burbage, to have overpowered the pubescent apprentice who played the Duchess. After all, notes David Carnegie, early modern boy actresses were 'junior in the theatrical hierarchy to the adult actors'. Carnegie reminds us that the Duchess's role is substantially shorter than Bosola's and ends in Act IV; 'Elizabethan and Jacobean dramaturgy', he opines, 'skillfully presents women whose importance, even dominance, is substantially assisted by the speech and action of the men'.[14] Yet Middleton and Rowley explicitly remember the speech and action of the Duchess herself, not that of the men around her. For these spectators, at least, the apprentice more than held his own opposite the most prominent shareholders in the company. The performance dynamics, as well as the plot, of *The Duchess of Malfi* can thus be seen as challenging normative boundaries between high and low.

Another early spectator of *The Duchess of Malfi* in performance saw the play as attacking the most high and reverend figures of his own society and in the process engaging my second definition of low culture (as that which debases its audience) as well as my first. Orazio Busino, chaplain at the Venetian Embassy in London, appears to be thinking of *The Duchess of Malfi* when he complains of the anti-Catholicism of English actors. 'They showed', he fumes,

> a cardinal in all his grandeur, in the formal robes appropriate to his station, splendid and rich, with his train in attendance, having an altar erected in the stage, where he pretended to make a prayer, organizing a procession; and then they produced him in public with a harlot on his knee.[15]

The fact that low-bred actors dared so scurrilously to imitate the grandees of the Church presumably adds insult to injury. At the same time, Busino admits some admiration for the players he saw, recalling how the Cardinal going to war 'ha[d] his sword bound on and don[ned] the soldier's sash with so much panache you could not imagine it better done'.[16] A mere actor (perhaps Henry Condell, the first Cardinal) takes on the role of the bellicose churchman with enviable style; the splendour of the playhouse's representation of high ecclesiastical pomp cannot be denied. As in the Duchess's marriage, high and low mingle to enticing if disconcerting effect.

The Duchess of Malfi thus emerges as a play whose success in its own time rested partly on its social multivalence. Not only was it popular enough to be publicly revived by the King's Men a decade after its première, increasing its accessibility to a wide audience, but the company and their most exalted spectators also valued it highly enough for it to be performed at Inigo Jones' private Cockpit theatre at court in

1630.[17] John Downes' *Roscius Anglicanus* (1708) records its survival as a recognized public crowd-pleaser well into the Restoration. At a revival in September 1662 in which the celebrated tragedian Betterton played Bosola and his wife Mary appeared as the Duchess, writes Downes, 'This Play was so exceeding Excellently *Acted* in all Parts; chiefly, Duke *Ferdinand* and *Bosola*: It filled the House 8 Days Successively, it proving one of the Best of Stock Tragedies'.[18] Downes perceives the Duchess's brother and his intelligencer, rather than the Duchess herself as in Middleton's and Rowley's encomia, as the star turns of the play. But the play's status as a popular work in terms of its capability to 'fill the house' remains firmly in place. Documented revivals in 1668 and 1672 attest to its ongoing public marketability; a performance at the court of King James II in 1686 gives evidence of its continuing appeal to the social elite.[19]

Even so, doubts about the play's stageworthiness begin to creep in during this period. In his diary, Samuel Pepys records seeing Betterton and his wife in the play's first Restoration outing in 1662: 'after dinner we took coach and to the Dukes playhouse, where we saw *The Duchesse of Malfy* well performed, but Baterton [Betterton] and Ianthe [Mrs. Betterton] to admiration'.[20] In November 1668, however, he was less impressed by a stage revival: 'my wife and I to the Duke of York's house to see *The Duchesse of Malfy*, a sorry play'.[21] Whether Pepys's view of the play itself had changed or whether the 1668 revival was simply less pleasing in his eyes, other evidence suggests that *The Duchess of Malfi* was looking increasingly old-fashioned by the turn of the new century. In 1708, the fourth quarto edition of the play began to edit and adapt Webster's playtext to suit the times. 'Metre is sometimes regularized, and there is considerable modernizing and simplifying of words that were becoming archaic', notes Carnegie.[22] Within 25 years, a much more radical transformation of Webster's *Duchess* appeared on the London stage: one whose approach laid the foundations for a polarization between high and low cultural readings of the play.

'A Style Worthy of the *Corsican Brothers*'

Lewis Theobald's *The Fatal Secret* played at Covent Garden for only two nights in April 1733, but the fact that it was a flop cannot be blamed on Theobald's failure to adapt *The Duchess of Malfi* to his era's tastes. In his preface to the published version of *The Fatal Secret*, Theobald described Webster as 'a strong and impetuous Genius, but withal a most wild, and indigested one'.[23] *The Duchess of Malfi*, he opined, suffered from a particularly virulent form of the vulgar lack of classical construction that afflicted so many plays of its era. 'As for Rules', Theobald complains, Webster

> either knew them not or thought them too servile a Restraint. Hence it is, that he skips over Years and Kingdoms with an equal Liberty. (It must be confess'd, the Unities were very sparingly observ'd at the time he wrote; however, when any Poet travels so fast that the Imagination of his Spectators cannot keep pace with him, Probability is put quite out of Breath.)[24]

To combat this fault, Theobald chose to 'moderniz[e]' Webster's tragedy.[25] His Duchess has no children by Antonio to be born inelegantly during the act breaks. She is strangled tastefully offstage. In the end, the Cardinal and Ferdinand having murdered one another, Bosola reveals that he has hidden the Duchess, substituting a wax dummy for her body in order to deceive her brothers. The heroine and Antonio are reunited in a poetically just reward of their virtue, love and constancy, and Antonio embraces Bosola as a brother. Decorum, unity and poetic justice dominate. In revising *The Duchess of Malfi*, Theobald strove to square it with the high culture of eighteenth-century neo-classicism.

When next revived on the London stage, over a century after *The Fatal Secret*'s failure, *The Duchess of Malfi* would fall less clearly into one camp, but would instead mix high and low cultures in a new manner. As performed at the Sadler's Wells Theatre in 1850, the play was again extensively adapted to suit the tastes and expectations of a new audience. The tragedy's rapid succession of settings, so abhorrent to Theobald's neo-classicism, appealed greatly to the pictorial enthusiasms of the Victorian stage; audiences at 'the Wells' were treated to an opening image of 'a bridge in Malfi, with gardens beyond', the first of many such vistas.[26] The spectacle of such productions appealed to the dominant tastes of the burgeoning Victorian popular theatre. Yet where the Wells had been under its previous manager 'a struggling theatre, patronized by a notorious rabble, producing melodrama, equestrian and aquatic spectacle and pantomine',[27] Phelps's Wells set out to educate and even elevate its 'attentive, loyal and large local audience' by introducing them to lost gems of the early modern English theatrical repertoire.[28]

To help Phelps achieve this aim, the poet and dramatist R. H. Horne followed in Theobald's footsteps to offer a modernized *Malfi*. In the age of the realist novel and of well-defined stage archetypes, the play's key problem was not lack of unities, but erratic characterization. Horne declared that 'if this great tragedy was to be exhumed from its comparative obscurity, by representation on the stage, all the characters must be made consistent with themselves, and all the events proper to them [...] must be made coherent'.[29] In particular, Horne worked hard to clarify the notoriously mixed motivations of Daniel de Bosola, transforming the complicated starring role of Lowin and Betterton into a more straightforward villain. Webster's notoriously nameless Duchess became the virtuous Marina, her new soubriquet recalling the luminous heroine of Shakespeare's *Pericles* (also revived by Phelps). A repentant Ferdinand died with her name on his lips: 'Marina calls!' Taken up by a number of touring companies, this more 'coherent' version of Webster's tragedy held stages in Britain, Australia and North America for over 20 years.[30]

Once a plum role for the boy actresses of the King's Men, the Duchess now decisively took her place as one of the classical repertoire's finest women's parts. Isabella Glyn, whose 'gay, loving, and self-willed' Duchess gained 'grandeur' from her sufferings, first essayed the role in Phelps's production; she continued to perform it as a 'star vehicle' in London and the provinces for 20 years.[31] By 1859, her death was celebrated as 'a scene of elevated martyrdom'.[32] Glyn having proved its stage-worthiness, other actresses took up the role, notable among them Emma Waller, who first played the role in Australia in 1855 and went on to play it for two decades across the United States.[33] In their productions, Ferdinand emerged into joint prominence with his sister. Phelps, who was Glyn's first Ferdinand, was praised by one critic for his 'almost frantic emotions, not so much exploding as giving the appearance of a vain endeavour to suppress them'.[34] Another fêted Henry Marston for the clarity of 'the moment of the accession of madness' as his Ferdinand fell apart after the Duchess's death.[35]

Such a performance style, designed to highlight key emotional 'points', joined with scenic spectacle to bring Webster's play in line with the most popular of Victorian theatrical forms, melodrama. In keeping with the Gothic tropes often deployed by this genre, the Duchess's ghost became a fixture in stagings of the fifth act; one reviewer of an 1855 revival of Phelps's production explicitly compared the effect of her appearance to those common in Romantic melodrama, commenting that 'Miss Glyn [...] glides away as the ghost of herself in a style worthy of the *Corsican Brothers*'.[36] In a number of American stagings, the Duchess appeared reunited with Antonio in the heavens above the stage at the play's end as Ferdinand grovelled on the boards below, spectacularizing the conflict between good and evil in quintessential melodramatic fashion.[37]

Reviewing Phelps's 1850 production, G. H. Lewes identified such effects with the lowest of low culture. For him, such 'terrific *melodrame*' served only to 'delight the pit'.[38] At the end of the nineteenth century, the great theatre critic William Archer followed Lewes's lead in his article,

'Webster, Lamb, and Swinburne'. This hugely influential diatribe was inspired by William Poel's 1893 Independent Theatre Society production of *The Duchess of Malfi*, which aimed to restore much of Webster's original text. Archer's response damned the deficiencies of early modern theatrical taste and Webster's personal predilection for violence via references to the popular culture of the Victorian age. He declared 'that Webster was not, in the special sense of the word, a great dramatist, but was a great poet who wrote haphazard dramatic or *melodramatic* romances for an eagerly receptive but semi-*barbarous* public'.[39] In the same vein, Archer's friend Shaw famously dubbed Webster 'the Tussaud laureate'.[40] *The Duchess of Malfi* is doubly damned by such formulations: an example of early modern barbarity, it is also closely allied to crass modern entertainment. The 'higher' educational aims of both Phelps's and Poel's productions are nowhere in sight.

Poel struck back against Archer precisely on these grounds. He charged the critic with 'imperfect historical knowledge', arguing that Archer had unfairly maligned Webster's age by ignorantly applying to it the criteria of his own.[41] Webster's horrors, insists Poel, are not gratuitous but rather intended 'to give vital embodiment to the manners and morals of the Italian Renaissance, as they appeared to the imagination of Englishmen';[42] 'to see dramatic propriety and dramatic power in *The Duchess of Malfi*', he argues, there may be needed both critical and historical imagination'.[43] Poel's own production, which featured costumes influenced by Holbein and a quasi-Renaissance 'Dance of Death' for the masque of the madmen, strove to demonstrate just such imagination.[44] To stage and to understand *The Duchess of Malfi* was not to sink into the popular mire, but to evince the high culture of the well-educated modern subject.

This debate around *The Duchess of Malfi*'s cultural impact in performance was still alive when the Phoenix Society staged the play at London's Lyric Theatre in 1919 with Cathleen Nesbitt as the Duchess and Edith Evans as Julia. The critic A. E. Filmer commented approvingly on the edifying value of such revivals, calling it '[a] fine work, surely, to stage plays by Webster and Congreve and Dryden. If only for the sake of the English language, the old plays should be heard again and again'.[45] T. S. Eliot was less convinced of the production's high cultural credentials. In his view, the actors dragged Webster's Jacobean tragedy too far into the commercial sphere of the West End. Instead of simply 'transmit[ting] the lines', he complained, they interpreted them in a style more suitable to popular modern drama. Nesbitt played 'not the Duchess, but something like the respondent in a drama of divorce'.[46] The flirtatious scene between Julia and the Cardinal 'closely resembled a modern social comedy'.[47] 'We do not conclude', concluded Eliot disapprovingly, 'that any service has been done to *Art* by such performance'.[48] The moment for Webster's play to achieve high culture status on the modern stage had not yet come.

The Duchess Restored?

Arguably, that moment arrived in April 1945 when George Rylands directed *The Duchess of Malfi* at London's Haymarket Theatre. In Rylands's watershed production, Webster's tragedy attained a notable success onstage in a textual form closely resembling the first quarto edition for the first time since the seventeenth century. In the dying days of the Second World War, moreover, the play's horrors seemed far more prescient than they had to Archer and Shaw. *The Times*' review of the production appeared immediately under searing photographs from the Nazi death camps at Nordhausen and Buchenwald.[49] Edmund Wilson later recalled the particular power of the Duchess's torture and death scenes 'at the moment of the exposé of the German Concentration camps'. Wilson mentions Rylands's *Duchess of Malfi* alongside a production of *Richard III* in which he also found the authentic 'emotion of wartime'; at this moment, *The Duchess of Malfi* suddenly took on something of the profundity and timelessness more usually associated in this era with Shakespeare himself.[50]

The three leading performances in Rylands's production all received considerable critical applause. Peggy Ashcroft's highly feminine Duchess was girlishly playful with Antonio but dignified and composed in the face of her brothers' tortures. Cecil Trouncer's imposing and intelligent Bosola, cynical but conscience-ridden, returned the role to the prominence it had enjoyed under Lowin and Betterton. Perhaps most influential, however, was John Gielgud's Ferdinand. In one sense, Gielgud's performance stood firmly in the melodramatic tradition; James Agate complained that Gielgud tore the Duke's 'passion to tatters as though on Leontes' rage he were piling Othello's frenzy'.[51] But where Victorian actors had generally stressed Ferdinand's madness, Gielgud centred his interpretation upon the notion of the Duke's erotic obsession with his sister. This choice checked complaints about the character's muddy motivation, explaining Ferdinand's sadism for a post-Freudian age as a by-product of his jealous and inadmissible desire.

Following Poel's dicta, Rylands set the play firmly in the Italian Renaissance, using clothing and jewellery minutely to delineate the social positions of the characters as they fluctuated throughout the play.[52] The design of his production assured the audience that they were peering into an older and more exotic world than their own and that the bizarre events of the play could be explained according to the assumptions of this past culture. At the same time, it invited spectators to glimpse in this older world a mirror image of the depravities and horrors of their own time. Playing to primarily bourgeois audiences in the West End of a London still suffering under wartime deprivation, it offered some of the exclusivity of class and space associated with 'high' culture. Above all, however, it achieved 'high' culture status by striving to enlighten its spectators, offering them both a window on the Renaissance past and a mirror in which to view more clearly the psychic agonies of the tortured present.

Just as Phelps's production in 1850 had begun a decades-long performance tradition, so Rylands's combination of Renaissance setting and Stanislavskian psychologically realist acting established an approach to *The Duchess of Malfi* that would dominate leading English-speaking stages for half a century. Between 1960 and 1995, at least six major productions built upon this approach. They included Donald McWhinnie's version of the play at the Royal Shakespeare Company in 1960; Jean Gascon's staging for the Stratford Festival, Ontario, in 1971; Clifford Williams's production for the Royal Shakespeare Company in the same year; the 1980 production at the Royal Exchange, Manchester, directed by Adrian Noble; Bill Alexander's Royal Shakespeare Company staging of 1989; and Philip Franks's interpretation of 1995, which began life at Greenwich Theatre and transferred to Wyndham's Theatre, London. The design of most of these productions featured stylized Renaissance elements. In McWhinnie's, for instance, gigantic set pieces (a curtained bed for the Duchess, a throne for the Cardinal) suggested the public status and inner desires of the leading figures. On the bare thrust stage of the Festival Theatre, Gascon's Stratford Festival production used costumes to symbolize both power and violence: 'To one critic the courtiers' sumptuous robes looked like crusted blood; at the other end of the social spectrum, Bosola's initial costume looked as if it had been eaten away by corrosive acid'.[53] Such visual elements drew the very picture of a corrupt Italian Renaissance that Poel had stressed in his apologia for the play.

Each of these productions also strove in good realist fashion to render Webster's characters comprehensible and humanly sympathetic to their modern spectators. Bosola tended to appear, not as the simple villain of the Victorian stage, but as a blunt and desperate ex-soldier who struggled adequately to react to the mounting insanity around him. In 1960, Patrick Wymark played him as 'a man who has been driven to brutality. Circumstances have made him what he is; he starts as a boorish ruffian and ends with our sympathy'.[54] In 1980, similarly, Bob Hoskins portrayed a 'soldier of fortune driven to villainy by his trade'.[55] Such Bosolas clashed reluctantly with, and were ultimately transformed by, thoroughly likeable Duchesses increasingly imbued with the spirit of second-wave feminism. Critics praised Judi Dench, Williams's Duchess in 1971, for her 'beautiful loving directness', her 'gentle laughter and warm passionate love'.[56] At the Stratford Festival, Galloway played an aristocrat of 'diamond-cool distinction'[57], but 'not without human pride, wilfulness, lust, and a sense of humour'.[58] In 1980, Mirren was a sensualist, 'playful, lascivious, and vain'[59], noisily slurping up Bosola's apricots; but her Duchess discovered 'at the cruel end a dignity in adversity'.[60] In Franks's production, Stevenson's Duchess was 'much more human than princely: playful, un-aloof and knowing in the opening acts, falling into a grim but far from heroic recognition of her fate at the end'.[61]

As these descriptions suggest, the realist acting approach established by Rylands's production ended by nudging *The Duchess of Malfi* away from the rigid class hierarchy associated with my first definition of high culture. Hence, we find Bill Alexander remarking of Harriet Walter's Duchess in his production that '[i]n many ways the Duchess is an ordinary woman and that is precisely her problem [...] She is like an aristocrat, a leader, of whom much is expected but who essentially is a very motherly, housely, wifely sort of person'.[62] To match this construction of the Duchess, these productions consistently represented Antonio as a thoroughly kind and loving, if fundamentally rather ordinary, person; '[h]e is never a heroic figure, sometimes the reverse; he is merely a decent man', wrote Emrys Jones of Mick Ford's Antonio in 1989.[63] Even Ferdinand figured in this levelling as Gielgud's desire-haunted Duke became the norm. In the Stratford Ontario version, remarks Lois Potter, 'Ferdinand seems hardly to have kept his hands off the Duchess in their scenes together'.[64] In 1995, Simon Russell Beale as Ferdinand began uncontrollably to grope his sister as they stood in the dark together in Act IV, Scene One; her disgusted rejection of his fumbling advances prompted him to pass her the dead man's hand.[65] Frank Whigham has argued that the Duke's obsession with his sister's purity would have appeared to early modern audiences 'a desperate expression of the desire to evade degrading contamination by inferiors',[66] but in these versions it spoke more closely to mass-market twentieth-century conceptions of sexual neurosis. *The Duchess of Malfi*'s mixture of high and low was still visible, albeit in a new form.

Nevertheless, the main thrust of this period's dominant reading of Webster's tragedy was a move away from forms and styles perceived as base, common and popular. To say that a production 'concentrated on emotional realism in acting, and [...] carefully avoided any hint of melodrama' became a high compliment.[67] To say, conversely, that audience members tittered in the mass slaughter of the final scene was an insult;[68] death is a serious business in high culture spectacle. The detailed Renaissance costumes and sets married with the Stanislavskian performance style of this tradition assured audiences that they were watching not a mere 'morbid tragedy' full of 'crowd-pleasing schlock moments',[69] but rather a piece of cultural heritage that both reflected the glories of the past and offered timeless insights into human nature. Some critics retained their doubts: Williams's production, opined Milton Shulman, would 'please those audiences who are not overawed by its classical pretensions and don't take it too seriously'.[70] Even so, *The Duchess of Malfi* edged closer to high cultural prestige in this period than ever before.

Alternative Duchesses: Brechtian and Baroque

At the same time, two counter-traditions strove to combat the dominant twentieth-century interpretation of Webster's play. The first interpreted the tragedy as an anti-naturalistic work of social and moral criticism: a critique, rather than an affirmation, of high cultural class and aesthetic norms. Bertolt Brecht, who spent a number of years in the late thirties and early forties working alongside the poet W. H. Auden on an adaptation of the play for the actress Elisabeth Bergner, was the progenitor of this approach. Like other theatre artists of his time, Brecht stressed the specifically Renaissance nature of the play, but his adaptation emphasized the class-based economic determinants of the action. In Brecht and Auden's version, *The Duchess of Malfi* depicted 'a family caught in a historical dialectic between old notions of aristocratic image and a new individualism associated with the bourgeois period of history'.[71] Brecht strove to make of *The Duchess of Malfi* a popular play in a Marxist sense by speaking to 'the people' of the socio-economic processes that could lead to their liberation.

Brecht and Auden's innovations largely sank from view when Elisabeth Bergner, impressed by the success of George Rylands's London production, invited him to direct her in *The Duchess of Malfi* in New York in 1946. Rylands was 'appalled by the hash, as he saw it, that Brecht and Auden had made of the play' and excised most of their adaptations.[72] Brecht, in his turn, was revolted by Rylands's 'pernicious practice of stressing the "eternally human" element' at the expense of the socio-economic specificity of the characters and their actions.[73] Most critics ascribed the subsequent failure of the production to Brecht's and Auden's tinkering and to weak acting, particularly by Canada Lee as Bosola.[74] But these criticisms are themselves susceptible of Brechtian analysis. Lee was one of the first African-American actors to achieve success in the 'legitimate' theatre on Broadway and, as Bosola, one of the first black actors to play a white character in whiteface on the 'Great White Way'.[75] When Mary McCarthy complained that 'the character of Bosola is brutalized by Canada Lee's acting' and that Webster's Bosola is a complex human being, 'not a nature-devil',[76] her rhetoric had unmistakable racist implications and re-inscribed unquestioned realist assumptions about character. The complex spectacle of an African-American actor taking on the role of a 'devilish' early modern galley slave in a manner that stressed the socially constructed nature of the villain's part might have worked brilliantly in a genuinely Brechtian production to question both popular stereotypes and high cultural assumptions about the timelessness of Renaissance drama.

The late 1960s and early 1970s saw a cluster of relatively small-scale productions that utilized Brecht's *verfremdungseffekt* less to encourage critical thinking about economics and ideology than to defy the dominance of realist acting. Brian Shelton at Scotland's Pitlochry Festival (1967), the Freehold Company at the Young Vic, London (1970), and Peter Gill at the Royal Court, London (1971) all explored a performance style that distanced the audience from Webster's characters rather than encouraged identification. Shelton retained the Renaissance costumes of the dominant contemporary tradition but emphasized the formality and meta-theatricality of *The Duchess* instead of its psychological intimacy. Freehold eliminated vast swathes of the playtext's rhetoric in favour of an intensely expressionistic physical theatre approach that aimed to conjure the seething corruption and violence of Webster's court. Gill's scenography featured only an array of broken down doors 'for men to take their exits' (*Duchess* 4.2.212), a number of kitchen chairs and a bare plywood table. Alongside the main actors, who wore simplified Renaissance dress, a chorus of eight performers in loose yellow pyjamas took on a range of subsidiary roles and lurked onstage to observe the action. The Royal Court in this period was known for offering counter-cultural, highly experimental 'people's theatre'; a mere two years after Gill's production it staged the world premiere of the soon-to-be cult classic *Rocky Horror Picture Show*.[77] By abandoning the emotional realism that had proved so well able to assert Webster's high culture credentials, Gill's production came in for harsh criticism. Because it represented 'Webster's nightmare [...] coolly and without involvement', objected Irving Wardle, 'the passions and carnage [...] appear as lifeless and absurd as a series of waxwork *tableaux*'.[78] The spectre of the 'Tussaud laureate' had returned.

The second alternative approach to *The Duchess of Malfi* also reminded critics of Shaw's critique. Where the dominant 'Renaissance realist' interpretation of the tragedy strove to tone down the play's grotesquerie and to emphasize its humanity, this more baroque tradition brought the macabre centre stage. Perhaps the most controversial essays in the baroque style were those of Scottish director Philip Prowse, who directed *The Duchess of Malfi* three times: at the Glasgow Citizens Theatre in 1975 and 1978 and at the Lyttleton, Royal National Theatre, in 1985. Prowse was palpably inspired by T. S. Eliot's declaration that 'Webster was much possessed by death, / And saw the skull beneath the skin'.[79] The figure of Death, bearing a huge scythe, haunted the stage throughout the action of his National Theatre production. 'Everyone wears costumes, not clothes, mostly black and monstrous in size', remarked John Barber.[80] Dependent upon the large budgets associated with the elite National Theatre, Prowse's baroque extravaganzas could be read as high cultural spectacles; but most critics identified them instead with the despised excesses of a dated popular tradition. Reviewing the Lyttleton production, Barber frowned that the final image of the Duchess's ghost 'parading in a see-through nightie [...] provides a tasteless conclusion to a bloody melodrama'.[81] For Barber as for numerous other critics, Prowse's pretentious interpretation only succeeded in robbing the play of its hard-won high culture credibility and returning it to Victorian vulgarity.[82]

Despite such dismissals, the baroque reading survived into the new millennium to dominate Peter Hinton's staging of *The Duchess of Malfi* for Ontario's Stratford Festival in 2006. All of the costumes in this 'punk/goth' interpretation layered black upon black; many of them, like the Duchess's initial mourning costume of 'a stylized farthingale, a black veil that obscured her face, and an enormous, canoe-shaped black hat that sat crosswise on her head', were larger-than-life.[83] Spectators entered the Tom Patterson Theatre to be greeted by the haunting figure of Joyce Campion's Old Lady, her skull-like face 'absolutely ravaged by time'.[84] Kim Solga describes how Campion constantly appeared and disappeared on the sidelines of this highly stylized production: a 'living memento mori' in a death-obsessed world.[85] The other actors' performances were characterized by classical hauteur tinged with melancholy. Solga identifies the murders of the Duchess and Cariola as the only fully naturalistic moments in the production; in the baroque interpretation of Webster, death is the only absolute reality.

The Brechtian and baroque traditions in the modern performance history of *The Duchess of Malfi* came together in the Apricot Theatre Company's production of 2004. Apricot's *Duchess* was 'built around a textbook display of the Brechtian alienation effect, with the audience constantly reminded that it was watching a performance'.[86] As Thomas Larque describes the production,

> [t]he cast were made-up throughout with clownish white face-paint, broken only by black smears for eyebrows and mouths. Individual roles were both shared and doubled, with two female

> actors alternating the roles of the Duchess and the Cardinal, and one male and one female actor alternating the roles of Duke Ferdinand and Bosola. Each character was identified by a particular set of garments – a wrap-around skirt, or coat and hat – that was passed in full view of the audience from one actor to another as the actors changed roles.[87]

This *Duchess* was a literal bloodbath complete with prop buckets of stage blood, as if to satirize both human violence and human delight in the representation thereof. It overtly mocked the dominant reading of the Duchess's heroic though vulnerable femininity by replacing a live actress in her death scene with 'a traditional child's doll, its serene emotionless face, frozen in conventional prettiness, emphasising the Duchess's performance in death of the feminine passivity and self-sacrifice demanded of her by her society'.[88] Eschewing historical contextualization and realist characterization, Apricot read *The Duchess of Malfi* through the 'low' cultural idioms of black farce and Victorian Music Hall, re-asserting in the process the vibrancy of the popular aesthetic its immediate forebears had so often eschewed.

'The Tarantino of Jacobean Melodrama'

Apricot Theatre's experiment took place within the context of a small-scale touring production, its defiance of the high cultural interpretation of *The Duchess of Malfi* reaching relatively few audience members. By the time it appeared, however, another approach to *The Duchess of Malfi* had emerged that would speak to a broader audience and prove far more pivotal to the play's performance history. The key influence on this approach was Hollywood filmmaker Quentin Tarantino, whose gangster dramas *Reservoir Dogs* (1992) and *Pulp Fiction* (1994) took cinematic audiences by storm in the early nineties. Tarantino's plots featured criminal scheming, betrayals and counter-betrayals, sexual shenanigans, torture and occasional lashings of potent religious rhetoric. His signature style, often itself compared to that of Jacobean tragedy,[89] was blackly comic, exceedingly bloody and richly allusive to contemporary popular culture. From 1995 onwards, a Tarantino-esque approach, featuring twentieth- or twenty-first-century dress and prominent references to mainstream cinema, began to dominate stage revivals of *The Duchess of Malfi*.

The twentieth century had seen modern-dress, cinematic *Duchesses* before. As far back as 1957, Jack Landau had mounted the play at the Phoenix Theatre in New York in costumes that 'mixed Austro-Hungarian officers' uniforms, Edwardian evening dress, and

Mussolini-style blackshirts'.[90] As if to stress its kinship with Cold War era films noirs, Landau dubbed the play an 'Elizabethan [*sic*] thriller' in publicity materials. Decades later, Red Shift Theatre Company achieved considerable success with a touring production which set *The Duchess of Malfi* in 'the Italy of high finance, corruption and style created as an image in the cinematic styles of film noir and neo-realism and popularised by the success of the "Godfather" films'.[91]

Despite such antecedents, the 'modern cinematic' reading of *The Duchess of Malfi* definitively replaced the 'Renaissance realist' interpretation as the dominant one on the major stages of England and North America only in the 1990s. This important shift in the play's performance history was signaled by the appearance of Declan Donnellan's touring Cheek By Jowl production on the stage of Wyndham's Theatre in London mere months after it had been vacated by Philip Franks's transfer from Greenwich. Where Franks's *Duchess* had featured Renaissance dress, Donnellan and his partner Nick Ormerod set the play in a proto-fascist royal court in the early twentieth century. The production was rife with cinematic references: Anastasia Hille's chain-smoking, platinum blonde Duchess was likened by critics to a range of screen icons from Greta Garbo to Bette Davis, and George Anton's Bosola appeared to murder the Duchess in makeup reminiscent of *Cabaret*'s MC.[92]

Donnellan and his company slashed at the very foundations of the established twentieth-century approach to *The Duchess of Malfi*. Their production was sexually explicit: the Cardinal took Julia sadistically from behind in their first encounter and she in turn sodomized Bosola with her pistol in the final act. Even more controversially, Hille and Donnellan replaced the tender, sensual and motherly Duchess of tradition with a witty, glamorous and brittle alternative. *New York Times* critic Ben Brantley described her in terms usually reserved for Ferdinand as 'an emotional cripple warped by regal arrogance and torn by sexual urges she can never fully understand'.[93] 'This Duchess is not some virtuous alien from outer space, but a chip off the same block as her brothers', remarked Benedict Nightingale admiringly.[94] Where most Duchesses have cowered before Ferdinand's armed invasion of their bedchambers in Act III, Hille responded by slapping Ferdinand across the face, grabbing his dagger, menacing him with it, and then laughingly pouring herself a whiskey. Feminine vulnerability was displaced onto her twin brother Ferdinand, played by a boyish Scott Handy as the 'unruly kid brother'[95] of the family. Even the Duchess's 'low-rated love' for Antonio came in for revisionist treatment. Matthew Macfadyen's Malvolio-like steward was a 'degraded and cowardly opportunist' whose apparent primness was exposed as hypocrisy when he lunged for a half-naked Duchess with undisguised lust at the height of their courtship scene.[96] The union degenerated into unseemly squabbling long before it was decisively destroyed by Ferdinand's machinations. Although many reviewers were shocked by what they perceived as the production's neglect of Webster's intentions,[97] Brantley concluded that it had achieved 'something very rare: the rethinking of a well-known classic in a manner that will never let you look at it in the same way again'.[98]

As if to support this assertion, Gale Edwards's 2000 staging for the Royal Shakespeare Company, Phyllida Lloyd's 2003 version for the Royal National Theatre, Colin McColl's production for Auckland Theatre Company in 2005, Michael Halberstam's staging for Chicago's Writers' Theatre in 2006 and Philip Franks's exploration of the play for the West Yorkshire Playhouse in the same year all offered some variation on the 'modern cinematic' *Duchess of Malfi*. Each of them featured some version of twentieth-century dress. Each of them embraced, rather than toned down, the play's black humour and bloody violence. Most of them were sexually explicit, many mirroring Donnellan's decision to show the Cardinal and Julia copulating (preferably under a large crucifix). The name of Quentin Tarantino can be found in one or more reviews of most of these productions.[99] One review of Edwards's *Duchess* is memorably headlined 'The Tarantino of Jacobean Melodrama Goes to the Dogs',[100] its allusions to postmodern and Victorian forms immediately suggesting *The Duchess of Malfi*'s return from the restrained realms of high culture to a more popular theatrical arena.

In this new tradition, productions and critics often viewed the play through the lens of modern celebrity culture. The programme of Lloyd's production featured a photograph of Diana, Princess of Wales; the implied comparison between Webster's doomed heroine and the flawed but adored 'People's Princess' suited the period's dominant approach to the Duchess. In Lloyd's production, the statuesque Janet McTeer was 'a bold, striking, naturally impulsive duchess'[101] who tickled and giggled with her children on the floor of her bedchamber. Sophia Hawthorne, McColl's Duchess, was praised as 'beautiful, courageous, sexually bold'.[102] Imogen Stubbs was a 'glamorous Duchess' for Franks in 2006. Kevin Berry complimented her for bringing 'colour, passion and humanity to the part' while also giving 'glimpses of arrogance and violence'; he concluded that 'given the lady's family genes, she cannot be all shining light'.[103] Stubbs's Lana Turner-esque New Look costumes linked her to the *femmes fatales* of film noir: smart, tough and sexually independent, but dangerous to themselves and to others.

The cinematization of *The Duchess of Malfi* facilitated new approaches to other major characters, too. In Lloyd's *Duchess of Malfi*, Will Keen's 'pill-popping, wild-eyed' Ferdinand paced the stage in a slick black suit, barking at his hangers-on through a microphone.[104] Small, twitchy and frenetic, he strongly recalled Joe Pesci's volcanic mobsters in Scorsese's *Goodfellas* and *Casino*; drug abuse and mental illness served to explain his erratic behaviour in the twenty-first century rather as imbalances of choler and black bile might have done in the seventeenth. In Leeds in 2006, Sebastian Harcombe's critically acclaimed performance as Bosola engaged with cinematic tropes of the self-loathing gunman; his assassin was 'a brooding, film-noirish figure in a mac'.[105] The Victorian popular theatre had shifted Bosola's repentance to the more Romantic figure of the mad Ferdinand; now, the recollection of modern popular cinema tropes allowed Harcombe to portray the remorse of an 'outcast who discovers himself too late'.[106]

Where Renaissance-dress *Duchess*es had strived to give Webster's play the credibility more often associated with Shakespeare, these *mises-en-scène* aspired instead to give it the immediacy of cinema. Edwards's production boasted incidental music that reminded at least one critic of a film soundtrack.[107] In Lloyd's version, a reel of film took the place of the masque of the madmen; its disturbing images included shots of a suggestively leering Ferdinand, a dead Antonio, a bleeding child, the Duchess's mouth greedily consuming apricots and an array of glinting razors and knives. Lloyd cut Webster's text mercilessly to ensure that her production ran at two hours and twenty minutes with no interval. In Chicago in 2006, Michael Halberstam cut and adapted the work even further to achieve a 'pithy and compact' length of two hours and ten minutes: the approximate duration of many a contemporary movie. [108]

The Duchess of Malfi's only major appearance in a recent motion picture reinforces the dominant contemporary interpretation of the play. In Mike Figgis's 2001 film *Hotel*, a motley film crew led by arrogant director Trent Stoken (Rhys Ifans) struggle to make *Malfi*, a movie based upon Webster's tragedy. John Charley (Heathcote Williams), who plays Bosola in the film-within-a-film, is the main adaptor of the text; he tells one of his younger colleagues wearily that changes have been made 'in order to try and create a fast food McMalfi, as it were, that would be very easily digestible and accessible even to aspiring Hollywood stars'. Stoken, meanwhile, sharply repudiates both the period dress and the restrained realist acting associated with 'heritage' films and high culture versions of *The Duchess of Malfi*. He mocks one rehearsal by the actors playing the Duchess (Saffron Burrows) and Antonio (Max Beesley), cooing,

> I love the Merchant Ivory version you're doing at the moment. Sweet, pungent smell of rose meadows, Earl Grey, and a wet saddle on the back of a horse. That sort of thing. [*Barking*] It's fucking shit!

His own cinematic vision features glamorous, 'punk/goth' contemporary dress. It mixes graphically enacted sex and violence with overt artifice. The Duchess forcefully sodomizes Antonio until she is interrupted by labour pangs and gives birth to a plastic baby. Later, Ferdinand (Mark Strong) shows the Duchess Antonio's naked and obscenely tumescent body lying beside two blood-spattered kewpie dolls.

Like so many versions of *The Duchess of Malfi* before it, *Hotel* balances between high and low registers. It echoes recent theatrical versions of the play by serving up a gleefully iconoclastic take on early modern tragedy: pure low culture according to my second definition of the term. Pascale Aebischer convincingly reads it as 'oppos[ing] heritage with disinheritance [...] and nostalgia with a relish for seeing the Jacobean "classic" as something that is alien enough to be new'.[109] At the same time, as Gordon McMullan notes, it risks re-inscription of high cultural canons of taste by allowing hostile spectators, Archer-like, simply to dismiss Jacobean revenge tragedy as 'a degraded, unhealthy successor to the vigorous splendours of Shakespeare'.[110] Moreover, much of *Hotel*'s international cinematic release occurred at elite film festivals and not on the screens of popular multiplexes.[111] So, too, the millennial theatrical productions that viewed *The Duchess of Malfi* through a Tarantino-esque lens engaged low cultural vocabularies from within established high cultural theatrical institutions. Just as Webster's heroine is 'Duchess of Malfi still' (4.2.137), simultaneously rupturing and reaffirming social hierarchies, even so contemporary performances of Webster's tragedy follow their historical progenitors in simultaneously engaging high cultural norms and defying them in favour of more popular idioms. Constantly shifting to suit new ages and tastes, *The Duchess of Malfi* in performance remains a work in which high and low engage in an endless–and an endlessly beguiling–negotiation.

Notes

1. See, for example, John Russell Brown, Introduction, *The Duchess of Malfi* by John Webster (London: Revels Plays, 1964), pp. xxii–xxiv, and R. B. Graves, '*The Duchess of Malfi* at the Globe and Blackfriars', *Renaissance Drama*, 9 (1978), 193–209.
2. For the historical complexity and slipperiness of these terms, particularly of 'popular culture', see John Storey, *Cultural Theory and Popular Culture*, 3rd edn (Harlow: Prentice Hall, 2001), pp. 5–15.
3. See Andrew Gurr, *Playgoing in Shakespeare's London*, 3rd edn (Cambridge: Cambridge University Press, 2004), p. 69 *passim*.
4. Walter Benjamin plays upon this definition of 'high' culture when he contrasts the aura of artwork accessible only to elite viewers with the altered affect created by mass production. See 'The Work of Art in the Age of Mechanical Reproduction', *Illuminations*, trans. by Hannah Arendt (New York: Harcourt Brace, 1968), pp. 217–52.

5. Hence, in *Keywords: A Vocabulary of Culture and Society* (1976; New York: Oxford University Press, 1985), Raymond Williams notes that despite shifts in meaning the term 'popular culture' 'still carries two older senses: inferior kinds of work [...]; and work deliberately setting out to win favour' (p. 237).
6. John Webster, *The Duchess of Malfi*, ed. by Leah S. Marcus (London: Methuen, 2009): 1.1.37–8. All subsequent references to *The Duchess of Malfi* will be to this edition and will appear in parentheses in the text of the essay.
7. William Rowley, 'To his Friend Mr. *John Webster* Upon his Dutchesse of *Malfy*', in John Webster, *The Tragedy of the Dutchesse of Malfy* (London, 1623), A4v.
8. John Webster, *The Tragedy of the Dutchesse of Malfy* (London, 1623), A2v.
9. See David Carnegie, 'Theatrical Introduction to *The Duchess of Malfi*', in *The Works of John Webster*, ed. by David Gunby, David Carnegie and Antony Hammond, 3 vols (Cambridge: Cambridge University Press, 1995), I, 423–5 and 443, n. 26.
10. See David Grote, *The Best Actors in the World: Shakespeare and His Acting Company* (Westport and London: Greenwood Press, 2002), pp. 192–3, for a discussion of Lowin's known roles.
11. For the eulogy to 'Dick' Robinson's skills of female impersonation, see Ben Jonson, *The diuell is an asse: a comedie acted in the yeare, 1616, by His Maiesties seruants* (London, 1631), R3r.
12. For Robinson and Sharp, see David Kathman, 'How Old Were Shakespeare's Boy Actresses?', *Shakespeare Survey*, 58 (2005), 220–46 (pp. 232–3). For the theory that Robinson played the Duchess in the original production, see Brown, ed., *The Duchess of Malfi*, pp. xx–xxi.
13. Thomas Middleton, 'In the just Worth, of that well Deserver, Mr. JOHN WEBSTER, *and Upon this* Maister-peece of Tragoedy', in Webster, *The Tragedy of the Dutchesse of Malfy* (London, 1623), A4r.
14. Carnegie, p. 417.
15. This translation from Busino's *Anglopotida* of 17 February 1618 appears in G. K. and S. K. Hunter, eds, *John Webster: A Critical Anthology* (Harmondsworth: Penguin Books, 1969), pp. 31–2. The passage is cited in its original Italian in E. K. Chambers, *The Elizabethan Stage*, 4 vols (Oxford: Clarendon Press, 1923), III, 511.
16. Busino in Hunter and Hunter, eds, p. 32.
17. For the performance at the Cockpit, see G. E. Bentley, *The Jacobean and Caroline Stage*, 7 vols (Oxford: Clarendon Press, 1941), I, 27–8.
18. John Downes, *Roscius Anglicanus (1708)*, ed. by Montague Summers (London: Fortune Press, 1928), p. 25.
19. See Kathleen McLuskie and Jennifer Uglow, *Plays in Performance: The Duchess of Malfi* (Bristol: Bristol Classical Press, 1989), pp. 12–17, for a superb analysis of the play's fortunes on the Restoration and early eighteenth-century stage.
20. Samuel Pepys, *The Diary of Samuel Pepys*, ed. by Robert Latham and William Matthews, 11 vols (Berkeley: University of California Press, 1970), III, 209.
21. Samuel Pepys, *The Diary of Samuel Pepys*, ed. by Robert Latham and William Matthews, 11 vols (Berkeley: University of California Press, 1976), IX, p. 375.
22. Carnegie, 'Theatrical Introduction', p. 429.
23. Lewis Theobald, *The Fatal Secret. A Tragedy. As it is acted at the Theatre-Royal, in Covent-Garden* (London, 1735), p. viii.
24. Theobald, p. viii.
25. Theobald, pp. vi–vii.
26. McLuskie and Uglow, p. 28, offer a detailed discussion of the celebrated scenic and lighting effects in Phelps's production.

27. McLuskie and Uglow, p. 27.
28. McLuskie and Uglow, p. 25.
29. R. H. Horne, 'Preface to his edition of *The Duchess of Malfi, Reconstructed for Stage Representation*, 1850', in Hunter and Hunter, eds, p. 59.
30. For detailed discussions of these nineteenth-century productions of *The Duchess of Malfi*, see F. W. Wadsworth, 'Some Nineteenth-Century Revivals of *The Duchess of Malfi*', *Theatre Survey*, 8.2 (1967), 67–83; '"Shorn and Abated": British Performances of *The Duchess of Malfi*', *Theatre Survey*, 10.2 (1969), 89–104; and '"Webster, Horne and Mrs. Stowe": American Performances of *The Duchess of Malfi*', *Theatre Survey*, 11.2 (1970), 151–66.
31. Rev. of *The Duchess of Malfi* at Sadler's Wells, *The Times*, 21 November 1850.
32. Cited in McLuskie and Uglow, p. 30.
33. See Wadsworth, 'Some Nineteenth Century Revivals'.
34. Cited in McLuskie and Uglow, p. 28.
35. Rev. of *The Duchess of Malfi*, The Athenaeum, 31 March 1855.
36. This moment is described in detail in Wadsworth, '"Webster, Horne and Mrs. Stowe"'.
37. See Peter Brooks, *The Melodramatic Imagination: Balzac, Henry James, Melodrama, and the Mode of Excess* (1976; Yale University Press, 1995), p. 36, for the classic analysis of melodrama as a play of 'pure, exteriorized signs' of good and evil.
38. G. H. Lewes, Rev. of *The Duchess of Malfi* at Sadler's Wells, *The Leader*, 30 November 1850.
39. William Archer, 'Webster, Lamb and Swinburne', *New Review*, 8 (January 1893), 96–106, (p. 106); emphasis mine.
40. George Bernard Shaw, *Our Theatre in the Nineties*, 3 vols (London: Constable, 1932), III, 317.
41. William Poel, 'A New Criticism of Webster's *Duchess of Malfi*', *Library Review*, 2 (1893), 21–4 (p. 22).
42. Poel, p. 23.
43. Poel, p. 24.
44. See McLuskie and Uglow, pp. 31–5, for a detailed discussion of Poel's production, which 'pleased virtually no one' (p. 33).
45. A. E. Filmer, 'Sunday Shows', *Drama*, 3–4 (1925–26), p. 3.
46. T. S. Eliot, '"The Duchess of Malfi" at the Lyric, and Poetic Drama', *Art and Letters*, 3.1 (1920), 36–9 (p. 37).
47. Eliot, p. 38.
48. Eliot, p. 39.
49. *The Times*, 19 April 1945.
50. Edmund Wilson, 'Notes on London at the End of the War', in *Europe without Baedecker* (New York: Doubleday, 1947), p. 7.
51. James Agate, 'Words, Words, Words', in *The Contemporary Theatre 1944–45* (London: George G. Harrap and Co., 1946), p. 176.
52. See McLuskie and Uglow, p. 42.
53. Carnegie, p. 436.
54. 'E. G.', 'What will be the Impact on London of "Malfi"?' *Stratford-upon-Avon Herald*, 2 December 1960.
55. Irving Wardle, 'Clearing the Vital Hurdle Boldly', *Times*, 17 September 1980.
56. J. C. Trewin, Rev. of *The Duchess of Malfi*, dir. by Clifford Williams, *Birmingham Post*, 16 July 1971; 'S. E. W.', 'Stratford "Malfi" Ends in Bathos', *The Stage*, 22 July 1971.

57. Herbert Whittaker, 'Splendid Production of The Duchess of Malfi', *Toronto Globe and Mail*, 9 June 1971.
58. Carnegie, p. 437.
59. Herbert Whittaker, 'Splendid Production of The Duchess of Malfi', *Toronto Globe and Mail*, 9 June 1971.
60. Eric Shorter, 'Serious Malfi', *Daily Telegraph*, 17 September 1980.
61. Ian Shuttleworth, Rev. of *The Duchess of Malfi*, dir. by Philip Franks, *Financial Times*, 27 April 1995.
62. In Yumi Sato, '*The Duchess of Malfi* at Stratford' (unpublished MPhil thesis, Shakespeare Institute, University of Birmingham, 1991), pp. 224, 228; emphases Alexander's.
63. Emrys Jones, 'Irregular Passions', *TLS*, 22 December 1989.
64. Lois Potter, 'Realism versus Nightmare: Problems of Staging *The Duchess of Malfi*', *in The Triple Bond: Plays, Mainly Shakespearean, in Performance*, ed. by Joseph G. Price (University Park: Pennsylvania State University Press, 1975), pp. 170–89 (p. 172).
65. These observations are based upon my own viewing of Russell Beale in Philip Franks's production of *The Duchess of Malfi* at Wyndham's Theatre in June 1995.
66. Frank Whigham, *Seizures of the Will in Early Modern English Drama* (Cambridge: Cambridge University Press, 1996), p. 191.
67. Carnegie, p. 440.
68. See, for instance, Charles Lewson, Rev. of *The Duchess of Malfi* dir. by Clifford Williams, *Listener*, 22 July 1971; here, the failure of the production is clinched for the reviewer by the fact that 'the multiple deaths at the end were received with laughs'.
69. Jane Edwardes, '*The Duchess of Malfi*', *Time Out*, 14 December 1989.
70. Milton Shulman, Rev. of *The Duchess of Malfi*, dir. by Clifford Williams, *Evening Standard*, 16 July 1971.
71. McLuskie and Uglow, p. 45.
72. McLuskie and Uglow, p. 43.
73. Bertolt Brecht, 'Attempted Broadway Production of *The Duchess of Malfi*', in *Brecht: Collected Plays 7*, ed. by Ralph Manheim and John Willett (New York: Vintage Books, 1975), p. 425.
74. See Carnegie, p. 434, and McLuskie and Uglow, p. 43.
75. See Mona Z. Smith, *Becoming Someone: The Story of Canada Lee* (New York: Faber and Faber, 2005), pp. 192–227.
76. Mary McCarthy, 'Five Curios', in *Sights and Spectacles, 1937–58* (London: Heinemann, 1959), p. 92.
77. See Philip Roberts, *The Royal Court Theatre and the Modern Stage* (Cambridge: Cambridge University Press, 1999).
78. Irving Wardle, 'An Uninhabited Nightmare', *Times*, 19 January 1971.
79. T. S. Eliot, 'Whispers of Immortality', in *Complete Poems and Plays, 1909–1950* (New York: Harcourt Brace, 1980), p. 32.
80. John Barber, 'Sinister Tricks', *Daily Telegraph*, 8 July 1985.
81. Barber, 'Sinister Tricks'.
82. See Carnegie, pp. 439–40, and McLuskie and Uglow, p. 62, for similarly negative conclusions.
83. Kim Solga, *Violence Against Women in Early Modern Performance: Invisible Acts* (Houndmills: Palgrave Macmillan, 2009), p. 118.
84. Solga, p. 120.
85. Robert Cushman, qtd. in Solga, p. 118.

86. Thomas Larque, Rev. of *The Duchess of Malfi*, dir. by Mark Edel-Hunt, *Early Modern Literary Studies* 11.3 (January 2005). 8 August 2009 <http://extra.shu.ac.uk/emls/11-3/revlarq.htm>, par. 3.
87. Larque, par. 2.
88. Larque, par. 3.
89. See, for example, Mashey Berstein, '"Fiction": A Modern Jacobean Drama', *Los Angeles Times* 23 January 1993. 1 August 2009 <http://articles.latimes.com/1995-01-23/entertainment/ca-23287_1_pulp-fiction>.
90. Carnegie, p. 434.
91. McLuskie and Uglow, p. 59; see Susan Bennett, *Performing Nostalgia: Shifting Shakespeare and the Contemporary Past* (London: Routledge, 1996), pp. 85–6, for another illuminating discussion of this production.
92. See <http://www.cheekbyjowl.com/productions/theduchessofmalfi/ gallery.html> for an image of both actors. Much of the following information about Donnellan's production is taken from a more detailed analysis in Roberta Barker, *Early Modern Tragedy, Gender and Performance, 1984–2000: The Destined Livery* (Basingstoke: Palgrave Macmillan, 2007), pp. 55–82.
93. 'A "Duchess" Returns, Engulfed by Depravity', *New York Times*, 11 December 1995.
94. *The Times*, 24 October 1995.
95. Alastair Macaulay, *Financial Times*, 4 January 1996.
96. Peter J. Smith, 'Two Views of Malfi', *Cahiers Elisabéthains* 49 (April 1996), 77–81 (p. 79).
97. See, for example, John Peter, *Sunday Times*, 7 January 1996.
98. *New York Times*, 11 December 1995.
99. See, for example, Michael Billington, 'The Taming of the Duchess of Malfi', *Guardian* 13 November 2000; Matt Wolf, Rev of *The Duchess of Malfi*, dir. by Phyllida Lloyd, *Variety*, 2 February 2003 <http://www.variety.com/review/ VE1117919854.html?categoryid =33&cs=1>; and Natasha Hay, 'If You Want Blood', Rev. of *The Duchess of Malfi*, dir. by Colin McColl, *New Zealand Listener*, 30 July–4 August 2005. For an extreme example of the Tarantino-ization of *The Duchess of Malfi*, see the following online advertisement for a production by Mob Hit Theatre of Calgary: <http://thisisamobhit.com/ index.php?option=com_content&task=view&id=50> (accessed 5 August 2009).
100. Kate Bassett, *Independent*, 12 November 2000.
101. Michael Billington, Rev. of *The Duchess of Malfi*, dir. by Phyllida Lloyd, *Guardian*, 29 January 2003.
102. Natasha Hay, 'If You Want Blood'.
103. Rev. of *The Duchess of Malfi*, dir. by Philip Franks, *The Stage*, 27 October 2006. 8 August 2009 <http://www.thestage.co.uk/reviews/review.php/ 14687/the-duchess-of-malfi>.
104. Matt Wolf, Rev. of *The Duchess of Malfi*, dir. by Phyllida Lloyd, *Variety*, 2 February 2003. 9 August 2009 <http://www.variety.com/review/VE1117919854.html?categoryid=33&cs=1>.
105. Dominic Cavendish, 'A Marvellous, Malignant Malfi', *Daily Telegraph*, 30 October 2006.
106. Lyn Gardner, Rev. of *The Duchess of Malfi*, dir. by Philip Franks, *Guardian*, 30 October 2006.
107. Lizzie Loveridge, Rev. of *The Duchess of Malfi*, dir. by Gale Edwards, *Curtain Up*, November 2000. 9 August 2009 <http://www.curtainup.com/duchessofmalfi.html>.

108. Jonathan Abarbanel, Rev. of *The Duchess of Malfi*, dir. by Michael Halberstam, *Theatremania*, 25 May 2006. 8 August 2009 <http://www.theatermania.com/new-york/reviews/-05-2006/the-duchess-of-malfi_8325.html>.
109. Pascale Aebischer, 'Shakespearean Heritage and the Preposterous "Contemporary Jacobean" Film: Mike Figgis' *Hotel*', *Shakespeare Quarterly*, 60.3 (2009), 281–305 (pp. 282–3).
110. Gordon McMullan, '"Plenty of Blood. That's the Only Writing": (Mis)Representing Jacobean Tragedy in Turn-of-the-Century Cinema', *La Licorne* 2 (2008), 8 August 2009 <http://edel.univ-poitiers.fr/licorne/document.php?id=4274>.
111. See http://www.imdb.com/title/tt0278487/releaseinfo.

CHAPTER THREE

The State of the Art: Critical Approaches 2000–08

Dymfpna Callaghan

Precisely those qualities that gave rise to critical derision of Webster as a sensationalist earlier in the twentieth century – highly sexualized violence, cruelty, depravity and the misuse of political power – are in the new millennium understood to be Webster's prescient vision of the parlous fragility of love and innocence. There is a kind of postmodern horror about *The Duchess of Malfi* whose hyperbolic violence and macabre spectacle cannot begin to approximate the numbing and terrifying images that now saturate our most intimate domestic spaces. In the age of *Kill Bill*, even the archaic genre of revenge itself serves not so much to feed a nostalgia for primitive score settling, but instead, as Stevie Simkin argues in the New Casebooks *Revenge Tragedy* (2001)[1], to appeal to a longing for a rapid eradication of the bureaucratic impediments to justice. The critical ground has shifted decisively, and on it there is no place for outrage, disdain or charges of decadence. Indeed, such responses have been replaced by an assurance not only that the themes and preoccupations of *Duchess* resonate profoundly with the twenty-first century present, but also that Webster demonstrates an incisive dramaturgical and political vision. This sense of certainty about the play's urgent relevance and ethical core undergirds almost every critical contribution since 2000. Recurrent critical issues continue to include those listed by Simkin, namely, 'sexuality, the complex relations of gender and power, and the relationship between the individual and the state' as well as court corruption and violence (5–6).

Gender and Sexuality

The most crucial force shaping criticism of the play through the eighties and nineties was unquestionably feminism, which, rather than seeing the absence of a male protagonist as constituting nothing short of a fundamental structural flaw, valued Webster's feminocentric vision. Feminist critics tended to see Webster as sympathetic towards women rather than as a misogynist playwright who presented his female characters like daughters of Eve who got what they deserved. Arguing that *The Duchess of Malfi* posed a challenge for feminist and contemporary criticism alike, in *Woman and Gender in Renaissance Tragedy* (1989),[2] I sought to understand how the path of a female protagonist upturned conventional ideas of tragedy, both in the Renaissance and in modern criticism: 'Major female characters [...] may indeed repeat the historic transgression of Eve, but if they do, their transgression does not bring the downfall of humanity but rather [...] discloses the limits of moral and social codes' (96–7). I also argued that feminist criticism did a disservice to Webster's remarkable Duchess by trying to press her into a female version of a male paradigm (68), a kind of 'great man' in drag. Also in the late eighties, Mary Beth Rose made the case for a 'female heroics' (1988) arguing that marriage was itself a new field of heroic endeavour in Protestant England,[3] while R. S. White's 'The Moral Design of *The Duchess of Malfi*' (2000) insisted: '[T]he plot could hardly be more emphatic as an example of the tragedy of the innocent victim. I should stress once again that "victim" does not require a lack of assertiveness – far from it, in this case' (204).[4] My own New Casebook on the play in 2000 reprised feminist scholarship from the mid-eighties, which in general sought to contextualize ideas about widows, marriage, female rulers and mothers in the early modern period.[5]

On the basis of this critical foundation, the feminist perspective on the play has become so pervasive that almost every essay published in the last decade assumes it. Feminist viewpoints no longer need to announce themselves as such nor do they need to advocate for female characters. Rather, feminism is now very much an integral part of the mainstream critical discourse. 'Queen of Apricots: *The Duchess of Malfi*, Hero of Desire' (2002), an important essay by Linda Woodbridge, is an exception in this regard since it includes an avowed statement of her position as a feminist that the personal is political.[6] Taking issue with what she describes as endemic oversimplification about early modern discourses of sexuality (166) and especially the neglect of neoplatonic and Italian humanist thought, she strikes out against the tendency to reduce all affective relations and amatory discourse in literature to allegories of political power. Woodbridge makes the case that 'the Duchess is *both* erotic and political' (164). Arguing for complexity and contradiction in early modern thinking about sex and marriage, she shows that the play's inclusion of the view expressed by Ferdinand that 'They are most luxurious / Will wed twice' (1.2.213–14) is indicative of the multiple and often colliding discourses about marriage and sexuality generated by the residual Catholic opposition to remarriage and, in concert with the reformers' revaluation of marriage over celibacy, the Protestant support of it.

Jennifer Panek also takes up the theme of remarriage in an essay that provides an invaluable theatrical context for the representation of the Duchess as a widow. '"My Naked Weapon": Male Anxiety and the Violent Courtship of the Jacobean Stage Widow' (2000) addresses a range of mainly comic widows, especially those of *The Widow's Tears, Ram-Alley,* and Greene's *Tu Quoque.*[7] The lusty widows of these plays are often wooed by violence, and widows in Jacobean comedy are, in general, Panek claims, represented as welcoming the prospect of rape. In *The Duchess of Malfi*, of course, the threat of violence (though not of rape) emanates not from Antonio, who does not woo at all, but from Ferdinand who 'hurls the epithet "lusty widow" (1.2.259) at his sister' (324). But this play, like *Hamlet*, Panek argues, is an anomaly among the widow plays of the period depicting marriages of great political import that are geographically removed from England and from 'middle-class London' (324): '[T]he tragic effect of *The Duchess of Malfi* derives partly from the horrific aftermath of what *should* be the stuff of comedy and celebration: a rich and powerful widow succumbing to her desires and making the fortune of an obscure but deserving young man' (341). While Webster may well have been fascinated by the prospect of violence against women, he does not seem to have found it reason for laughter. In '*The Duchess of Malfi* and Widows' (2005), I also took up the matter of how much agency widows actually possessed in early modern England, arguing that the feminist revisionist idea of the young merry widow exercising sexual freedom was a cultural fantasy of widowhood that did not account for those instances where women were either coerced into second marriages or compelled to remarry in order to attain some degree of social (and sexual) protection.[8]

Like Panek, Kimberly A. Turner expresses a similar leeriness about feminism as 'victim studies' in 'The Complexity of Webster's Duchess' (2000).[9] The essay is essentially a critique of Christy Desmet's classic 1991 essay, '"Neither Maid, Nor Widow, Nor Wife": Rhetoric of the Woman Controversy in *Measure for Measure* and *The Duchess of Malfi*'.[10] Turner charges that Desmet is guilty of anachronism in viewing the Duchess as the victim of misogyny in the play. She claims, furthermore, that Desmet unwittingly confines the possibilities for both real women and female characters in the period, and especially the unconventional Duchess whose 'spirit remains intact' (397) despite the trials she is compelled to undergo and who remains 'free to express her sexuality' and is 'not defined or limited by Renaissance (or modern) conventions' (399). Chiding a feminist critic for pointing out Webster's representation of Renaissance misogyny – to which the play is not, incidentally, at all sympathetic– strikes me as misguided. However, Turner poses a compelling question about our interpretation of *The Duchess of Malfi* when she asks what would a complex and undiminished tragic female hero look like if not just like the Duchess (398). Diminishment is after all, a precondition of the genre.

Marliss Desens in 'Marrying Down: Negotiating a More Equal Marriage on the English Renaissance Stage' (2001)[11] is less optimistic than Turner about the Duchess's freedoms. She examines the attempts by female characters in a range of early modern dramas to negotiate their conjugal arrangements so as to achieve an unofficial, *de facto* equality within an institution that would seem to be predicated on its denial. Desens argues that the Duchess tries to use 'social difference to offset the gender difference' (241), but the necessity of concealing the marriage 'ultimately prevents the working out of the difference between gender and social rank' (242). Ina Habermann tackles the prospects of equality from the point of view of the judicial system noting that 'John Webster perhaps more than any other contemporary playwright used the stage to explore the relation between women and the law' (100).[12] '"She Has That in Her Belly Will Dry Up Your Ink": Femininity as Challenge in the "Equitable Drama" of John Webster' (2005) takes its title from *The Devil's Law Case* and the essay focuses on the historical and structural interactions between theatre and the law in the full range of Webster's plays. *The Duchess* in particular 'puts gender relations, rather than women, on trial' (116) and 'finally sublimate[s] the legal context in order to foreground the ethical dimension [...] transforming the audience's disposition for critical judgment into the tragic emotion of pity' (101). Taking up an entirely different aspect of gender relations, Reina Green's '"Ears Prejudicate" in Mariam and *Duchess of Malfi*' (2003)[13] moves away from the more typical feminist focus on the ways women characters are silenced to the related question of how they listen. Instead of viewing women's speech as a violation of the patriarchal injunction on female silence, Green argues instead that we might consider, before we assign them to mute passivity, that characters who are not talking are actively listening on stage, which she suggests is a form of obedience. After her death, the Duchess thus becomes 'the ideal listening wife' (467). The play may well echo Webster's concerns about his own audience, Green argues, because 'the playwright is forced to accept the repercussions of his audience's inattention'.

Theodore B. Leinwand's '*Coniugium Interruptum* in Shakespeare and Webster' (2005) addresses the issue of sexuality head on: '[W]hat, precisely, did marital sex offer?' (239).[14] It is a question that, at least in the early modern context, *The Duchess of Malfi*, with its emphasis on companionate marriage, is well poised to answer. Leinwand sets about that task in relation to the very ticklish matter of the relationship between the private and the public in nascent modernity in dialogue with Valerie Traub and Stanley Cavell, critics who both assess the meaning of private, domestic heteroeroticism for and against the public sphere. Leinwand observes that it is not only Antonio but also Cariola who sleeps with the Duchess, the latter complaining that her mistress is 'the sprawlingest bedfellow' (3.2.13). Next, Cariola flaunts her knowledge of what her mistress and Antonio take for intimacy when she asks him why it is that when 'you lie with my lady/ [...] you rise so early' (3.2.16–17). 'So much', Leinwand notes, 'for bourgeois notions of privacy' (249).

While the social dimensions of sexuality such as widowhood and marriage are still important in critical analyses of the play, another phenomenon that several recent critics agree to be peculiar to the articulation of specifically female-centred tragedy is the use of the discourses of anatomy and medical science whose proximity to surveillance, rape and torture are analysed repeatedly. Maurizo Calbi's '"That Body of Hers:" The Secret, the Specular, the Spectacular in *The Duchess of Malfi* and Anatomical Discourse' (2005) draws heavily on Lacanian psychoanalysis to examine the construction of gender and class via the regulatory apparatus of medicine and other forms of 'visual mastery'.[15] Calbi sees the 'double injunction to veil and unveil the female body' (1) as one of the play's controlling impulses. Covering some of the same ground as Calbi's theory-oriented illuminations on *Duchess*, albeit from a very different methodological angle, is Sonja Fielitz's 'Testing the Woman's Body: Subtle Forms of Violence in Jacobean Drama' (2001).[16] Fielitz argues that because in Jacobean drama 'it is women in particular who expose the tentativeness, fragility and vulnerability of the patriarchal order' (43), their submission becomes one of the central tasks in the exercise of political and social power. Men, Fielitz argues, intrude into domain of female reproductivity, the only physical power women possess, as they 'try to gain knowledge and control over female bodies and especially of the status of the reproductive organs' (44). Because it falls short of murder or rape, this violence is often unnoticed by critics, or is at best dismissed as an aesthetically dubious curiosity. However, 'tests' to establish virginity or pregnancy are but more subtle forms of practices deployed both in witch persecutions and the burgeoning empiricism of scientific inquiry – namely violence against women. These tests figure significantly in *The Duchess of Malfi* and three other Jacobean plays: John Fletcher's *The Faithful Shepherdess* (1608/09), which because it is a generic anomaly Fielitz does not treat; Thomas Middleton and William Rowley's *The Changeling* (1622) and *Hengist, King of Kent: or, the Mayor of Queenborough* (1619/20). While the Duchess is the unwitting subject of Bosola's apricot test, in the later plays women exercise much more agency using it to their own ends. In *The Duchess* Fielitz argues, the test shows how much the tragic protagonist is 'already in Bosola's hands' (49).

Historicizing questions of interiority and individuality is the central aim of 'Invasive Procedures in Webster's *The Duchess of Malfi*' (2003). Here, Ellen Caldwell suggests that women in Jacobean culture represent the mystery of 'the other', whose 'secret' is to be wrested from them by medical, anatomical, legal and religious practices, all of which tend towards violence.[17] In concert, especially with the voyeuristic aspects of anatomy, in Webster's play, the Duchess is under constant surveillance, never once alone on stage, and '[a]lthough she is not literally dissected, the pregnancy of the Duchess marks her [...] as an object of both reverent fascination and disgust [...]' (163). Ultimately, Caldwell argues, the protagonist is able to resist 'the invasive practices of church or state' (18). In her 2002 essay, 'Possets, Pills and Poisons: Physicking the Female Body in Early Seventeenth-Century Drama', Katherine A. Armstrong takes up yet another aspect of medical practice, namely juxtaposition of women and drugs in *The Duchess of Malfi*, John Marston's *The Malcontent* and William Rowley's *The Changeling*.[18] She argues that 'whenever women in these plays come into contact with drugs [...] the results are unpredictable and dangerous, and that this reflects fears about the inadequacy of contemporary epistemologies to explain, control or contain female sexuality' (43). In the body politic, the female body is a poison to be purged.

Recent criticism, then, has tended to regard the new science of anatomy and medicine as a somewhat sinister development, symptomatic of the incursion of power on that equally new category of subjectivity, the individual. There has been a profound consensus among critics that *Duchess*, as a postmodern play *avant la lettre*, is symptomatic of the emergent facets of modernity, especially the instantiation of private life as a refuge from state power. But just as critical theory has moved away from 'grand narratives', those big, overarching stories that tend to subsume all cultural detail and aesthetic particularity, Wendy Wall's remarkably innovative essay, 'Just a Spoonful of Sugar: Syrup and Domesticity in Early Modern England', (2006) interrogates these macro-historical assumptions in relation to previous scholarship.[19] Wall argues that the

Duchess's dying instructions for her children's care – '[G]iv'st my little boy / Some syrup for his cold' (4.2.196–7) – have been too readily read as signals of 'the West's move to modernity in the seventeenth century' and of 'the play as a whole, as instrumental in ushering in a conceptual schema of separate private and public spheres'(150). Instead, working from the perspective of material history, Wall takes minutiae rather than macro theory as her starting point. The syrup becomes the focus of her analysis, as she traces its uses as well as its contradictory significations through a diverse array of medical handbooks, cookbooks and literary texts. Who knew, for example, that Lady Grace Mildmay [*sic*] ground up human skulls to make the cough syrup she gave her children, or that the practice was not especially unusual (161)? Maternal care of this variety does not comport well with our sense that the Duchess and Mary Poppins might have treated sick children in similar ways. Wall concludes: 'The play will not truly fit neatly into well-known stories about the rise of modernity. Instead, the play's richly associative domestic meanings might point scholars to investigate the sheer uncanniness of the early modern everyday, that is, the reward for focusing on something as banal – and as literary – as syrup' (172).

Dead Bodies

While much criticism over the last decade has consolidated its defense of Webster against charges of decadence and sensationalism, Susan Zimmerman's 'Invading the Grave: Shadow Lives in *The Revenger's Tragedy* and *The Duchess of Malfi*' (2005) unapologetically addresses the play's graveyard ambience.[20] Zimmerman demonstrates that Webster drew on a widespread recognition in the period that the putrefied corpse was in a very real, material sense 'alive' rather than defunct and inert, and thus took on an indeterminate status, somewhere in the liminal territory between life and death. This lack of clarity about the status of the quick and the dead sat uneasily with post-Reformation theology as well as with the new science of anatomy. Zimmerman's compelling and fully theorized reading of the play (via Lacan and Benjamin among others) focuses on the 'unsettling, slippery images of the interstitial, the in-between: images of dung, poison and blood; of wolf-men, wax figures, witches and lunatics; of mandrakes, hyenas and basilisks; of echoes, shadows and evanescent stains in snow' (143) and on the significance of the Duchess as herself a corpse. Likewise Thomas Anderson's less visceral 'The Art of Playing Dead in Revenge Tragedy' (2006) argues that the representation of death on the Renaissance stage enacts 'a crisis of inheritance for generations of history's survivors intent on overcoming the past' (125).[21] Taking issue with Foucault's argument in *Discipline and*

Punish that the mutilated corpse 'did not re-establish justice; it reactivated power' (125), Anderson argues instead for 'the pressing claims of the dead in the aftermath of the Reformation through the form and logic of revenge' (126). *The Duchess of Malfi*, among other plays of this genre, participates in the debate over the place of the dead in society. Garrett A. Sullivan, on the other hand, considers not the Duchess's dead body, but, intriguingly, her sleeping one.[22] Going to bed in 'Sleep, Conscience and Fame in *The Duchess of Malfi*' (2005) thus signals much more (or perhaps less) than merely lustful pleasures (119). Sullivan argues that sleep is central to the formation of subjectivity in Webster's play, and he examines the different significations of sleep that variously connote 'self-division or self-dispersal' (117) or a 'sleepy conscience' (120). Sullivan ultimately suggests that the Duchess's death, as a form of final sleep, reasserts the integrity of her subjectivity and assures her fame.

The scene of death is also the subject of recent work on the play. In an innovative contextualization of a range of plays including *The Winter's Tale* and *The Duchess of Malfi*, Philip D. Collington examines the affective and cognitive response of audiences to the plight of women in prison.[23] 'Pent-up Emotions: Pity and the Imprisonment of Women in Renaissance Drama' (2003) argues that the Duchess's imprisonment, reminiscent of the protracted incarceration of Mary Queen of Scots, is 'a remarkably ambivalent theatrical experience, in that as her plight becomes increasingly pathetic, she becomes more adamant that witnesses *not* pity her' (170). When she compares her state of abjection to that of 'the tanned galley-slave' (4.2.28), she has become 'masculine, even *muscular* in her ability to withstand pain and sorrow' (170). Collington claims that Webster sent 'mixed messages' to his audience about his executed female hero, and that in this he is unlike Shakespeare, who clearly establishes the innocence of Hermione, his royal female prisoner (185). Richard Madelaine considers another space associated with death in '"The dark and vicious place": The Location of Sexual Transgression and its Punishment on the Early Modern English Stage' (2005).[24] In those texts from Kyd to Ford that explore the interconnections between lust, tyranny and death, the 'dark and vicious place' is a generic location that connotes both illicit desire and the grave. Where exactly these sites of both sexual transgression and murder are located on the stage is seldom specified in the text, though they can only serve their purpose if clearly visible to the audience.

Albert H. Tricomi's 'The Severed Hand in Webster's *Duchess of Malfi*' (2004) does not deal in prostheses, but it does adduce a new source for John Webster's *The Duchess of Malfi* (albeit one challenged by Brett D. Hirsch two years later in *Notes and Queries*), namely, Henry Boguet's extremely popular *Discours Exécrable des Sorciers*.[25] Boguet's chapter

'Of the Metamorphosis of Men into Beasts' provides a strong link to the dead-man's hand episode in *The Duchess* as well as to Webster's representation of lycanthropic possession throughout the play. Hirsch, on the other hand, suggests that Simon Goulart's *Admirable and Memorable Histories* is a more likely source. Roberta Barker, in '"Another Voyage": Death as Social Performance in the Major Tragedies of John Webster' (2005), considers the dead body not so much as an object on the stage as a performance by a living actor.[26] Barker argues that Webster's thoroughly metatheatrical death scenes function as dramatic transactions which unsettle the categories of 'actor, character, and spectator' (36). Her focus is not only on the playtext but also on early modern conditions of performance signalled, for example, by the tributes to individual performers in printed version of the plays.

Theatre and Performance

Barker's work returns us to the analysis of *Duchess* not just as an intriguing work on the page, but as a performance for the stage. In recent years, there have been a number of important attempts to place Webster's play in the context of other Elizabeth and Jacobean dramas, including Barbara Correll's 'Malvolio at Malfi: Managing Desire in Shakespeare and Webster', (2007), an essay that 'hypothesizes a transgeneric afterlife for Malvolio in Webster's *Duchess of Malfi*' (65).[27] In the realization of his ambitions to marry his aristocratic mistress, Malvolio is regenerated as Antonio. This surprising premise finds its justification in an item from Webster's biography. He joined the Middle Temple in 1598 and was thus potentially in the audience for a performance of Shakespeare's play in 1602. This is not the only evidence, of course; many of the connections Correll draws between Shakespeare's comedy and Webster's tragedy come from the plays themselves. For example, the Duchess speaks of her last will and testament (*What You Will*) as a prelude to her marriage proposal to her steward (79). Webster's Antonio, however, does not reflect the sour discontent of Shakespeare's misfit, which, Correll argues, is transposed onto Bosola, Webster's 'brooding intelligencer' (65). This is because the pattern that Correll rightly sees as being reiterated is the fulfillment of the cross-class marriage of mistress and servant about which Malvolio fantasizes in *Twelfth Night*, and which, more than any of his other behaviours, makes him ridiculous. Correll argues that 'Webster was attuned to the historical liminality of the steward, that he used Malvolio's erotically inflected relation to a female aristocrat to sharpen issues of social transition, service, class formation and conflict introduced in Shakespeare's play' (65). Thus a crisis of power is rendered as a crisis of the exchange of women between men. Whereas *Twelfth Night* establishes some degree of social and erotic stability at the end, 'Webster's investment in the tragic dissolution of the beleaguered marriage, attended by deaths, mental disintegration, and dismemberment, constitutes an interesting response to the social and heteronormative stakes – or the homosexual panic – of *Twelfth Night*'s comic marriage festivity' (66). Correll takes issue especially with Frank Whigham's influential interpretation of the play that blames the Duchess for sexual exploitation of her steward as the 'the alienated nocturnal sex worker who furtively exits before morning' (71). In Correll's reading, Antonio, Bosola and the Duchess, are all figures who push the social limits (85): 'Following Malvolio's threat and dramatically developing its social-erotic dimension, Webster stages tragic consequences with a socially provocative potential' (92).

Another theatrical juxtaposition, this time on the theme of female disobedience, is Julia Schmitt's 'Sisterly Transgression: An Examination of Evadne from *The Maid's Tragedy* and the Duchess from *The Duchess of Malfi*' (2002).[28] Schmitt draws out the connection between the two plays, arguing that the dire consequences of a sister's disobedience to her brothers does not in fact support gender roles by demonstrating the punitive consequences that await women who do not toe the line, but rather subverts them, showing the irrational injustice of such limitations on women. Further, Schmitt claims that the Duchess and Evadne both play the woman's part with an insistently theatrical self-consciousness that undermines orthodox notions about female sexuality as well as the rigid gender categories that subtend them: 'I account this world a tedious theatre/, For I do play a part in't 'gainst my will' (4.1.81–2). While Ferdinand condemns his sister's body with 'Damn her! that body of hers,' (4.1.118) she is able to recuperate it in death: 'Dispose my breath how please you, but my body / Bestow upon my women' (4.2. 220–1).

Given the paucity of Webster performed on stage, relative to Shakespeare at least, there are few approaches to *The Duchess* from the perspective of performance. Roberta Barker's work is an exception. In 'An Actor in the Main of All: Individual and Relational Selves in *The Duchess of Malfi*' (2007),[29] Barker examines the Duchess's relationships with the play's male characters in the context of performance, specifically, Bill Alexander's 1989 production for the RSC and Declan Donnellan's 1995–96 production for Cheek by Jowl. The two productions offer significantly different interpretations of Webster's play – Alexander's is wholly sympathetic to the Duchess whose erotic choices amount to heroism, while for Donnellan, she is a 'regal overreacher' (69) who marries a reluctant Antonio and counts on having the power to transgress in private without public consequences. For all their differences, both productions foreground the Duchess's tragic subjectivity and her negotiations of power and identity. What modern productions fail to grasp, however, Barker claims, is the refusal of early modern acting styles to 'body forth the stable inner realities that define men and women'. Barker presents the 'Character of an Excellent Actor', long ascribed to Webster, as evidence of this difference: 'what hee doth fainedly that doe others essentially: this day one plaies a Monarch, the next a private person. Heere one Acts a Tyrant, on the morrow an Exile [...] and so of divers others' (81).

Ben Spiller also addresses the matter of modern performance in 'Inconstant Identities on the South Bank: *The Duchess of Malfi* and the Homeless Visitor' (2003).[30] Commercial runs of the play included the West End production of 1995 with Juliet Stevenson in the title role. As Stevie Simkin has pointed out, revivals of Webster are for the most part 'only state-subsidised theatre companies (usually the Royal Shakespeare Company or National Theatre)', only to be 'locked securely away again for another ten years' (4). Spiller's essay is an account of an interview with the director, Phyllida Lloyd, of a production of *The Duchess* performed at Lyttelton Theatre in early 2003. Lloyd's production (bearing out the arguments of Lisa Hopkins and Thomas Rist below) staged the action of the play in the present, and had dead characters sit on a staircase that ran the width of the performance space for the remainder of the play: 'Janet McTeer's Duchess, who had accepted her death as an almost welcome release from the hell she was living, sat centre-stage and constantly reminded us of her continuing, post-death influence on the play'. According to Spiller, the Duchess is 'enigmatic' (25), passive, and devoid of focused identity (27).

The success of *Duchess* in performance gives the lie to the longstanding mid-century consensus that Webster's plays are episodic and structurally flawed. While that line of argument has been ignored in favour of gender, sexuality and the like, it was not directly addressed or countered until David Gunby's '"Strong Commanding Art": The Structure of *The White Devil*, *The Duchess of Malfi*, and *The Devil's Law-Case*' (2004).[31] Gunby's riposte is important because instead of making the spurious claim that in the postmodern critical moment structure is irrelevant, he shows, by careful and sustained attention to the text itself, that the argument was misguided in the first place. So for example, when Ferdinand vows at the end of Act II to discover the identity of his sister's lover, by Act III, despite her now multiple pregnancies, he still does not know. It is precisely these significant time gaps between each Act that are the focus of Gunby's discussion. Far from being accidental and signs of Webster's ineptitude in the matter of structure, these gaps, he argues, demonstrate that the playwright's use of time is in fact self-conscious and an artful deployment of a system of parallels, echoes and repetitions. This is evident, for example, in the way that Webster emphasizes the time gap between Acts II and III, providing 'a thirty-five line dialogue between Antonio and Delio in which time is constantly at issue' (215). Gunby argues the three plays identified in his title are marked by the same 'two-movement structure' (219), which suggests artistic unity and progression as well as a highly sophisticated sense of dramatic structure. This argument is corroborated by Jeremy Lopez's work on 'Managing Asides' (2003).[32] In a brief section on *The Duchess of Malfi* in his chapter, Lopez focuses on the opening of Act III, when Delio and Antonio joke about the passage of years in plot-time, and of minutes in actual theatre time: 'within this half hour' (3.1.7). Like Gunby, Lopez argues that this is an intentional moment of self-conscious theatricality. In a similar vein, Richard A. Levin, in '*The Duchess of Malfi*: What's to Come is Still Unsure' (2001), also defends Webster's dramatic design on the grounds that the opacity of its schemes 'function to place us within the world of the play, an uncertain world demanding discernment as well as caution' (109).[33] By closely following the positions of the critically neglected characters of Delio and Pescara within the play's fluctuating network of power relationships, Levin argues that both characters show themselves to be adroit, if hesitant, participants in court politics. Examining the way in which the emblematic and the psychological are carefully interwoven in Webster's tragedy, Leslie Thomson's 'Fortune and Virtue in *The Duchess of Malfi*' (2000) provides an account of the play's remarkable indebtedness to emblem books.[34] From the point of view of this tradition, the characters take on an emblematic role reminiscent of their theatrical antecedents in morality plays. The Duchess in particular is figured as Fortune when she says to Antonio 'I would have you lead your Fortune by the hand / Unto your marriage bed' (1.2.401–2). Like conventional emblematic treatments of Fortune and Love, she is ultimately and invariably defeated by Death.

Religion

A number of important critical contributions over the last decade treat Webster's play as a post-Reformation phenomenon written during a more settled period of the established Anglican Church. However, English Protestantism still found its identity in relation to the faith it had renounced, namely Catholicism, whose home was Italy where Webster sets *The Duchess*. In 'Action and Confession, Fate and Despair in the Violent Conclusion of *The Duchess of Malfi*' (2001), John C. Kerrigan explores the transition between the two religions as a context for the violence in *The Duchess of Malfi*: 'the act 5 setting of the abbey in ruins seems an allusive reminder of England's own recent past – the plundering and abandonment of the monasteries in the late 1540s' (251).[35] In the midst of the doctrinal flux of the period, Kerrigan reminds us, Protestant antipathy towards auricular confession was especially significant. The late sixteenth century had seen the consolidation of the Protestant doctrine of grace within the Anglican Church. Since grace superseded even the most heinous misdeeds, confession, hitherto an important and sacramental practice, became superfluous. However, the idea that grace might provide a loophole in allowing people to sin as they pleased was an ideologically unworkable idea, and so contradictions around contrition, and penitence remained to trouble Anglican theology and practice. Thus, violence in *The Duchess of Malfi*, Kerrigan argues, 'may be read as the frustration resulting from the lack of an outlet for expressing guilt and the inability to confess' (251). Highlighting the pervasive language of confession in the play, he draws attention to a striking but hitherto unnoticed facet of the Duchess's character, namely her sincere personal piety: 'What is perhaps most remarkable about the Duchess's character is her faith' (252). In contrast, other characters, Bosola in particular, must resort to the rhetoric of fate, rather than faith, because they face despair as the only alternative to the free and redeeming confession of their misdeeds.

Other writers on *Duchess* are similarly alert to the residual presence of Catholicism in the play. Thomas Rist's 'Melodrama and Parody: Remembering the Dead in *The Revenger's Tragedy*, *The Atheist's Tragedy*, *The White Devil* and *The Duchess of Malfi*' (2008) contends that early modern revenge tragedies are 'suffused with remembrances of the dead' (97).[36] While *Antonio's Revenge*, *The Spanish Tragedy*, *Titus Andronicus* and *Hamlet* are marked by persistent traditionalism and pro-Catholic bias, the later tragedies listed in his title present a Protestant ethic that, nonetheless, does not shy away from nuanced presentations of mourning and remembrance. In the section devoted to *The Duchess of Malfi*, Rist argues that the play is initially very explicit in its anti-Catholic bias. However, by the time the Duchess and Antonio are objects of pursuit, the iconography of Catholicism is recalled in a favourable light. Ultimately, Rist suggests that the play's religious bias can be interpreted along the axis of appropriate and inappropriate remembrance.

Another key element of Catholicism that surfaces in *Duchess* is the presence of the Blessed Virgin. However, as her title '"Black but Beautiful": *Othello* and the Cult of the Black Madonna' (2007) suggests, *The Duchess of Malfi* is not the focus of this author's argument.[37] Nonetheless, Lisa Hopkins raises a fascinating and little-studied dimension of the play centring upon Our Lady of Loreto, to whose shrine the Duchess ostensibly repairs to escape her murderous brothers. Like Rist,

Hopkins believes, *The Duchess* is 'a text which generally has little time for Catholicism', and yet for all that, Webster presents the sanctity of the shrine as something that should not be trifled with (77):

> In my opinion,
> She were better progress to the baths at Lucca
> Or go visit the Spa in Germany;
> For, if you will believe me, I do not like
> This jesting with religion, this feigned pilgrimage. (3.2.316–20)

Furthermore, Cariola's forebodings are borne out by the play, and the shrine's holiness is corroborated by the First Pilgrim: 'I have not seen a goodlier shrine than this, / Yet I have visited many' (3.4.1–2). This otherworldly alignment of power and femininity, a reflection and refraction of the Duchess's own, is explored more generally in Hopkins's examination of the various proposed origins of the Black Madonna, and their contested significance, especially during the Reformation. In another essay on the play, 'Women's Souls: *The Duchess of Malfi* and *'Tis Pity She's a Whore*' (2002), Hopkins points out that '[t]he intensity of early seventeenth-century interest in the body by no means precluded an equally eager interest in the soul' (118).[38] While the corporeality of female protagonists is underscored in these plays, she argues, the spirit or soul remains the feature that most defines their heroism. Hopkins points out that both men and women in *The Duchess* are understood to possess interiority, and in men, this 'inner nature is not a feminized threat, but an essential part of human make-up' (120). That Webster ultimately privileges interiority, she suggests, is why the Duchess dies in Act IV. This early death serves not to diminish or truncate her role as tragic protagonist 'but to confirm her status as the encapsulation of the ethos of interiority which the play has so energetically propounded' (131).

In their analysis of religion, critics have not focused, however, on God alone. Albert H. Tricomi gives the devil his due in 'Historicizing the Imagery of the Demonic in *The Duchess of Malfi*' (2004). Tricomi argues that critics have taken refuge from the charged world of the demonic and supernatural of the seventeenth century in the more comfortable language of the symbolic, the allegorical and the psychological. He contends that 'Webster's mimetic art in *The Duchess of Malfi* needs to be rendered in terms of the indeterminate horizon of early modern religious beliefs and intuitions' (349).[39] Importantly, Tricomi's approach is concerned not with establishing Webster's position on the spectrum of post-Reformation theology but rather with the insistent presence in the play of an all-pervasive, unseen world. Along with *The Witch of Edmonton*, he contends, Webster's *Duchess* is 'the most important dramatic realization we have of the intersubjective experience of demonism in Tudor-Stuart drama' (366).

Sovereignty

The examination of female power in a more secular vein is the subject of Hester Lees-Jeffries's chapter on 'The Public Fountain: Elizabethan Politics and the Humanist Tradition', in her book-length study of ornamental water features.[40] Lees-Jeffries provides an architectural context for the *Duchess of Malfi*'s important opening metaphor of the head of state as fountainhead, suggesting the implicit shadow of Elizabeth. The chapter opens with the description of a medal by the Flemish immigrant engraver Stephen van Herwijk bearing the traditional image of Elizabeth in profile on its face and, on the back, the feminine figure of Fides sitting by a fountain with a cross clasped to her bosom. This image carries the Greek inscription, 'The divine fountain of the realm'. The design and motto of the medal were by the Flemish poet Charles Utenhove, who also sent a poem in French on the same topic to William Cecil, which described the Queen as '*la Divine fontaine / En vertu, en savoir, en beauté*'. 'These are staunchly Protestant sentiments, yet the fountain as a political symbol of power and authority', the author argues, 'was specifically associated with Elizabeth I in subtle, yet increasingly complicated and ambivalent ways' (198). Among others, Ben Jonson's *Cynthia's Revels* (1601), Sir Thomas Elyot's *The Image of Governaunce* (1556) and Erasmus's *The Education of a Christian Prince* (1516) and Anthony Fletcher's, *Certaine Very Proper, and Most Profitable Similies* (1595) used a political context for the fountain image, whose classical source was Plutarch's *Moralia.* Webster's language is very close to Fletcher's own: 'Euen as a brooke doth follow the nature of the fountaine, from whence it commeth: So people do follow the disposition of their prince: the fountaine being troubled, the brooke is troubled also, and the prince disquieted, the people finde no peace' (201). But the fountain device was also embroidered on Elizabeth's clothes and worked into her emblematic jewellery. The danger of pollution, however, especially in relation to a female head or source (women were – Elizabeth's sieve portrait notwithstanding – the ultimate leaky vessels) complicates this image, and Lees-Jeffries reminds us that the ravished Lavinia in Shakespeare's *Titus Andronicus* (1595) is also imaged as a fountain: 'a crimson river of warm blood, / Like to a bubbling fountain stirred with wind' (2.2.22–3). Thus in deploying this image, Webster and his contemporaries implicitly solicit 'an analogous consideration of these concepts and principles in the culture of the Elizabethan court' (217).

Milagro Ducassé-Turner similarly takes up the contradictions arising from female government in early modern England in 'Gods on Earth: Usurping Kingly and Godly Authority in Shakespeare's *Macbeth* and Webster's *The Duchess of Malfi*' (2005).[41] This theme was earlier addressed by Theodora Jankowski in 'Defining/Confining the Duchess: Negotiating the Female Body in John Webster's *The Duchess of Malfi*' (1990), an essay which argued for the slippage between public and private selves.[42] Similarly drawing on theory of the King's two bodies and a 1623 sermon by Donne, from which she derives her title, Ducassé-Turner examines the conflict between the authority of kings and the God they purport to serve. Ducassé-Turner structures her argument around three tropes she identifies as common to both *Macbeth* and *The Duchess of Malfi*: the ideal prince's court, tyrannical imposture and the traitor. Sid Ray's 'So Troubled with the Mother', on the play's politics of pregnancy (2007), claims that Webster was sufficiently ahead of his time to endorse, among other things, 'female sovereignty, participatory government and merit-based inheritance' (27).[43] The grounds for this interpretation lie in the relation between the pregnant body of the play's female ruler and theory of the king's two bodies. While Elizabeth emphasized the masculinity of her corporeal body through virginity, the Duchess of Malfi's power is predicated on her fertility and her literalization of the two-body metaphor. Ray also compares Webster's *Duchess of Malfi* with its source material to show how Webster deliberately foregrounds the correspondence of pregnancy and authority. Angela Woollam takes up several of the themes addressed by Lees-Jeffries, Ducassé-Turner and Ray, but in specific relation to language.[44] 'The Stakes of Semantic Significance in *The Duchess of Malfi*' (2003) assesses 'what is ultimately and potentially at stake in different assumptions about language that were current in Early Modern England by depicting their ramifications on conceptions of authority, experience, and selfhood' (24). Finally, Jill Ingram Philips in 'The "Noble Lie": Casuistry and Machiavellism in *The Duchess of Malfi*' (2005) identifies the Duchess as a 'virtuous machiavel' and analyses the play as a demonstration of the complex dialectic between political survival and Christian morality.[45] Drawing on early modern *ars moriendi* manuals, Ingram suggests that the moment and the manner of her death renders the Duchess's deceptions benign in contrast with those of her brothers, which are demonstrably sinful.

Wolves, Madness, etc.

It has been a perennial topic of fascination among Webster critics that as a sufferer from lycanthropia Ferdinand believes he has 'hair on the inside'. The wolf-man angle is also somewhat symptomatic of the vast and eclectic range of possible interpretations the play has produced.

In 2000, David W. Cole examined the play's equine imagery, while in 2002 Robert Palter took on what turns out to be the surprisingly significant issue of early modern fruit.[46] Another contribution that does not fit easily into any organizational rubric is Keith Botelho's '"Into Russian Winter:" Russian Extremes in *The Duchess of Malfi*' (2005). This essay historicizes the discursive production of Russia in the early modern English imagination and argues that the frequent allusions to Russia in the latter acts of the play help to create a 'dizzying, tyrannical, and often half-imaginary world'.[47] Courtney Lehmann's and Bryan Reynolds's essay, 'Awakening the Werewolf Within: Self-Help, Vanishing Mediation, and Transversality in *The Duchess of Malfi*' (2006) is inspired directly by Ferdinand's madness.[48] Ostensibly an analysis of Ferdinand, the essay is also a meditation on ways of conceptualizing identity. The whole gamut of theorists, from Adorno to Žižek, makes an appearance here; surprisingly, so too does Tony Robbins' self-help treatise, *Awaken the Giant Within* (1992). The overarching framework of this diverse array of texts brought to bear upon *The Duchess* is that of 'transversal theory', which 'sees everything and, quite literally refers to everything present or absent, real or imaginary, material or immaterial, and is only interested in differentiating among these terms conditionally and as circumstances, ethical or unethical, encourage doing so, depending on the particular purpose and stakes' (235). With that knotty point clarified, the authors conclude: 'Webster has become a vanishing mediator for a self-help ethos that is the product of totalitarian fantasies, the interstices of which speak to the ongoing reality of werewolf syndrome' (238).

A more strictly historical account of madness in the play is Ken Jackson's '"Twin' Shows of Madness": John Webster's Stage Management of Bethlem in *The Duchess of Malfi*' (2005).[49] Jackson takes his cue from R. S. White's path-breaking analysis of the moral design of *The Duchess of Malfi*, which argued that the death of the Duchess unequivocally works to create sympathy for her rather than – as earlier critics had somewhat perversely maintained – grounds for her condemnation. He argues similarly that Webster orchestrates his audience's reception of madness and by that means elicits pity for the Duchess: 'Webster thus gives two "twin" shows of madness, the Duchess and Ferdinand's, and directs two opposing responses, one charitable, one mocking' (197). Manic laughter is also the subject of Arthur Lindley's 'Uncrowning Carnival: The Laughter of Subversion and the Subversion of Laughter in *The Duchess of Malfi*' (2006).[50] Like Brian Gibbons, whose 2001 edition of the play notes the Jacobean trend towards the tragic hybrid, Lindley focuses on the play's grotesque, carnivalesque laughter.[51] Lindley argues that *The Duchess of Malfi* deconstructs the opposition between Bakhtinian carnival and Augustinian carnival as the play represents the reciprocal nature of carnival and Lent.

As this account of the critical work over the past several years has tried to suggest, Webster's *Duchess* constitutes an extraordinarily rich vein that is unlikely to dry up any time soon. But what of the work that remains to be done? While the themes and issues raised above are sure to continue on all fronts – theoretical, historical, medical, religious, theatrical and performance oriented – there remains much to do if we are to recover the context of Webster's writing and to understand exactly why he chose in *Duchess* and in *The White Devil* to put a woman at the centre of his plays. Important scholarly labour has been invested in three editions of the play since 2000 – that by Brian Gibbons, mentioned above, another by Leah Marcus and the edition of the play that forms part of the new *Complete Works* whose three volumes were finished in 2008.[52] David Gunby's contribution of the playwright's biography in the latter volume as well as his entry in the *New Oxford Dictionary of National Biography* points to an important gap in the field, namely a full-length critical biography of Webster, which we have not had since C. R. Forker, *Skull Beneath the Skin: The Achievement of John Webster* (1986) and M. C. Bradbrook, *John Webster: Citizen and Dramatist* (1980).[53] One could only wish that the kind of energy that has been invested in Marlowe and Shakespeare biography might be put into Webster. For there is surely more to tell about how he came to compose this magnificent tragedy.

Notes

1. Stevie Simkin, ed., *New Casebooks: Revenge Tragedy* (Basingstoke: Palgrave, 2001).
2. Dympna Callaghan, *Woman and Gender in Renaissance Tragedy: A Study of 'King Lear,' 'Othello,' 'The Duchess of Malfi,' and 'The White Devil'* (Brighton: Harvester, 1989).
3. Mary Beth Rose, *The Expense of Spirit: Love and Sexuality in English Renaissance Drama* (Ithaca: Cornell University Press, 1988).
4. R. S. White, 'The Moral Design of *The Duchess of Malfi*' in *New Casebooks: 'The Duchess of Malfi'*, ed. by Dympna Callaghan (New York: St. Martin's 2000), pp. 201–216.
5. Dympna Callaghan, ed., *New Casebooks: 'The Duchess of Malfi'* (New York: St. Martin's Press, 2000).
6. Linda Woodbridge, 'Queen of Apricots: The Duchess of Malfi, Hero of Desire', in *The Female Tragic Hero in English Renaissance Drama*, ed. by Naomi Conn Liebler (New York: Palgrave, 2002), pp. 163–84.
7. Jennifer Panek, '"My Naked Weapon": Male Anxiety and the Violent Courtship of the Jacobean Stage Widow', *Comparative Drama*, 34, 3 (2000), 321–44.
8. Dympna Callaghan, '*The Duchess of Malfi* and Widows', in *Early Modern English Drama: A Critical Companion*, ed. by Patrick Cheney and Garrett Sullivan (Oxford: Oxford University Press, 2005).
9. Kimberly Turner, 'The Complexity of Webster's Duchess', *Ben Jonson Journal*, 7 (2000), 380–400.

10. Christy Desmet, '"Neither Maid, Nor Widow, Nor Wife": Rhetoric of the Woman Controversy in *Measure for Measure* and *The Duchess of Malfi*', reprinted in Callaghan (1991), 46–60.
11. Marliss Desens, 'Marrying Down: Negotiating a More Equal Marriage on the English Renaissance Stage', *Medieval and Renaissance Drama in England*, 14 (2001), 227–55.
12. Ina Habermann, '"She Has That in Her Belly Will Dry Up Your Ink": Femininity as Challenge in the "Equitable Drama" of John Webster', in *Literature, Politics and Law in Renaissance England*, ed. by Erica Sheen and Lorna Hutson (New York: Palgrave, 2005), pp. 100–20.
13. Reina Green, '"Ears Prejudicate" in *Mariam* and *The Duchess of Malfi*', *Studies in English Literature*, 43, 2 (Spring 2003), 459–74.
14. Theodore B. Leinwand, '*Coniugium Interrutptum* in Shakespeare and Webster', *English Literary History*, 72 (2005), 239–57.
15. Maurizio Calbi, '"That Body of Hers": The Secret, the Specular, the Spectacular in *The Duchess of Malfi* and Anatomical Discourses', in *Approximate Bodies: Gender and Power in Early Modern Drama and Anatomy* (New York: Routledge, 2005), pp. 1–31.
16. Sonja Fielitz, 'Testing the Woman's Body: Subtle Forms of Violence in Jacobean Drama', in *The Aesthetics and Pragmatics of Violence: Proceedings of the Conference at Passau University* 15–17 March 2001.
17. Ellen Caldwell, 'Invasive Procedures in Webster's *The Duchess of Malfi*', in *Women, Violence, and English Renaissance Literature: Essays Honoring Paul Jorgensen*, ed. by Linda Woodbridge and Sharon Beehler (Tempe: University of Arizona Press, 2003), pp. 149–86.
18. Katherine A. Armstrong, 'Possets, Pills and Poisons: Physicking the Female Body in Early Seventeenth-Century Drama', *Cahiers Elisabéthains*, 61 (2002), 43–56.
19. Wendy Wall, 'Just a Spoonful of Sugar: Syrup and Domesticity in Early Modern England', *Modern Philology*, 104, 2 (2006), 149–72.
20. Susan Zimmerman, 'Invading the Grave: Shadow Lives in *The Revenger's Tragedy* and *The Duchess of Malfi*', in *The Early Modern Corpse and Shakespeare's Theatre* (Edinburgh: Edinburgh University Press, 2005).
21. Thomas Anderson, 'The Art of Playing Dead in Revenge Tragedy', in *Performing Early Modern Trauma from Shakespeare to Milton* (Burlington, VT: Ashgate, 2006).
22. Garrett A. Sullivan, 'Sleep, Conscience and Fame in *The Duchess of Malfi*', in *Memory and Forgetting in English Renaissance Drama* (Cambridge: Cambridge University Press, 2005).
23. Philip D. Collington, 'Pent-up Emotions: Pity and the Imprisonment of Women in Renaissance Drama', *Medieval and Renaissance Drama in England*, 16 (2003), 162–91.
24. Richard Madelain, '"The dark and vicious place": The Location of Sexual Transgression and its Punishment on the Early Modern English Stage', *Parergon*, 22, 1 (2005), 159–83.
25. Albert H. Tricomi, 'Historicizing the Imagery of the Demonic in *The Duchess of Malfi*', *Journal of Medieval and Early Modern Studies*, 34.2 (2004), 345–72; Brett D. Hirsch, 'Werewolves and Severed Hands: Webster's *The Duchess of Malfi* and Heywood and Brome's *The Witches of Lancashire*', *Notes and Queries*, 53, 1 (2006), 92–4.
26. Roberta Barker, '"Another Voyage": Death as Social Performance in the Major Tragedies of John Webster', *Early Theatre*, 8, 2 (2005), 35–56.
27. Barbara Correll, 'Malvolio at Malfi: Managing Desire in Shakespeare and Webster', *Shakespeare Quarterly*, 58, 1 (2007), 65–92.

28. Schmitt, Julia, 'Sisterly Transgression: An Examination of Evadne from *The Maid's Tragedy* and the Duchess from *The Duchess of Malfi*', *Selected Papers from the West Virginia Shakespeare and Renaissance Association*, 25 (2002), 58–69.
29. Roberta Barker, 'An Actor in the Main of All: Individual and Relational Selves in *The Duchess of Malfi*', in Barker, *Early Modern Tragedy, Gender, and Performance, 1984–2000: The Destined Livery* (New York: Palgrave, 2007).
30. Ben Spiller, 'Inconstant Identities on the South Bank: *The Duchess of Malfi* and the Homeless Visitor', *Renaissance Journal*, 1.8 (2003), 25–31.
31. David Gunby, '"Strong Commanding Art": The Structure of *The White Devil, The Duchess of Malfi*, and *The Devil's Law-Case*', in *Words that Count: Essays in Early Modern Authorship in Honor of MacDonald P. Jackson*, ed. by Brian Boyd (Newark: University of Delaware Press, 2004), pp. 209–21.
32. Jeremy Lopez, 'Managing Asides', *Theatrical Convention and Audience Response in Early Modern Drama* (Cambridge: Cambridge University Press, 2003).
33. Richard A Levin, '*The Duchess of Malfi*: "What's to Come is Still Unsure"', in *Shakespeare's Secret Schemes: The Study of an Early Modern Dramatic Device* (Newark: University of Delaware Press, 2001).
34. Leslie Thomson, 'Fortune and Virtue in *The Duchess of Malfi*', *Comparative Drama*, 33 (1999–2000), 474–94.
35. John C. Kerrigan, 'Action and Confession, Fate and Despair in the Violent Conclusion of *The Duchess of Malfi*', *Ben Jonson Journal*, 8 (2001), 249–51.
36. Thomas Rist, 'Melodrama and Parody: Remembering the Dead in *The Revenger's Tragedy, The Atheist's Tragedy, The White Devil* and *The Duchess of Malfi*', in *Revenge Tragedy and the Drama of Commemoration in England* (Burlington, VT: Ashgate, 2008), pp. 97–144.
37. Lisa Hopkins, '"Black but Beautiful": Othello and the Cult of the Black Madonna', in *Marian Moments in Early Modern British Drama*, ed. by Lisa Hopkins and Regina Buccola (Burlington, VT: Ashgate, 2007), pp. 75–86.
38. Lisa Hopkins, 'Women's Souls: *The Duchess of Malfi* and *'Tis Pity She's a Whore*', in *The Female Hero in English Renaissance Tragedy* (New York: Palgrave, 2002).
39. Albert H. Tricomi, 'The Severed Hand in Webster's *Duchess of Malfi*', *Studies in English Literature*, 44, 2 (2004), 347–8.
40. Hester Lees-Jeffries, *England's Helicon: Fountains in Early Modern Literature and Culture* (New York: Oxford University Press, 2007).
41. Milagro Ducassé-Turner, 'Gods on Earth: Usurping Kingly and Godly Authority in Shakespeare's *Macbeth* and Webster's *The Duchess of Malfi*', *Anglophonia*, 17 (2005), 35–49.
42. Theodora Jankowski, 'Defining/Confining the Duchess: Negotiating the Female Body in John Webster's *The Duchess of Malfi*', (1990) reprinted in Callaghan (2000), pp. 80–103.
43. Sid Ray, '"So Troubled with the Mother": The Politics of Pregnancy in *The Duchess of Malfi*', *Performing Maternity in Early Modern England*, ed. by Kathryn Moncrief and Kathryn McPherson (Burlington: Ashgate, 2007), pp. 17–28.
44. Angela Woollam, 'The Stakes of Semantic Significance in *The Duchess of Malfi*', *English Studies in Canada*, 26, 1 (2003), 11–28.
45. Jill Ingram Philips, 'The "Noble Lie": Casuistry and Machiavellianism in *The Duchess of Malfi*', *Explorations in Renaissance Culture*, 31, 5 (2005), 135–60.
46. David W. Cole, 'Webster's *The Duchess of Malfi*', *The Explicator* 59, 1 (2000), 7–8; Robert Palter, *The Duchess of Malfi's Apricots and Other Literary Fruits* (Columbia: University of South Carolina Press, 2002).

47. Keith Botelho, '"Into Russian Winter": Russian Extremes in *The Duchess of Malfi*', *English Language Notes*, 42, 3 (2005), 14–18.
48. Courtney Lehmann and Bryan Reynolds, 'Awakening the Werewolf Within: Self-Help, Vanishing Mediation, and Transversality in *The Duchess of Malfi*', in *Transversal Enterprises in the Drama of Shakespeare and His Contemporaries*, ed. by Bryan Reynolds (New York: Palgrave, 2006).
49. Ken Jackson, '"Twin Shows of Madness": John Webster's Stage Management of Bethlem in *The Duchess of Malfi*', *Separate Theaters: Bethlem ('Bedlam') Hospital and the Shakespearean Stage* (Newark: University of Delaware Press, 2005), pp. 183–284.
50. Arthur Lindley, 'Uncrowning Carnival: The Laughter of Subversion and the Subversion of Laughter in *The Duchess of Malfi*', *Journal of the Australasian Universities Modern Language Association*, 106 (2006), 105–21.
51. Brian Gibbons, ed., *The Duchess of Malfi*, by John Webster (New York: A&C Black, 2001).
52. David Gunby, David Carnegie, Antony Hammond and MacDonald P. Jackson, eds., *The Works of John Webster* 3 vols (Cambridge: Cambridge University Press, 1996–2007).
53. C. R. Forker, *Skull Beneath the Skin: The Achievement of John Webster* (Carbondale: University of Illinois Press, 1986); M. C. Bradbrook, *John Webster: Citizen and Dramatist* (New York: Columbia University Press, 1980); David Gunby, 'Webster, John (1578–1638?)', *Oxford Dictionary of National Biography*, online edition.

CHAPTER FOUR

Staging Secret Interiors: *The Duchess of Malfi* as Inns of Court and Anticourt Drama

Curtis Perry and Melissa Walter

Much of the best recent work on *The Duchess of Malfi* has focused on Webster's depiction of domesticity, building on Catherine Belsey's influential account of the play as a 'fable of emergent liberalism'.[1] Arguing that the play draws a sharp distinction between the private sphere, as represented in the domestic scenes shared by Antonio and the Duchess, and 'a newly differentiated public world of state power, law, and politics' represented by Ferdinand and the Cardinal, Belsey suggests that it 'anticipates the system of differences which gives meaning to the discourse of liberalism'.[2] Subsequent critics have refined and challenged this argument by emphasizing the difference between privacy and secrecy: the latter requires active exclusion and is thus inherently social in a way that the private, as a constitutive category of modern liberalism, pretends not to be.[3] The distinction between secrecy and privacy is, moreover, especially vexed in the context of the inevitable public significance of a ruler's domestic arrangements. This is, of course, fundamental to the plot of Webster's play, and so it is by no means clear that its political and domestic spheres can ever be said to be differentiated.

These distinctions – between privacy and secrecy or between the domestic and the political – are exploited in *The Duchess of Malfi* to great effect. Witness its playful, metadramatic handling of theatrical time. Insofar as the Duchess and Antonio are able to live together in a state of personal contentment over a period of time without effecting meaningful change in the public, political world – as they ostensibly do – one might almost imagine them as a private nuclear family. But since our apprehension of the Duchess's married life is framed by multiple scenes in which the Cardinal and (especially) Ferdinand focus upon their sister's secrecy with an intensity that one cannot imagine being sustained over several years, the dramatic effect of the story *as staged* is at odds with its reported timeline. Students reading the play are inevitably surprised by the passage of time recorded at the beginning of Act III ('since you last saw her, / She hath had two children more' [3.1.6–7]), and Webster himself makes a joke there about how incongruous this passage of time feels to a theatrical audience ('verily I should dream / It were within this half-hour' [3.1.10–11]). One might explain this tension in terms of Webster's need to fit the story of Giovanna d'Aragona to conventions of Italianate Senecan tragedy, which emphasize extremities of passion and spectacular violence. But that means that the play's depiction of the Duchess's family life always exists in tension with, and as contextualized by, a set of dramatic conventions better suited to depict the secrets of the great than private domesticity.

Webster's fascination with political aspects of the distinction between privacy and secrecy derives from unresolved tensions built into Jacobean orthodoxy concerning the secret lives of rulers who are, as King James put it, 'publike persons':

> Kings being publike persons, by reason of their office and authority, are set [...] upon a publike stage, in sight of all the people; where all the beholders eyes are attentively bent to looke and pry in the least circumstance of their secretest drifts: Which should make Kings the more carefull not to harbor the secretest thought in their minde, but such as in the owne time they shall not be ashamed openly to avouch; assuring themselves that Time the mother of Veritie, will in the due season bring her owne daughter to perfection.[4]

James here advocates for a fantasy that is in some ways antithetical to the modern liberal idea of privacy, and one that underscores the profound conceptual difficulties concerning the nature of monarchical domesticity that *The Duchess of Malfi* brilliantly explores. On the one hand, monarchs like James and Elizabeth had privy chambers that were open only to a select few, and so it would not have been controversial to assert that a ruler should be allowed to control access to her own chambers. But, on the other, James's advice reminds us that the ruler's chambers are guaranteed to provoke scrutiny and he urges the ruler to eschew privacy. Webster's play is about the intense, corrosive scrutiny that royal privacy generates, and one could read the Duchess's story as an instantiation of the truism that the secrets of the great must eventually come to light.

We aim here to revisit the political dimensions of the dramatic representation of privacy and secrecy in *The Duchess of Malfi*. To do so, we wish to focus in particular upon the way the play imagines the architectural spaces in which its action takes place.[5] This, we argue, undergoes a transformation in Webster's play as control of the dramatic action is seized away from the Duchess by her brothers. As this happens, Webster avails himself of a manner of imagining the court as a dramatic locale that, as a shorthand, we will call the proto-gothic: a conception of courtly space in which hidden places like secret chambers, vaults and passageways stand in some metaphorical or allegorical relation to the murky and dangerous psychological and/or somatic interiors of the tyrants and schemers who inhabit them. This politicized conception of space and/as character will be familiar to readers of Jacobean and Caroline tragedy – from plays like *The Changeling* (1622), for example – and it will likewise be self-evident that a conception of court as a hive of secret spaces has a political dimension in relation to the ideological fantasy of kings as 'publike persons'. Our reading of *The Duchess of Malfi* hinges on the idea that the play interrogates the categorical confusion surrounding royal secrecy by means of a metadramatic competition over the imagination of architectural space that takes place as the play moves from the Duchess's household to the spaces associated with Ferdinand and the Cardinal.

In order to understand what is at stake in the proto-gothic conception of court that comes to dominate Webster's play-world, it will be necessary to locate *The Duchess of Malfi* within a thumbnail literary history of the mode's English deployment. To do this, we will here trace interconnections between three related plays from three quite different micro-political moments. They are, respectively, the early Inns of Court tragedy *Gismond of Salern*, first performed before Elizabeth in the mid to late 1560s, Webster's mid-Jacobean masterpiece, which has a great deal in common with *Gismond* and almost certainly draws upon it, and William Davenant's early Caroline play *The Cruel Brother* (1627), which is closely modelled upon *The Duchess of Malfi* but which is also very much about the problematic figure of the Duke of Buckingham.

We argue here that thinking about the early provenance of this proto-gothic manner of imagining courts can – by helping to clarify political stakes that would once have been implicit in the form – enrich our understanding of the Jacobean and Caroline plays where we encounter it most often. In particular, we want to argue that reading *The Duchess of Malfi* as part of this tradition can allow us to recover political implications implicit in its dramaturgy and available to contemporary audiences that have not always been adequately recognized in criticism of the play. Even more broadly, we are also interested in exploring the interplay between literary form and political circumstance within the literary historical story these plays allow us to tell, a story about how an early Elizabethan insider language of political advice used by Inns of Courtiers to address their queen becomes over time a staple of anticourt fantasy.

* * *

Gismond of Salern – written by several members of the Inner Temple for performance before Queen Elizabeth in 1566–68 – marks the point at which lurid stereotypes concerning the secret interior spaces of court enter the bloodstream of English vernacular drama. This play, adapted from the first tale of the fourth day of Boccaccio's *Decameron*, hinges upon the secret love affair of Gismond, a young widow, princess of Salern, who is discovered by her father Tancred with tragic consequences.[6] The play has two movements, each organized around an architectural conceit that allegorizes the unruly passions of its human actors. The first half of the play, introduced by Cupid, depicts Gismond's love affair, which is facilitated by a secret vault and passageway through which she is able to smuggle her lover into her bedroom. This hidden passage, allowing access to Gismond's chambers, mirrors the way love itself is said to enter Gismond by 'creeping through all her veines within' (1.1.63).

Compared to Boccaccio's novella, which grants Gismond's desire for a lover considerable dignity, the Inns of Court play emphasizes the disorderliness of Gismond's passion as a parallel to her father's. When Gismond's love affair is discovered by the over-loving, semi-incestuous Tancred – who hides in his daughter's bedroom and watches as the affair is consummated – Cupid departs and the Senecan fury Megaera takes over. Tancred, in the play's second movement, has his daughter's lover killed in a prison that is described as the last remaining portion of a ruined tower, a 'strong turrett compact of stone and rock / hugie without, but horrible within' (5.1.61–2). This description seems to allegorize the relationship between Tancred's power and what the play calls 'the horror of his furious breast' (5.1.71). Tancred's servants kill the lover and cut out his heart, which is then delivered to Gismond in a golden chalice. And Gismond completes the tragedy by weeping into the cup, adding poison and drinking the mixture off.

Thinking of *Gismond of Salern* as a point of origin for the proto-gothic depiction of court corruption in English drama puts us in position to hazard some remarks about the mode's literary provenance. *Gismond* is the first of many English tragedies to be adapted from stories lifted from the novella tradition, and like many other plays, it borrows from these stories not only their plots but also motifs of enclosed space that serve as metaphors for body and self.[7] *Gismond of Salern* also draws on a neo-classical Dido play by Lodovico Dolce, the same Dolce whose version of Euripides forms the basis of Gascoigne's and Kinwelmersh's *Jocasta* (1566), another early Elizabethan Inns of Court play. And finally, *Gismond*, with its Fury, its numerous lines lifted directly from *Thyestes*, and its stichomythic scenes of counsel spurned, is part of the remarkable early-Elizabethan renaissance of Senecan drama which included the publication of translations of at least seven of the ten plays then attributed to Seneca between 1559 and 1567 as well as the performance of Senecan-style tragedies like *Gorboduc* and *Gismond*.

Ultimately, the proto-gothic imagination of *Gismond of Salern* can be traced all the way back to Seneca's description of the secret grove in which Atreus commits his murders in *Thyestes*:

> On the summit of the citadel is a section of the House of Pelops that faces south. Its outer flank rises up like a mountain, hemming in the city and holding in its range a populace defiant to its kings. Here is a vast gleaming hall, room enough for a multitude, its gilded roofbeams supported by columns with conspicuous varied markings. Behind these public rooms, where whole peoples pay court, the wealthy house goes back a great distance. At the farthest and lowest remove there lies a secret area that confines an age-old-woodland in a deep vale – the inner sanctum of the realm.[8]

This 'inner sanctum' is where Atreus murders his nephews, and it is depicted by Seneca as a kind of pre-Cartesian allegory of somatic interiority: the hidden secret inside correlating to autocratic power and public magnificence. We might think of this, especially, as a classical analogue for Tancred's forbidding 'turrett'. But in *Gismond* this space appears in relation to Gismond's room, a more explicitly feminine space of a kind that is exuberantly elaborated in the many Italian novellas that narrate various ways to grant and deny access to a woman's room and sexual body.[9] In the archive underpinning *Gismond*'s architectural imagination, Senecan tragedy, Italian tragedy and the novella tradition all inform each other before being poached by the Inns of Courtiers, who draw on what Michele Marrapodi describes as a 'Senecan-Boccaccian tradition' that is developed in Italian theatre and travels to England via both prose and drama.[10]

The play combines classicism and Italianate learning in a display of self-conscious erudition directed to political ends. Jessica Winston has suggested that early Elizabethan Inns of Court writers were drawn to Senecan drama both because of Senecan tragedy's interest in tyranny and failed counsel and also because Seneca himself, as both dramatist and advisor to Nero, was a classical exemplar for the kind of politically engaged authorship to which they themselves aspired.[11] If so, it is not surprising that these same Inns of Courtiers should also have been drawn to novella collections. For, though Boccaccio's tales are not framed overtly as political discourse, already in 1476 Masuccio Salernitano's *Novellino* is made up of tales individually dedicated to courtiers in Aragonese Naples, so that by the sixteenth-century *Novelle* of Matteo Bandello the storytelling scene has been recast to reflect authorial self-consciousness about literary advising and access to elite society: each of Bandello's tales – including that of the Duchess of Malfi – is framed by a dedicatory letter recounting when Bandello first heard the story told, usually among Italian ladies and gentlemen passing the time in courtly conversation, often in the context of authorial commentary on social mores. Bandello portrays a social space of power that is negotiated through the exchange of fictions.

William Painter, a gunner and clerk at the Tower of London whose influential anthology of translations of Italian, French and classical stories was published in 1566, signals his interest in this space, and imagines it architecturally, when he titles his collection *The Palace of Pleasure*. The architectural image allows Painter to map his book onto the elite space of the Elizabethan court, as in this rhetorical question, from the dedicatory epistle to the 1575 reprinting of the *Palace*:

> who is he that more condignelye doth deserue to be possesst in a Palace of Pleasure, than he that is daily resiant in a Palace of renowmed fame, guided by a Queen adorned with most excellent beauty indued and garnished with great learning, passing vertues and rare qualities of minde.[12]

Yet although his dedication imagines a virtuous Queen, many of the stories in the collection hinge on secrecy, violence and unruly passions. Painter's architectural conceit makes literal both a desire for access to the palaces of the great and a pessimism about their secrets, and both attitudes figure prominently in the broader 'Senecan-Boccaccian tradition' that provides the source material for *Gismond of Salern*.

The immediate political concerns animating *Gismond of Salern* are the succession and the plight of Lady Catherine Grey, a potential claimant to the throne who had been imprisoned for her secret marriage to

Edward Seymour.[13] But more generally, the play comments, via a cautionary tale hedged by profuse flattery, upon Elizabeth's peremptory refusal to accept counsel about marriage and succession. Its authors emphasize Gismond's erotic incontinence in order to distance her from the chaste queen of England, but the play's real political concerns have more to do with Tancred's tyrannical reaction to his daughter than with the politics of dynastic marriage per se. In *Gismond*, as in Seneca, the secret dungeon where Tancred has his daughter's lover killed represents something like the interiority of tyranny, and much is made in the second half of *Gismond of Salern* of the abject servitude of the functionaries who perform Tancred's commands. The play, in other words, features an architecturally allegorized anatomy of tyranny as unchecked passion that is facilitated by the lack of any real conciliar independence.

Written from the perspective of Inns of Courtiers – would-be advisors who are concerned about Elizabeth's refusal to listen to advice concerning marriage and succession – *Gismond of Salern* is a cautionary tale concerning the political imbalance and tyranny that can overtake a realm when proper counsel is dispensed with.[14] It therefore allows us to see how the proto-gothic imagination of court space operates as a political trope, simultaneously allegorizing the immoderate passions within the tyrant's breast and linking the psychophysiology of tyranny to an architecture designed to provide the literal secrecy required for nefarious schemes. That is, the secret interiors that dominate the play's architectural landscape represent the hidden promptings within the human breast that can manifest themselves as immoderate love or as tyranny and at the same time speak to what happens to government when it moves out of council chambers and into the ruler's 'inner sanctum'. What *Gismond* allows us to see, therefore, is how the proto-gothic imagination of court adopted by Inns of Courtiers from a 'Senecan-Boccaccian tradition' served as a figural language for corruption in a political milieu that put a premium on counsel and imagined that a ruler should be 'carefull not to harbor the secretest thought'.

In 1591, one of *Gismond*'s original authors, Robert Wilmot, allowed a stylistically updated version of the play to be printed as *The Tragedie of Tancred and Gismund*. This belated print publication implies that the play had an enduring reputation, and lends credence to Michael Neill's estimation that the Inns of Courtier John Ford – whose *'Tis Pity She's a Whore* features several motifs reminiscent of *Gismond* – would have been aware of the earlier play as 'one of the more celebrated amateur successes to have emerged from the Inns of Court in the generations preceding his own'.[15] The same might be said of Webster if one accepts (as we do) that he is most likely the same John Webster who entered the Middle Temple in 1598. In fact, since Webster was likely a Middle Templar, and since Davenant, at the time when he wrote his early tragedies was a member of the household of Middle Templar Fulke Greville, it begins to seem as though the proto-gothic imagination of court with which we are concerned may in fact be a dramatic vocabulary associated throughout our period with the Inns of Court. Noting this helps make sense of the otherwise uncanny way in which *Gismond of Salern* seems to anticipate the characteristic atmosphere of later plays like *The Duchess of Malfi*: there is a tradition here, one which associates Italianate tragedy, a proto-gothic style of somatic/architectural allegory and a would-be advisor's avid concern with political tyranny and corruption.

* * *

The Duchess of Malfi also comes from a novella: in this case one of Bandello's novelle that is translated in Painter's *Palace of Pleasure*. Webster's version of the story, moreover, features several episodes and motifs not present in Painter that seem indebted in a more general way to the 'Senecan-Boccaccian tradition'.[16] We think that *The Duchess of Malfi* is indebted specifically to *Gismond of Salern*, too, since both plays are about the amatory desires of young widows and about the incestuous impulses of male family members seeking to control them.[17] Webster, as an Inns of Court writer, would likely have been familiar with *Gismond of Salern*, and he probably also knew the story of Tancred and Gismond from Painter's collection as well. He may also have been reminded of *Gismond of Salern* because he was interested in parallels between Catherine Grey's situation and that of Arbella Stuart. Stuart, of course, was a potential claimant to the throne who had been imprisoned for a secret marriage to William Seymour in 1610. Their clandestine marriage, escape and her subsequent recapture, it has been argued, is a contemporary topical analogue for the secret marriage, flight and eventual capture of Webster's Duchess.[18] Stuart's husband, William Seymour, was in fact the grandson of Catherine Grey and her clandestine husband, Edward Seymour, and there is evidence that some of Webster's contemporaries considered these two cases as historical echoes of one another.[19] Since *Gismond* was originally composed to comment upon Grey's case, perhaps Webster, thinking about Stuart's case as a kind of re-enactment of Grey's, likewise thought of the earlier play.

Antonio's famous panegyric to the French royal household (1.1.4–22) frames the action of *The Duchess of Malfi* in terms of the political meaning of the privacy or secrecy of rulers, praising the French king for eschewing the intimacy of 'flattering sycophants' (8) and insisting upon the overriding importance to his 'blessed government' of 'a most provident council' (16–17). The emphasis on the importance of independent council is a truism, one shared by the Inner Templars who composed *Gismond of Salern* as a study of secrecy, tyrannical passion and advisorial sycophancy. And by framing his play explicitly in terms of the importance of free and independent council, Webster in effect aligns his own play with a quasi-republican ethos popular with would-be councillors at the Inns of Court. Since the play later adopts something like the same proto-gothic sense of court corruption deployed by *Gismond*'s authors, we can perhaps understand Antonio's speech as a generic marker as well: it announces the play's participation in a tradition of politicized drama designed to comment upon court corruption from the specifically conciliar perspective associated with the Inns of Court.

It does so even as concerns about the politics of intimacy and council become increasingly urgent during the first decade of King James's reign. Queen Elizabeth's chambers had been staffed by women who enjoyed informal authority by virtue of their access to the queen but who were prevented by their gender from holding political office. When James ascended to the English throne, he retained most of the Elizabethan machinery of government but staffed his Bedchamber with Scottish associates who were also entrusted with considerable official authority. There is nothing unprecedented or inherently corrupt (by pre-bureaucratic standards) in this arrangement, but one can see how emphasizing the political power of the Bedchamber might seem to threaten the ideal of conciliar independence that Antonio articulates.[20] There was certainly grumbling, from the beginning of James's reign, about the wealth and influence granted to Bedchamber favourites, and this only intensified as difficulties concerning crown finances (and thus royal patronage) came to a head after the failure of Robert Cecil's Great Contract in 1610. Cecil's death in 1612 seemed to shift the balance of power away from the Privy Council and towards the Bedchamber, which had come to be dominated by the Scottish favourite Robert Carr, Earl of Somerset. The premature death of Prince Henry later that same year also deprived those unhappy with James of hope for a brighter future. These events, leading up to the failure of the so-called Addled Parliament, all contributed to what has recently been called 'the crisis of 1614'.[21]

Written during the uncertain period leading up to this crisis, *The Duchess of Malfi* registers a growing uneasiness with the Jacobean politics of favouritism and intimacy. Looked at this way, it becomes possible to see in Webster's play – which begins with Antonio's long speech on healthy royal households and ends with multiple murders in the Cardinal's darkened chambers – a specifically mid-Jacobean quality of anxious foreboding. This is presumably part of what J. W. Lever meant when he declared, some years ago, that 'the court of Amalfi presents in miniature the court of Whitehall'.[22] It would be more accurate, though, to say that *The Duchess of Malfi* explores questions concerning secrecy and tyranny that felt increasingly urgent during 1612–14, and that it does so while deploying a proto-gothic figural language, understood to be appropriate for such questions, with a long pedigree. More specifically, *The Duchess of Malfi* captures this mid-Jacobean foreboding by imagining the kind of secret interior space derived from plays like *Gismond of Salern* as an outsider's fantasy of court corruption, projected by Ferdinand, Bosola and others onto the Duchess's privy chambers, that then becomes true when the Duchess is supplanted by her tyrannical brothers.

The play opens in the 'presence' chamber of the Duchess's palace (1.2.1), the equivalent of what Seneca describes as 'public rooms, where whole peoples pay court'. Antonio introduces the Duchess and her brother by describing the differences between their outward personae and their putatively hidden interiors. The Cardinal, we learn, has some courtly elegances that he displays for show, but 'his inward character' is melancholy and jealous (1.2.74–78); as for Ferdinand, 'what appears in him mirth is merely outside' (1.2.88). The Duchess, however, is described as a figure of perfect integrity, morally constant even when alone: 'her nights – nay more, her very sleeps – / Are more in heaven, than other ladies' shrifts' (1.2.120–1). There is already something allegorical about the play's conception of architectural space and bodily or psychological interiority, and the opening of the play provokes curiosity about both even as it prepares to move into more private areas of the palace.

After the play enters the Duchess's privy domain, it emphasizes the gap between what actually happens there and the far more lurid ways in which privacies are imagined by those on the outside. The Duchess's brothers generate much of the play's nosey curiosity about the Duchess's secret domain, but the play also demonstrates how rumours get generated about the Duchess without any specific referent save secrecy itself. When the Duchess, to hide the delivery of her child, puts her palace into lock-down, a rumour is shown to emerge spontaneously about 'a Switzer in the Duchess's bedchamber' with a pistol in his codpiece as part of a French assassination plot (2.2.37), and later a rumour circulates that Antonio is a 'hermaphrodite', and unable to 'abide a woman' (3.2.221–2). Bosola speculates that the Duchess may have been the victim of sorcery (3.1.63–5), and Antonio tries to put Bosola off the scent by hinting that the Duchess may have been poisoned (2.3.30–1). The point seems to be that the privy chambers of the great are productive of almost random talk, endless variations on a few basic themes. In using a plot featuring secret pregnancies, Webster maps the tendency of women's (potentially) birthing bodies to provoke suspicion – exemplified also in the rampant Elizabethan rumour-mongering about secret pregnancies hidden and delivered on progress – onto curiosity about the secrets of the great.[23] This allows him to offer a symptomatic analysis of what the play itself calls 'Pasquil's paper bullets, court calumny', which is seen as 'a pestilent air, which princes' palaces / Are seldom purged of' (3.1.50–51).

When Ferdinand and the Cardinal imagine their sister's secrecy as moral incontinence, they are, of course, participating in a long-standing discursive tradition associating patriarchal anxieties about the secrets of women's bodies with unruly or ungoverned interiority. And (as in *Gismond of Salern*) the brand of unruly or over-passionate inwardness that the brothers ascribe to the Duchess is likewise readily associated with the personal misrule of the tyrant. But although Ferdinand claims that the Duchess's passions are disorderly, Webster uses her ability to regulate the space of her household as an index to her capacity for both government and self-government. This is clearest, perhaps, in the birth scene, where Bosola's misogynistic observations concerning the Duchess's intemperate appetites and apparent pregnancy are countered by the ability of the Duchess and Antonio to 'shut up the court gates' (2.2.29). In that scene, the sense of corporeal leakiness or incontinence that one might expect to find associated with childbirth in a misogynistic Renaissance tragedy is displaced onto Antonio, whose inopportune nosebleed (2.3.41) seems to register in somatic terms the breach of security represented by his encounter with Bosola.[24] Elsewhere, the Duchess uses an architectural metaphor to describe to Antonio the virtue she recognizes in him:

> If you will know where breathes a complete man
> (I speak it without flattery) turn your eyes,
> And progress through yourself. (1.2.346–48)

When Antonio promises to be 'the constant sanctuary / of [the Duchess's] good name' (1.2.370–1), she confidently shelters him within her 'circumference' (1.2.378). Webster, in a sly reversal of gender stereotypes, makes his widowed Duchess capable of self-governance, shows her household space to be well-regulated and represents her lover-favourite as a public servant worthy of regard.

The brothers' initial attitudes towards their sister read like a parody of James's injunction against harbouring secrets: they threaten her with the erasure of her privacy ('your darkest actions – nay, your privatest thoughts, / Will come to light' [1.2.231–2]), and also with enclosure ('the marriage night / Is the entrance into some prison' [1.2.239–40]). But it is when Bosola gives Ferdinand 'a false key / Into her bed-chamber' (3.1.80–1), that the Duchess begins to lose control of her body, her household and her realm.[25] Ferdinand's incursion into the Duchess's chamber likewise inaugurates a striking transformation in the way the play imagines the hidden space of power, a shift towards the political-architectural register we have been calling the proto-gothic. Ferdinand (who is himself characterized as a haunted house [3.1.23–4]) tells the Duchess that if she wants to protect her husband, she must 'build / Such a room for him as our anchorites / To holier use inhabit' (3.2.100–2), perverting the language of shelter that she offered Antonio before. And in what follows the play is dominated more and more by the unnamable manias of Ferdinand and the Cardinal and located, increasingly, in secret, labyrinthine, and macabre interiors.

Beginning with the moment that Ferdinand, Tancred-like, invades the bedchamber, Webster's pervasive, metadramatic interest in the conventions governing the representation of secret interiors finds expression in a conceptual battle between the Duchess and her brother over the meaning of the spaces they both inhabit. Political control brings with it the ability to control the spaces of the play: where the play's first two acts emphasize the Duchess's ability to control her privy chambers, her sometimes-pregnant body and the meaning of what takes place within the 'circumference' of the embrace she offers to Antonio (1.2.378), its characteristic settings from this point on seem increasingly to allegorize the murky and unregulated passions of the play's fraternal tyrants even as they provide the kind of secrecy required for them to commit their atrocities. As Ferdinand seizes power, compelled to commit atrocities by inner passions that remain secret even to himself, the play moves into a new secret space, bathed in darkness, a space that contains the sister who has become for him both the focus of obsessive attention and the object he feels he must avoid.

The literature of tyranny commonly associates a tyrant's disorderly personal passions with illegitimate and violent rule in the body politic, and we can think of the proto-gothic mode, which represents the murky interiority of the tyrant by means of the physical space of his court, as a trope for this kind of analogical thinking: the ruler's body mirrors his household which in turn represents the body politic. Part of the attraction (and horror) of imagery that links the hidden spaces of court to the ruler's own body lies in the way it can project corrupted interior states outward. A court full of gossips and spies, a court where the rule of the legitimate monarch is abrogated, becomes a court where the spaces that should be harmoniously aligned with the monarch's orderly energies and intentions become disordered, alienated, haunted, gothic. Such disturbed spaces both stand for the monarch's body and are spaces that people can walk through or hide or be trapped in: rooms, prisons, closets. Threatening, quasi-animated spaces like the Duchess's prison in Act IV offer a vivid way of imagining corruption as a quality that pervades an entire dramatic environment without necessarily being directly attributable at all times to any individual's agency. When her brother summons the chorus of madmen to serenade the Duchess's prison in Act IV, the effect is to surround the Duchess with an atmospheric insanity that is at once Ferdinand's own and something more pervasive.

The proto-gothic space of the prison reflects at once Ferdinand's attempts to torment and control his sister, his own disordered psyche and the play's metatheatrical registering of usurpation and tyranny. It is also the Duchess's 'last presence chamber', (4.2.164), and the relationship between the two siblings continues to involve an imaginative battle over the meaning of this space. Believing that she is looking at the corpses of her husband and child, the Duchess wishes that 'they would bind me to that lifeless trunk, / And let me freeze to death' (4.1.66–7). In so saying, she reframes as an act of mercy the 'immoderate cruell punishmente' offered to an unfaithful wife from Bandello's novellas, known as 'A Lady of Turin' in Painter's *Palace*, who is walled up with her lover's corpse. In other words, she replaces her brother's punishment for illegitimate sexuality with an act of willing self-sacrifice of the type associated with heroic wives.[26] The Duchess's continued opposition to her brothers, along with the contrast between the orderly, sheltering spaces of her rule and this space of mutilation and murder, reminds the audience that this chamber is a perversion of what we saw of her court as the play opened.

The play's crazy finale, which takes place primarily inside the Cardinal's chambers, is staged as a kind of farcical re-enactment of its earlier action; this time, both Antonio and Bosola have been granted secret access. Antonio signals a parallel between this scene and the earlier one where Ferdinand appears in the Duchess's chambers, declaring,

> I have got
> Private access to his chamber, and intend
> To visit him about the mid of night,
> As once his brother did our noble Duchess. (5.1.63–6)

The scene also recalls the earlier birth scene, because everyone in the household is again confined to their rooms. The Senecan trope of a building with deceptively magnificent exteriors recurs as a way to describe the tyrant in Bosola's description of the Cardinal: 'wherefore should you lay fair marble colours / Upon your rotten purposes to me' (5.2.282–3). In contrast to the well-managed domestic intimacy shared in secret by Antonio and the Duchess, the later scenes in the Cardinal's chambers show Julia's sudden and immoderate lust for Bosola (declared behind locked doors), the Cardinal's murder of Julia, Ferdinand's insanity (manifested as lycanthropic rage at false insides) and the stabbing deaths of Antonio, the Cardinal and Bosola. The mistaken identity plot – in which Bosola accidentally murders Antonio – and the brutal gest by which none of the Cardinal's associates are willing to respond to his cries of help at the end – convey the impression that the Cardinal's rooms are as dark and labyrinthine as their chief inhabitant.

When the Cardinal advises Julia that the holders of prince's secrets 'had need have their breasts hooped with adamant / To contain them' (5.2.246–7), his use of a spatio-bodily image for secrecy anticipates the murder by which he reduces her person to a silent space, 'a grave dark and obscure enough / For such a secret' (5.2.257–8). Then, when the Duchess's voice speaks from the grave in the echo scene (in 5.3), the play once again uses the spatial possibilities of the stage to contrast the Duchess's legitimate rule with her brothers' tyranny. Stripped of political authority, the Duchess's voice appears as an echo in a ruined building, contributing to the proto-gothic atmosphere of the play's last two acts. As with the ruined fortress that houses Tancred's turret in the second half of *Gismond of Salern*, the association of the Duchess's voice with architectural ruins calls up associations of cultural decay that have political implications for the world of the play. The effect is to extend the metadramatic contest over the play-world's space beyond the Duchess's death, but also to underscore the tenuousness of what remains of the Duchess in an imagined political milieu that is now more conducive to secrecy and scandal than to any 'provident council' (1.1.17).

Since both the Duchess's use of heroic, masculine language and the evocative theme of secret, royal pregnancies seem designed to evoke memories of Elizabeth, it is possible that the play's atmosphere of decay expresses a cultural pessimism related to the passing of Prince Henry and the collapse of the programme of self-conscious Elizabethan nostalgia that he fostered. But the crucial point is that the horrors that take place in the play's second movement – in darkened, secret spaces, perpetrated by tyrants who are themselves figured as grand edifices with dangerous secrets inside – beggar the imagination demonstrated earlier in the play by producers of court calumny. In this sense, the play explicitly charts a process by which its own lurid reality overtakes the imagination of rumour-mongers, a process by which tyranny overtakes legitimate government and the secret spaces of the great become worse than they could ever have been imagined to be. Read this way,

The Duchess of Malfi becomes legible as a brilliantly evocative response to mid-Jacobean pessimism, one that uses a set of motifs and images borrowed from the 'Senecan-Boccaccian tradition' in order to capture a sense that anticourt stereotypes in circulation for decades might now be coming true.

* * *

Shortly *after* the first performances of Webster's play, suspicions concerning Jacobean secrecy received spectacular confirmation in the scandalous revelations of the Overbury murder trials which, as Alastair Bellany has shown, had an enormous and lasting impact upon the way early Stuart subjects thought about court corruption.[27] The sensational trials of 1615–16, in which the king's favourite Somerset and his wife were convicted of conspiring to poison Overbury in the Tower of London, reminded observers of plays like Webster's and made it seem that, with regard to lurid court secrecies at least, reality had caught up with fiction.[28]

Bellany, who reads *The Duchess of Malfi* as an indicator of English paranoia concerning royal courts on the eve of the Overbury trials, notes that 'the pressure of contemporary events could infuse traditional stereotypes of court corruption with an intense political energy'.[29] This is what seems to have happened to the proto-gothic imagination of court secrecy in the years following the initial performances of Webster's play: a mode of dramatic representation that had once offered Inns of Courtiers an oblique way to comment upon the linkage between tyranny, secrecy and counsel without specifically accusing the English monarchy of anything became a vehicle for topically pointed representation of an explicitly anticourt variety. We can see this transformation by turning briefly to William Davenant's earliest staged play, *The Cruel Brother*, which, though not especially well-known, is interesting specifically as an early Caroline imitation of *The Duchess of Malfi*. One has the sense, reading these plays for their shared figural vocabularies, that the pessimism one can detect behind Webster's play has been replaced by a more overtly critical anticourt discourse by the time Davenant composes his.

Davenant's debt to Webster is clear from the overall dramatic structure of his play: like *The Duchess of Malfi*, *The Cruel Brother* begins in a comparatively realistic political setting in which outsiders spread libellous rumours about the secrecies of the court only to undergo a transformation in mode that involves adopting the proto-gothic sense of court space that we have been discussing. The first two acts of *The Cruel Brother* make much of the mundane realities of patronage and access in a court dominated by Lucio, the virtuous favourite of the duke of Sienna. In one episode (1.1.120–220), Lucio's virtuous underling Foreste is shown denying a request for a monopoly patent; in another (1.2), Lucio converses with the duke while suitors clamour offstage for attention.[30] The duke's privy chambers are private, and are therefore understood as a space set apart from the play's more common venues, but there is no sense that what goes on in these hidden chambers is anything scandalous.

The play's transformation occurs at the end of Act II, when the affection which had initially drawn the duke to his favourite gets transferred (in a scene specifically reminiscent of Ferdinand's change of heart after his sister's death) to the favourite's wife. When this happens, the duke is transformed from a flighty, besotted and somewhat irresponsible ruler, more interested in his favourite than in the business of statecraft, into a brooding and malevolent tyrant capable of rape. And as the duke changes, so does the way the play depicts the architecture of his court. By Act V, the duke's privy chambers have been re-imagined (in a manner strikingly reminiscent of the finale of *The Duchess of Malfi*) as a network of secret passages surrounding the duke's bedchamber in which the characters skulk around with dark lanterns and secret master-keys and ambush one another. This alteration in the play's architectural imagination is strongly associated with the duke's psychological transformation and so can be read in terms of the same proto-gothic conception of secrecy and tyranny on display in both *Gismond of Salern* and the second portion of Webster's play.

The Cruel Brother invites topical, political reading much more overtly than does Webster's play, adopting the proto-gothic sense of space that it shares with *Gismond* and *The Duchess of Malfi* to comment upon early Caroline firestorms surrounding the Duke of Buckingham, whose career was understood both as the source of court corruption and as a product of the overextension of royal prerogative. Or, to be more precise: the gossip that the duke's privy chambers generate during the play's opening acts indexes the rumour and innuendo surrounding Buckingham before his assassination in 1628. But the transformation of the play after the end of Act II shifts the blame away from the favourite, offering instead an anatomy of tyranny that traces the roots of political outrage to the ruler's own lack of self-government. By locating his play's denouement in the kind of proto-gothic setting associated at once with the failure of counsel and with tyrannical excess, Davenant comments upon the problem of favouritism in such as way as to offer up a striking and intentional reversal of an official language of complaint that blamed the favourite while exculpating the king.[31]

Since *The Cruel Brother* is in some ways derivative of *The Duchess of Malfi*, and since it uses its proto-gothic conception of the royal household in an overtly political manner, to comment upon the intensifying controversy surrounding Buckingham and King Charles ca. 1627, we can read Davenant's play as offering confirmation of our argument about the always-already political nature of this mode of dramatic representation. For *The Cruel Brother*, as for *The Duchess of Malfi* and *Gismond of Salern*, the proto-gothic court offers at once an allegory of the psychology of the kind of tyrannical ruler who dispenses with provident counsel and a lurid manner of imagining the space of political secrecy that replaces public governance. Strikingly, though, for all of *The Cruel Brother*'s overt topical resonance, its proto-gothic manner of depicting tyranny and corruption ultimately involves repurposing a figural vocabulary, borrowed from Webster, that was originally conceived of as an Elizabethan vehicle for delicate political advice.

Notes

1. Catherine Belsey, *The Subject of Tragedy: Identity & Difference in Renaissance Drama* (1985; rpt London: Routledge, 1991), p. 197. For a resumé of subsequent criticism dealing with the play's depiction of domesticity, see Wendy Wall, 'Just a Spoonful of Sugar: Syrup and Domesticity in Early Modern England', *Modern Philology*, 104.2 (2006), 149–72.
2. Belsey, *The Subject of Tragedy*, pp. 199–200.
3. See, e.g., Frances Dolan's essay in this volume, and the essays on secrecy cited therein. Lena Cowan Orlin's *Locating Privacy in Tudor London* (Oxford: Oxford University Press, 2007) reminds us that modern notions of privacy rely upon modern arrangements of domestic and institutional space.
4. King James VI and I, *Political Writings*, ed. by Johann P. Somerville (Cambridge: Cambridge University Press, 1995), p. 4.
5. On space in Webster's play see especially Judith Haber, '"My Body Bestow upon My Women": The Space of the Feminine in *The Duchess of Malfi*', *Renaissance Drama*, n.s. 28 (1999), 133–59, and Lisa Hopkins, 'With the Skin Side Inside: The Interiors of *The Duchess of Malfi*', in *Privacy, Domesticity, and Women in Early Modern England*, ed. by Corinne S. Abate (Aldershot: Ashgate, 2003), pp. 21–30.
6. See John W. Cunliffe, '*Gismond of Salerne*', *PMLA*, 21 (1906), 435–61, John Murray, '*Tancred and Gismund*', *The Review of English Studies*, o.s. 14 (1938), 385–95, and Melissa Walter, 'Shakespeare's News: Autonomy, Authority and the Symbolic Vocabulary of European Novellas in Early Modern England', (Unpublished Doctoral Thesis, University of Wisconsin, 2004), pp. 147–86. Our text is from Cunliffe's *Early English Classical Tragedies* (Oxford: Clarendon Press, 1912). Citations will be given parenthetically.
7. See Melissa Walter, 'Shakespeare's News', 'Dramatic Bodies and Novellesque Spaces in Jacobean Tragedy and Tragicomedy' in *Transnational and Transcultural Exchange in Early Modern Drama: Theater Crossing Borders*, ed. by Robert Henke and Eric Nichols (Aldershot: Ashgate, 2008), pp. 63–77, and 'Drinking from Skulls and the Politics of Incorporation in Early Stuart Drama' in *At the Table: Metaphorical and Material*

Cultures of Food in Medieval and Early Modern Europe, ed. by Timothy J. Tomasik and Juliann M. Vitullo (Turnhout: Brepols, 2007), pp. 93–105.

8. Seneca, *Tragedies*, ed. and trans. John G. Fitch, 2 vols (Cambridge: Harvard University Press, 2002–04), II, 286.
9. Walter, 'Dramatic Bodies', p. 63.
10. Marrapodi, 'Retaliation as an Italian Vice in English Renaissance Drama: Narratives and Theatrical Exchanges', in *The Italian World of English Renaissance Drama: Cultural Exchange and Intertextuality*, ed. by Marrapodi and A. J. Hoenselaars (Newark: University of Delaware Press, 1998), pp. 190–207.
11. Winston, 'Seneca in Early Elizabethan England', *Renaissance Quarterly*, 59 (2006), 29–58.
12. *Palace of Pleasure*, ed. Joseph Jacobs, 3 vols (1890; rpt. Honolulu: University Press of the Pacific, 2002), I, 6.
13. See, e.g., Marie Axton, *The Queen's Two Bodies: Drama and the Elizabethan Succession* (London: Royal Historical Society, 1977), pp. 56–8.
14. For a more fully elaborated version of this reading of the play see Curtis Perry, '*Gismond of Salern* and the Elizabethan Politics of Senecan Drama', forthcoming in *Gender Matters*, ed. by Mara R. Wade (Amsterdam: Rodopi).
15. Neill, '"What Strange Riddle's This?": Deciphering *'Tis Pity She's a Whore*', in *John Ford: Critical Re-Visions*, ed. by Michael Neill (Cambridge: Cambridge University Press, 1988), pp. 153–79. The quotation is from p. 158. See also Marrapodi, 'Retaliation'.
16. See R. W. Dent, *John Webster's Borrowing* (Berkeley: University of California Press, 1960), and Gunnar Boklund, *The Duchess of Malfi: Sources, Themes, Characters* (Cambridge: Harvard University Press, 1962).
17. Frank Whigham's account of Ferdinand's incestuousness as status-based and encoding a wish for perfected endogamy (*Seizures of the Will in Early Modern Drama* [Cambridge: Cambridge University Press, 1996], pp. 188–201) also helps explain the incestuous coding of Tancred's relation to his daughter.
18. Sara Jayne Steen, 'The Crime of Marriage: Arbella Stuart and *The Duchess of Malfi*', *Sixteenth Century Journal*, 22 (1991), 61–76.
19. See Sara Jayne Steen, ed., *The Letters of Lady Arbella Stuart* (New York: Oxford University Press, 1994), pp. 82–3.
20. See the essays collected in David Starkey, ed., *The English Court: From the Wars of the Roses to the Civil War* (London: Longman, 1987).
21. Stephen Clucas and Rosalind Davies, ed., *The Crisis of 1614 and the Addled Parliament: Literary and Historical Perspectives* (Aldershot: Ashgate, 2003).
22. Lever, *The Tragedy of State* (London: Methuen, 1971), p. 87. See also Albert H. Tricomi, *Anticourt Drama in England, 1603–1642* (Charlottesville: University Press of Virginia, 1989), pp. 110–20.
23. On late medieval and early modern discourses concerning the maternal body's secrets see for example Katharine Park's *Secrets of Women: Gender, Generation, and the Origins of Human Dissection* (New York: Zone Books, 2006), pp. 121–59.
24. See also Haber, 'My Body', p. 143.
25. Haber reads Ferdinand's invasion as rape ('My Body', p. 144).
26. Painter, *Palace of Pleasure*, I, 241.
27. Bellany, *The Politics of Court Scandal in Early Modern England: News Culture and the Overbury Affair, 1603–1660* (Cambridge: Cambridge University Press, 2002). Webster knew Overbury, and may have served as something like his literary executor (see Charles R. Forker, *The Skull Beneath the Skin: The Achievement of John Webster* [Carbondale: Southern Illinois University Press, 1986], pp. 120–22).

28. See Muriel Bradbrook, 'Webster's Power Game' in *The Artist and Society in Shakspeare's England* (Sussex: The Harvester Press, 1982), pp. 51–58. On contemporary comparisons between the Overbury scandal and plays, see Bellany, *The Politics*, p. 74.
29. Bellany, *The Politics*, p. 5. On Webster's play see pp. 1–7.
30. Davenant, *The Cruel Brother*, in *Eros and Power in English Renaissance Drama: Five plays by Marlowe, Davenant, Massinger, Ford and Shakespeare*, ed. by Curtis Perry (Jefferson, NC: McFarland, 2008).
31. See Curtis Perry, *Literature and Favoritism in Early Modern England* (Cambridge: Cambridge University Press, 2006), pp. 163–73.

CHAPTER FIVE

The Duchess's Marriage in Contemporary Contexts

Leah S. Marcus

During Act I Scene Two of *The Duchess of Malfi* we, along with the Duchess's lady-in-waiting Cariola, observe as Antonio and the Duchess exchange marriage vows and then retire to consummate their union. After the harmonious, reciprocal language of the vows themselves, Cariola's reaction, which ends the scene, may come as a bit of a shock:

> Whether the spirit of greatness or of woman
> Reign most in her, I know not; but it shows
> A fearful madness. I owe her much of pity. (1.2.410–12)

According to Cariola, the Duchess's marriage is an act of courage and magnanimity ('spirit of greatness') but also of folly, inconstancy and incontinence, according to proverbial saws about women ('spirit [...] of woman'). It is also an act of 'fearful madness', and this final judgement tips the balance of Cariola's assessment decidedly towards the negative.

For whom does Cariola speak? Many readers and critics of the play have assumed that her assessment is culturally normative, and that early viewers or readers of the play would have agreed with her. Webster's main source, the second tome of William Painter's *Palace of Pleasure* (London, 1567), takes an equally dim view of the Duchess's match, calling it but 'a Maske and coverture to hide hir follies & shamelesse lusts' (p. 357). Painter's view of the match may reinforce our tendency to believe Cariola. In modern editions of the play, Cariola speaks after the

Duchess and Antonio have exited and thus gets the last word in the first act, which gives her comments the weight of a broad, cumulative moral judgement of the clandestine marriage that has just taken place.

In the first quarto of the play, however, which was published in 1623 and which serves as the base text for all modern editions, Antonio and the Duchess do not formally exit before Cariola makes her remarks. They are still on stage as she speaks, and all three exit together. The final stage direction reads '*Exeunt*', not '*Exit*'. Of course, early quartos of early modern plays are known to be unreliable, and Q1 *Duchess of Malfi* has enough irregularities in its printing that we cannot take its stage directions to be infallible.[1] Nor can we assume a direct correspondence between the play as printed and the play as performed on stage, or that the play, which was revived in London several times between its initial performances in 1612–13 and its first printing in 1623, remained static in its staging. We have strong evidence that it did not.[2] In my Arden Early Modern Drama edition of the *Duchess of Malfi*, I elected to preserve the first quarto's '*Exeunt*' at the end of the marriage scene. Entertaining the possibility that the scene can be staged differently than it has traditionally been opens up our evaluation of the Duchess's marriage to points of view other than Cariola's.

Having the Duchess and Antonio available on stage to hear Cariola's sentiments allows for an altered dynamic in performance. The two newlyweds may, for example, laugh off Cariola's dire language in a way that makes her look fairly ridiculous, or they may give her an incredulous stare. Or they may be so wrapped up in each other that they fail to hear her. Elsewhere in the play, when Cariola expresses an opinion strongly at odds with the Duchess's, we tend to side with the Duchess. At the end of 3.2, for example, when Cariola condemns the plan for the Duchess and her family to escape from Amalfi to Ancona under the pretext of a religious pilgrimage, Cariola protests, 'I do not like / This jesting with religion, this feigned pilgrimage' and the Duchess responds by calling her a 'superstitious fool' (3.2.319–21). As it turns out, Cariola is right to advise against travel to Ancona, where the Duchess falls into the Cardinal's carefully orchestrated trap, but her reasoning is nonetheless suspect: to feign a pilgrimage in the interests of saving a family is not necessarily 'jesting with religion'. In 4.2, even more forcefully, our sympathies are with the Duchess rather than with her lady in waiting. The Duchess dies in almost preternatural nobility and calm while Cariola flails out desperately to find some way of staying alive – within the space of a few lines, she demands a trial, claims spiritual unreadiness, asserts that she is pregnant, and claims to be contracted to be married. Her hysterical reaction to her impending death may be very human, but it scarcely inspires confidence in her judgement, particularly since it contrasts so markedly with the Duchess's transcendent serenity. If the Duchess and Antonio are onstage at the end of 1.2 to undercut Cariola's pronouncement upon their marriage with some sort of dismissive gesture, then Cariola's reaction can potentially be seen as overly conservative or unnecessarily fearful, like some of her reactions later in the play, rather than culturally normative.

This essay will consider the Duchess's marriage in terms of contemporary contexts that may, like the stage direction at the end of 1.2, expand our view of how the play resonated with its early readers and audiences. Of course, early opinion is finally unrecoverable, but it is nevertheless worth investigating, if only for its potential to help move us out of a recurrent tendency on the part of readers and literary critics to equate the play's final moral stance towards the Duchess and the choices she makes with some of the most negative judgements of her that are expressed within it (see Fran Dolan's survey of critical opinion in the present volume). What would seventeenth-century viewers have thought of the Duchess's clandestine marriage, assuming that they did not automatically agree with Cariola? The most important issue is its legitimacy: were the Duchess and Antonio legally married or were their children, as Duke Ferdinand suggests more than once, bastards? As Fran Dolan's contribution to the present volume suggests, in England itself the issue of what constituted valid marriage was complicated and contested at the time. And in Italy, where the play is set, what constituted marriage would depend on which state one happened to be married in and the date of one's marriage contract. After the Council of Trent ruled on the matter in 1563, marriages in Roman Catholic countries had to be performed in public before a parish priest to be valid.[3] But the date of the Duchess's marriage as specified in the play is a year or two before 1504, the date of the horoscope Antonio draws for their first child (2.3.55–62), and therefore well in advance of the Council of Trent. Before 1563 in Italy, clandestine marriage was accepted as valid in some areas but not in others. As Christiane Klapisch-Zuber has pointed out, marriage in Rome required participation of the church even in the early sixteenth century, but in other areas such as Florence, and probably also Amalfi, marriage was almost entirely domestic and outside the control of the church: a couple could marry by exchanging vows and rings and then consummating the marriage, provided that they also acknowledged the marriage in public.[4]

It is unlikely that many members of the audience in early London performances had the detailed knowledge of Italian customs and history required to be able to evaluate the status of the Duchess's marriage in Italian terms with the required degree of local and historical specificity. They were far more likely to judge the matter in light of English ecclesiastical law of their own period, and even then they would be likely to respond in a broad spectrum of ways, depending on their views of the Church of England's efforts, parallel to those of the Catholic Church in Europe, to extend its control over the institution of marriage. To put the matter in a nutshell, the more hostile a viewer was to Catholicism and to highly ritualized religious practices in general, the more receptive he or she would likely be to the Duchess's unorthodox marriage.

It is always hazardous to attempt to gauge audience response from a time far distant from our own, but as it happens we do have a report by an early viewer of Webster's play, who interpreted it as a savage indictment of Catholicism. Horatio Busino, a Catholic priest who served as chaplain to the Venetian Ambassador in London in 1617–18, witnessed a performance of *The Duchess of Malfi*, probably in early 1618. The English, he complained 'deride our religion as detestable and superstitious, and never represent any theatrical piece [...] without larding it with the vices and iniquity of some Catholic churchman, which move them to laughter and much mockery'. At the performance of Webster's play the actors

> represented the pomp of a Cardinal in his identical robes of state, very handsome and costly, and accompanied by his attendants, with an altar raised on the stage, where he pretended to perform service, ordering a procession. He then re-appeared familiarly with a concubine in public. He played the part of administering poison to his sister [Businos error for mistress; his diary had earlier complained that it was difficult for him accurately to describe distant things because of his short-sightedness (138)] upon a point of honour, and moreover, of going into battle, having first gravely deposited his Cardinal's robes on the altar through the agency of his chaplains. Last of all, he had himself girded with a sword and put on his scarf with the best imaginable grace. All this they do in derision of ecclesiastical pomp which in this kingdom is scorned and hated mortally.[5]

The performance that Busino witnessed was admittedly a revival some five years after *The Duchess of Malfi* was first staged, and it may have ramped up the play's anti-Catholic satire more than some other productions did. Then too, Busino himself may have been slightly paranoid as a result of his marginal status as a Catholic priest in Protestant London during a time of rising anti-Catholic sentiment related to James I's unpopular pro-Spanish views, his fostering of ecclesiastical policies that were perceived by many as scandalously 'Popish', and his plan, from 1614 onwards, to marry Prince Charles with the Spanish Infanta.

Nevertheless, Busino's reaction is the best evidence we have about how an early audience received the play in performance.

When John Webster's *Duchess of Malfi* was published in 1623, London Hispanophobia was at its height. Prince Charles and his favourite the Earl of Buckingham travelled secretly to Madrid to secure the Spanish match; when they returned without the Infanta London burst into celebration, with bonfires and jubilant crowds in the streets.[6] Two of the three poets who wrote laudatory verses for Webster's first quarto edition of *The Duchess of Malfi*, Thomas Middleton and William Rowley, were also involved in the scurrilously anti-Spanish and anti-Catholic play *A Game at Chess*, performed a year later in 1624 to great applause in London and shut down by the authorities after a spectacular nine days' run. Middleton wrote the play and Rowley likely played the Archbishop of Spalato.[7] Busino's response to the *The Duchess of Malfi* in performance in 1618 picks up something that was probably true of other performances as well: its portrayal of the Cardinal, a thoroughly corrupt and sexually active *bon vivant* who can toss off his religious vocation as easily as he removes his cardinal's robes, was pitched not as an indictment of a single individual but as a satiric indictment of Catholicism in general. In Act V of Webster's play, the Cardinal uses a bible or some other sacred book to poison his mistress Julia, who dies because she kisses it devoutly in response to the Cardinal's request. This sacrilegious gesture on the Cardinal's part enacts contemporary Protestant views of the Catholic hierarchy as contemptuous of scripture and deliberately withholding it from the faithful – as though direct access to holy writ could poison them spiritually in the same way that reverence for the holy book causes Julia's death.

Similarly, Webster's portrayal of Ferdinand, if interpreted in terms of its early cultural contexts, resonates strongly with English Protestant fears of Catholicism. It is important that Ferdinand and the Cardinal are Spaniards, members of the House of Aragon: even more than the Italians, the Spaniards were feared in England for their imperialist ambitions, as in the attempted invasion by the Spanish Armada in 1588 to restore England to the Catholic fold, and in their later efforts (or so many Protestants interpreted them) to seduce James I into an alliance that would eventually restore England to Catholicism. The name of the Duchess of Malfi's twin brother in the historical narratives on which the play is based was Carlo, not Ferdinand. Webster may well have chosen the name Ferdinand because of its resonance with Ferdinand of Spain, a member of the House of Aragon who, along with his queen, Isabella, was more widely known for his unscrupulous tactics in defense of Catholicism than for his sponsorship of Columbus's voyages to America. Machiavelli famously praised Ferdinand for his great and extraordinary successes in *The Prince*, chap. 21:

> [...] always in the name of religion, he resorted to a pious cruelty, despoiling the Marranos and driving them from his kingdom. There could be nothing more pitiful or unusual than this. Under the same cloak of piety he attacked Africa; he undertook his Italian campaign; and lastly he has made war on France. Thus, he has always planned and executed great things which have filled his subjects with wonder and admiration [....][8]

For Machiavelli, it was Ferdinand's use of religion to cloak his political ambitions that made him particularly admirable as a tactician. But in England, Machiavelli's praise would have registered as the inverse: the Italian political thinker was widely hated and feared in England as a proponent of ruthless amorality: we may think of the villainous Richard of Gloucester (later Richard III of England) and his resolve in Shakespeare's *King Henry VI, Part 3* to 'set the murtherous Machevil to school' (3.2.193).[9] For early audiences, the resonant name and tyrannical behaviour of Webster's character Ferdinand may have evoked a similar Machiavellian Catholic *realpolitik*.

As Ferdinand gradually descends into lycanthropy after his sister's death, he takes on subhuman attributes that Reformation Protestant culture associated with Catholic spiritual predation. These associations are more subtle than the blatant anti-Catholicism surrounding the portrayal of the Cardinal, but they may have resonated for some members of the play's early audiences, particularly since the two brothers often appear together on stage, act in concert and have the same basic agenda of persecuting their sister. According to Protestant polemic, echoing Christ's teachings in the Sermon on the Mount about wolves in sheep's clothing (Matt. 7.15), the wolf is specifically associated with Catholicism: cf. the 'grim Wolf with privy paw' who devours the helpless sheep in John Milton's *Lycidas* (lines 125–9), or the image of the wolf in emblem literature,[10] or for a text contemporary with Webster's play, Thomas Adams's famous London sermon on 'Lycanthropy, or the wolf worrying the lambs' (ca 1615), which associates the wolf with Catholicism and also with the emerging Laudian wing of the English church, whose ritualism and preservation of Catholic institutions were becoming anathema to radical Protestants.[11] In the play, in addition to becoming a predatory wolf-man, Ferdinand shows a predilection for manipulating ritualized fragments that may, for contemporary audiences, have suggested the Catholic reverences for images: a dagger, a severed hand, the waxwork bodies of 4.1, his attempts, in the Duchess's words, to keep her 'cased up like a holy relic' (3.2.137).

The Duchess herself is sister to the Cardinal and Ferdinand, and therefore also of the Spanish House of Aragon. But she and Antonio act in defiance of her brothers and adopt language and attitudes that may well have resonated for some members of early London audiences with Protestant as opposed to Catholic values. Antonio is at one point called 'precise' (2.3.65), a code term for Puritans during the period. Antonio complains of the Cardinal, 'He should have been Pope, but instead of coming to it by the primitive decency of the church, he did bestow bribes so largely and so impudently as if he would have carried it away without heaven's knowledge' (1.2.80–4). 'Primitive decency of the church' is also language closely associated with Protestant critique of Catholicism: for Protestants who distrusted Catholic ritualism, 'popish' liturgy and ecclesiastical governance were a later corruption of the 'primitive decency' of early Christianity rather than a direct inheritance from the early church. The Cardinal complains in 5.2 that Antonio has atheistic tendencies and fails to go to mass: he considers 'religion / But a school-name', or mere empty words (5.2.122–3). As William Empson suggested long ago, perhaps Antonio is instead a proto-Protestant who shuns Catholic ritual because he perceives it as meaningless noise.[12]

The Duchess, similarly, seems to distrust empty rituals. She defends her marriage as 'a sacrament o'th' church' and warns Ferdinand that he will 'howl in hell' for violating it (4.1.38–9), but she does not in any way feel bound to make use of ecclesiastical ceremony or affirmation by a priest to insure the validity of her marriage. She and Antonio exchange a set of vows that have a liturgical element of repetition in that they begin with 'That', like liturgical responses in the Church of England,[13] but they are freely improvised rather than following a set form: 'That we may imitate the loving palms, / [...] That fortune may not know an accident' (1.2.392–5). They are not echoing the language of the church; rather, according to the Duchess, ''tis the church / That must but echo this' (1.2.398–9).

We have circled back to the question of the validity of the Duchess's marriage. In England, as previously noted, the Duchess's marriage would have been considered illegal, but not necessarily for that reason invalid. In 1597 and 1604, the English church issued new canons tightening up what constituted legal marriage with the goal of discouraging clandestine marriage. The canons of 1604, in particular, clarified the definition of marriage. Any marriage was 'clandestine' if it, in Martin Ingram's words,

> neglected one or more of the canonical regulations governing the solemnization of matrimony. After 1604 this meant a marriage without the threefold publication of banns or the issue of a valid licence, a ceremony conducted outside the diocese in which the

> couple dwelt, or a marriage performed during certain prohibited seasons or outside certain set hours, or in any circumstances save within a lawful church or chapel and in the presence of a properly constituted minister of the church of England.[14]

The Duchess's marriage is clearly clandestine by this definition. In fact, under the provisions of English canon law, it may not have counted as a marriage at all because ecclesiastical law required clandestine marriages to be performed in front of not one, but two, witnesses. However, she and Antonio are clearly satisfied of its validity. As she says, 'I have heard lawyers say a contract in a chamber / *Per verba presenti* is absolute marriage' (1.2.385–6). Although she and Antonio never use the prescribed language 'I marry you' or 'I thee wed' in the present tense their intent is clearly to be married 'by words in the present'. Under the canons of 1604 in England, she and Antonio could have been punished for their neglect of the proper legal formulae: they could have been hauled before the ecclesiastical courts and forced to pay a heavy fine, perhaps even do public penance, for violating the canons of the church. Cariola could also have been prosecuted by the church courts as a witness to clandestine marriage.[15] Even after the 1604 canons forbidding clandestine marriages, such marriages were still practised, particularly by couples who were of unequal status, or in the case of widows who wanted to protect their income from their first marriages, or among those who refused to acknowledge the jurisdiction of the ecclesiastical courts on the basis of principle. All of these three motives apply to the Duchess and Antonio.

Beginning at least in 1613, if not considerably earlier, there were even 'lawless' churches in London that were outside the jurisdiction of the bishops and that married couples in defiance of the ecclesiastical courts (Outhwaite, pp. 25–8). People could get into trouble for clandestine marriage, but it was not ordinarily a crime that was punished with loss of life, as it is in Webster's play. There was one prominent case in which a clandestine marriage was handled with particular severity: the case of Lady Arbella Stuart, who was in the line of royal succession and therefore needed the permission of James I to marry. Webster may have had her in mind in constructing his play about the Duchess. When the king refused to marry Lady Arbella off she took matters into her own hands and secretly married William Seymour. The two lovers attempted to escape and Lady Arbella was caught. She was thrown into the Tower of London, where she eventually went mad and died.[16] But even Lady Arbella, unlike the Duchess of Malfi, was not executed for the crime of marriage outside the canonical regulations.

Londoners who were seriously alarmed about Spanish and Catholic encroachment in England were also usually worried about the English ecclesiastical courts. Since the courts were based in the canon and civil law of the Roman Catholic Church, they were, to many in England, yet another contamination of the purity of the English church. According to one contemporary critic, the operation of the church courts ensured that 'the pope hath his horse ready saddled and bridled, watching but the time to get up again'.[17] Others called the 'Popish' canons 'the very handes of that Hellish *Cerberus* of Rome, and the synews of his tyrannicall authoritie'; or, in language that strikingly resembles the language of lycanthropy in Webster's play, the officers of the courts 'mad men, greedie & devouring Wolves' that 'fed' on the people 'with delight'.[18] The ecclesiastical courts, their canons and procedures, came under increasing criticism in England during the early seventeenth century from an alliance of Puritans and common lawyers who disputed their jurisdiction. By the 1640s the courts were so hated that they were abolished, along with other structures of episcopacy, 'Root and Branch', according to a famous act of Parliament.

Given that non-clandestine marriage in the early seventeenth century required compliance with the ecclesiastical canons, we can see how, for some in Webster's audience, the Duchess's clandestine marriage might have appeared not as a reckless and intemperate evasion of law but as a retreat into virtue. She and Antonio are surrounded by a corruption that is portrayed in the play as so closely linked to the prying, intrusive presence of the Cardinal and Ferdinand that the only way she can create a life for herself free of their contamination is by contracting a private marriage and living it out in a confined world that her brothers have not managed to violate. On such a reading, her marriage is not the act of unbridled lust that her brothers and a number of modern critics portray it to be, but rather an act of heroic resistance. She describes it in terms that suggest the Protestant 'Heroics of Marriage': 'as men in some great battles / By apprehending danger have achieved / Almost impossible actions', so she will marry, 'through frights and threatenings, will assay / This dangerous venture'. She is 'going into a wilderness / Where [she] shall find nor path nor friendly clue' (1.2.259–75).[19] The Duchess attempts to enact a strategy that was used by actual English families during the Jacobean period, withdrawing 'into [themselves] rather than associating with sin'.[20] Her tragedy is not that she makes the attempt through her clandestine marriage, but that she is not allowed to succeed.

We can see the relative radicalism of Webster's treatment of clandestine marriage in *The Duchess of Malfi* by comparing it with Shakespeare's *Measure for Measure*, another play that takes on the topic but from a different point of view. Shakespeare's play was first performed in 1604 – the same year in which the newly strict canons on marriage were adopted by the English church and also, not coincidentally, the year in which James I made peace with Spain.[21] The play centres on two clandestine marriages: between Juliet and Claudio and between Mariana and Angelo. Both marriages have been interrupted. Juliet and Claudio are, in their own view, married by a 'true contract' and have consummated the union (1.2.145–6). They have therefore taken the same steps towards clandestine marriage as the Duchess and Antonio; they have not declared their marriage openly because the dowry has not been settled, and they have therefore come under Vienna's draconian laws punishing fornication with death. According to canon law, the impediment of an unsettled dowry would not nullify the marriage because its consummation rendered prior limitations to the contract null and void (Ingram, p. 190). They are nevertheless in severe jeopardy because the tyrannous Angelo has sentenced them to death.

In *Measure for Measure*, however, the good and bad characters are reversed in terms of their ecclesiastical affiliations. In *The Duchess of Malfi* the Cardinal, a representative of the Catholic Church, persecutes the Duchess and Antonio and helps to instigate the Duchess's execution. In *Measure for Measure* the Duke of Vienna disguised as a Friar, a representative of the Catholic Church, rescues Juliet and Claudio from their condemnation by Angelo. In *The Duchess of Malfi* the 'precise' Antonio, who is associated with Puritan or at least strongly Protestant values, is one of the relatively good and trustworthy characters who is persecuted by the Arragonian brothers. In *Measure for Measure* the 'precise' Angelo (1.3.50), associated like Antonio with Puritan or strongly Protestant ideals, is the chief villain, a deeply dyed hypocrite who uses a public mask of sanctimony to hide his secret vice. In Webster's play, the role of chief hypocrite is instead played by the Cardinal, who flaunts his own ecclesiastical vows of celibacy at the same time that he attempts to enforce celibacy on his sister. The clandestine marriage in *The Duchess of Malfi* stands sufficient without any validating ecclesiastical ceremony, despite the Duchess's brothers' attempts to undermine it: at the end of the play, the eldest son of the Duchess and Antonio stands poised to take over his mother's title, though Delio realizes that making the case for the son's inheritance may not be easy. In *Measure for Measure* the clandestine marriages of Juliet and Claudio and Angelo and Mariana must be ratified at the end of the play by public weddings before a priest, according to the provisions of the 1604 canons. The banns have not been said nor a licence procured, but the Duke's word serves as the ultimate 'licence' to authorize the unions. If Shakespeare's play is interpreted in terms of contemporary London controversy, *Measure for Measure* can usefully be read as a celebration of the relative merits of English canon law in general over a competing common-law jurisdiction, and of the 1604 marriage canons in particular, ultimately backed as they are in the play by the word of the ruler, whose equivalent in England was also the head of the church. *The Duchess of Malfi*, by contrast, shuns the ecclesiastical hierarchy and associates its representatives with tyranny. Neither play is unequivocal, of course. By pointing out one set of contrasts between the two plays, I do not mean to suggest that either can be reduced to contemporary critique. But the ideological gap between them is wide.

Whether or not they recognized and responded to the play's hostile treatment of Catholic institutions, during the early decades of *The Duchess of Malfi*'s performance in the seventeenth century audience sympathy would appear to have been solidly with the Duchess. Middleton's commendatory poem in the play's first quarto calls it a '*masterpiece of tragedy*' and asks rhetorically, 'who e'er saw this Duchess live and die / That could get off under a bleeding eye?' – that is, without eyes bloodshot from weeping (Marcus, ed., p. 123). It is not only her death, according to Middleton, that inspired universal pity; it was also her life. Middleton was of the same anti-Spanish and anti-Catholic bent as was Webster himself, and therefore perhaps prejudiced in the Duchess's favour. But we have other evidence suggesting that even in its own time the play, like all great art, transcended the immediate milieu and ideology of its creation. *The Duchess of Malfi* was revived at court in 1630, where it was performed at the Cockpit theatre and perhaps also during the same season in the public theatres. A manuscript poem by William Heminges, son of John Heminges, a shareholder in the King's Men, the company that had staged Webster's play, wittily refers to continuing interest in the Duchess circa 1632, after the recent revival. Heminges's poem is a mock elegy mourning the 'death' of poet Thomas Randolph's little finger, which had been severed during a brawl. Heminges quips that the company of London poets wishing to give the finger proper burial applied to John Webster's brother Thomas for coaches, since Thomas ran the Webster family's London coaching business, only to find that all had been conscripted for the funeral of the Duchess of Malfi:

> but websters brother would nott lend a Coach:
> hee swore thay all weare hired to Convey
> the Malfy dutches sadly on her way.[22]

It is a graceful compliment in the middle of a witty and irreverent poem. Despite – or because of – her clandestine marriage and its aftermath, the Duchess of Malfi aroused a sympathetic response among many Londoners even decades after the work in which she appears was written and first performed. We would do well to bear that in mind as we construct our own readings of the play.

Notes

In all citations, u/v and i/j are normalized to modern usage.

1. See John Russell Brown, ed., *The Duchess of Malfi*, Revels Plays (Cambridge, Mass.: Harvard University Press, 1964); David Gunby, David Carnegie and Macdonald P. Jackson, eds., *The Duchess of Malfi* in *The Works of John Webster*, vol. 1 (Cambridge: Cambridge University Press, 1995); and Leah S. Marcus, ed., *The Duchess of Malfi*, Arden Early Modern Drama (London: Arden, 2009), pp. 61–91.
2. Antonio's description of changes at the French court, for example, almost certainly postdates the initial performances of the play (1.1.4–13). See Marcus, ed., p. 94.
3. Martin Ingram, *Church Courts, Sex and Marriage in England, 1570–1640* (Cambridge and New York: Cambridge University Press, 1987), p. 132.
4. Christiane Klapisch-Zuber, *Women, Family, and Ritual in Renaissance Italy*, trans. by Lydia G. Cochrane (Chicago: University of Chicago Press, 1985), pp. 178–212. Since the Duchess and Antonio do not publicly acknowledge their union, they do not fulfill the final Italian requirement for clandestine marriage. See Marcus, ed., pp. 32–8.
5. *In The Journals of Two Travellers in Elizabethan and Early Stuart England: Thomas Platter and Horatio Busino*, ed. by Peter Razzell (London: Caliban, 1995), pp. 145–6.
6. See Thomas Cogswell, *The Blessed Revolution: English Politics and the Coming of War, 1621–1624* (Cambridge: Cambridge University Press, 1989).
7. See *A Game at Chess*, ed. by Gary Taylor, in *Thomas Middleton: The Collected Works*, ed. by Gary Taylor and John Lavagnino (Oxford: Clarendon, 2007), pp. 1773–1885.
8. Cited from *The Prince and Selected Discourses*, trans. by Daniel Donno (New York and London: Bantam Books, 1966; rpt. 1971), p. 77.
9. This and subsequent citations of Shakespeare are from the *Riverside Shakespeare*, ed. by G. Blakemore Evans, 2nd edn (Boston and New York: Houghton Mifflin, 1997).
10. See Marcus, ed., pp. 28–32.
11. Thomas Adams, *The Works of Thomas Adams* (London, 1630).
12. William Empson, 'Mine Eyes Dazzle', in Norman Rabkin, ed., *Twentieth Century Interpretations of The Duchess of Malfi: A Collection of Critical Essays* (Englewood Cliffs, N J: Prentice-Hall, 1968), pp. 90–5.
13. See Brown's notes to the marriage scene, which in his edition occurs as part of Act I, Scene One.
14. Ingram, p. 213. See also R. B. Outhwaite, *Clandestine Marriage in England, 1500–1850* (London: Hambledon, 1995).
15. See R. H. Helmholz, *Roman Canon Law in Reformation England* (Cambridge and New York: Cambridge University Press, 1990), pp. 71–3.
16. See Sara Jayne Steen, 'The Crime of Marriage: Arbella Stuart and *The Duchess of Malfi*', *Sixteenth-Century Journal*, 22 (1991), 61–76.
17. Cited in Ingram, p. 6 from Brian P. Levack, *The Civil Lawyers in England, 1603–1641* (Oxford: Clarendon, 1973), p. 159.
18. Richard Cosin, *An apologie for sundrie proceedings by jurisdiction ecclesiasticall* (London, 1593), sigs. C1v–C2r. Many of Cosin's citations come from James Morice, *A briefe treatise of oathes exacted by ordinaries and ecclesiasticall judges* (Middelburg, 1590).
19. See Mary Beth Rose, *The Expense of Spirit: Love and Sexuality in English Renaissance Drama* (Ithaca and London: Cornell University Press, 1988), pp. 93–177. See also

Eileen Allman, *Jacobean Revenge Tragedy and the Politics of Virtue* (Newark and London: Associated University Presses, 1999).

20. Susan D. Amussen, 'Gender, Family and the Social Order, 1560–1725' in *Order and Disorder in Early Modern England*, ed. by Anthony Fletcher and John Stevenson (Cambridge: Cambridge University Press, 1985), pp. 196–217.
21. My argument here recapitulates some of chap. 4 in Leah S. Marcus, *Puzzling Shakespeare: Local Reading and Its Discontents* (Berkeley and London: University of California Press, 1988), pp. 160–211. Readers who would like more documentation of some of the controversies discussed here will find it in that much fuller treatment.
22. G. C. Moore Smith, ed., *William Heminges's Elegy on Randolph's Finger* (Oxford: Blackwell, 1923), p. 12.

CHAPTER SIX

'Can this be certain?': The Duchess of Malfi's Secrets

Frances E. Dolan

The Duchess of Malfi is famous for its remarkable, indeed improbably sustained, secrets: a clandestine marriage concealed even from a resident spy; three pregnancies whose paternity remains unknown to most members of the household; and, more generally, overdetermined and thus obscured motives. Why do the Duchess's brothers oppose her second marriage so vehemently? Why doesn't she grasp how deadly serious their prohibitions are? The play offers us glimpses of intimate moments – bedtime banter between lovers, maternal solicitousness – but those peeks at a cherished but imperiled familial life raise as many questions as they answer. The play freights the Duchess and Antonio's interactions with meaning, teasing us with brief disclosures and drawing our attention to their relationship in large part by making it a secret. But we cannot be sure what we are seeing or what it means, not just because the play withholds this information but because, I will argue, the play insists that one can never be sure about other people's intentions and relationships.

While the play marks what happens between the Duchess and Antonio as deeply interesting to the audience as well as to Ferdinand and to a lesser extent the Cardinal, their relationship is secret rather than private, as several critics have pointed out. Dympna Callaghan describes their marriage as 'perpetually clandestine'. Wendy Wall describes that clandestinity as 'the Duchess's idiosyncratic choice'.[1] Although the audience is in on the fact that the Duchess and Antonio are married, the couple's experience of or feelings about their marriage remain almost as unknowable to viewers and readers as they are to the Duchess's dangerous brothers. The play, in its emphasis on the excessively and eccentrically secretive, draws our attention to the ways in which all intimate relationships are, to some extent, clandestine, mysteries to their participants as well as to the most zealous observer.

Research into privacy in the early modern period has tended to emphasize that it did not yet exist as we now understand it. The early modern household was embedded in larger networks of relationship and accountable to them; it was vulnerable to scrutiny and intervention from within and without; its walls were riddled with fissures through which co-habitants and neighbours peeped and listened – and then often reported what they'd learned; even its beds and bedchambers were routinely shared. In the play, for instance, Cariola confesses that she 'lies with' the Duchess 'often' and finds her 'the sprawlingest bedfellow' (3.2.11, 13). She depicts this sleeping arrangement as unremarkable. Many households were filled with relatives and servants like Cariola who not only witnessed but participated in the most intimate of interactions. As Wall points out, for instance, 'all four of the primary conjugal husband-wife scenes that critics see as showing the heightened emotional intensity of marital intimacy include Cariola as an active participant'.[2]

Given such material conditions, Lena Orlin argues, 'For most Elizabethans, privacy was less a material condition than a consensual act'. That is, privacy did not automatically attach to a particular place, utterance, action or relationship. It required a conscious choice, and often a contested one. While many scholars have assumed that privacy was emerging as a new value in this period, Orlin emphasizes that, if so, it was suspected more than desired: 'to many [...] privacy seemed a menace to public well-being. It threatened to deprive people of knowledge to which they thought they were entitled and about which they felt a sense of social responsibility'.[3] This entitlement justified vigilant inquiry into what happened behind closed doors. In *The Duchess of Malfi*, Ferdinand insists he is entitled to knowledge of his sister's sexual conduct and that it cannot be kept from him. As he warns her, 'Your darkest actions – nay, your privatest thoughts, / Will come to light' (1.1.231–2). Apparently, he wants her dark actions and private thoughts to be revealed to him, but not to others. He later complains that she was 'too much i' th' light' (4.1.41) – too exposed by her 'own choice' and her 'own way' to public talk (1.2.233, 237). As the play shows, while the contested and compromised nature of 'privacy' ensured that secrets usually came to light, there were also epistemological barriers to interpreting the meaning of those secrets. Even when Ferdinand spies on the

Duchess talking to Antonio at bedtime, he fails to ascertain Antonio's identity. More to the point, he cannot understand the nature of their attachment. And neither, really, can we. In Ferdinand, then, the play depicts an entitlement to knowledge as both destructive and doomed to failure. Drawing our attention to the relationship between the Duchess and Antonio and thwarting our attempts to understand it, the play both provokes our desire to know and invites us to question that desire.

Much critical ink has been spilled about the Duchess and Antonio's marriage, which the two transact between them with Cariola as witness. Are they really married? Although the play is set in Italy, many critics focus on trying to reconstruct the attitudes towards such a marriage in the play's first English audiences. By the seventeenth century in England, it was widely accepted that marriages should be advertised in advance by the calling of banns three times, solemnized in open church by a minister, and recorded in the parish register. Still, many marriages were transacted outside of these rules and they remained binding nonetheless. Such couples might be brought before a church court for their 'irregularity' and punished for their conduct by excommunication, penance or a fee. But unless one spouse or the other was already married to someone else, the marriage could not be dissolved, especially if the couple had children. So if Antonio and the Duchess both agree that they are married and that he is the father of their children, and Cariola stands as their witness, as do members of the audience (as Huston Diehl points out), then their marriage would probably have seemed valid to most people who saw the play whether or not they thought it advisable.[4] Moreover, the Duchess's action under clearly exceptional circumstances harks back to older Catholic modes of solemnizing marriage and anticipates the actions of religious non-conformists who resisted the regulation of marriage by the Church of England.

Although the audience is invited into the secret that the Duchess and Antonio are married, we are also shown that the legitimacy of this marriage is illegible to everyone who lives with them except Cariola. The spouses are themselves the sole authorities on their status. For characters who have not witnessed the secret marriage, as we in the audience have, the uncertainty of their marital status raises doubt as to whether they are married or merely living in sin and casts doubt on their children's legitimacy. They can adduce no minister or document to make their case. No one in the play can know for sure; everyone must take the couple's word for it. Such an undocumented marriage helps us understand why a system of public solemnization, licensing and registration emerged in this period – without it a marriage is open to dispute. As we see in *The Duchess of Malfi*, her brothers can intervene because it is not absolutely clear to everyone that she is married and to whom. If

Antonio disputed the marriage – in a different kind of tragedy – the Duchess would have only Cariola to help support her side of the story.[5]

But if their circumstances are distinctive, their leap of faith is not. Marriage, the play suggests, is always a 'dangerous venture' (1.2. 263). The future is unscripted, unpredictable, a 'wilderness' without path or guide (even when one behaves conventionally) (1.2.274–6). Many critics have argued that the play affirms the ideal of companionable equality between spouses, 'ordinary earthly sexual desire', and maternal care.[6] But even when critics agree that the relationship between the Duchess and Antonio is a love match, they disagree as to whether we should admire or censure the Duchess for setting so high a priority on her own happiness. For a Duchess, is this 'dangerously naïve' or even irresponsible, as an earlier generation of critics argued?[7] Or is insisting on love a visionary, progressive, or even subversive insistence on an emergent and better ideal?[8] The Duchess demands of Ferdinand, 'Why might not I marry? / I have not gone about, in this, to create / Any new world or custom' (3.2.108–10). But for many critics the Duchess's insistence on marrying a second time, choosing her own mate and preferring her steward is innovative and therefore admirable. From this perspective, the Duchess's insistence on what she presents as normative and unremarkable becomes oppositional whether she wants it to be or not.

How best might one describe the relationship between the two once they are married? Some critics emphasize that the Duchess sustains the advantage of her rank throughout the marriage; she remains Duchess of Malfi still, and mistress of her household, while Antonio remains her steward still. She is always the one who initiates action. 'I have fashion'd it already' she advises him, having in seconds and without consultation devised the plan to slander and separate from him (3.2.158). As Theodore Leinwand argues, 'Where we might expect conjugal affect, a caress, we instead find hierarchical relations. Their banter hints that mastery and subjection temper, perhaps structure, their nights together [...] Of course theirs is, famously or infamously, a marriage that began with the woman on top'. Perhaps, at best, they achieve 'reciprocity between unequals' to use Frank Whigham's phrase.[9]

Or perhaps their arrangement suits them both even if it does not conform to modern expectations that companions should be side by side rather than top and bottom (whoever plays each role). Distinguishing attitudes towards remarrying widows in post-reformation England from those in the Catholic Mediterranean, some critics have suggested that the Duchess's decision to remarry would not have seemed scandalous to many people in an English audience.[10] It would certainly not have been a justification for murder. Tragedies set in Catholic countries often exaggerate cultural differences so as to dismiss certain views or practices as obsolete, irrational or excessive.[11] In *The Duchess of Malfi*, Linda Woodbridge suggests, Webster invites us to ask what is wrong with being or marrying a lusty widow.[12] Many widows remarried; many texts depicted a widow as a particularly attractive marriage prospect. In various representations of remarrying widows, Jennifer Panek finds the possibility of 'orderly inversion', a possibility that might apply to the Duchess's marriage to Antonio. Asking 'to what extent might the widow's position of power from which she enters a second (or third or fourth) marriage remake the conditions of marriage itself?', Panek suggests that 'a certain set of circumstances [...] may have created a space where a wife's government of her husband could be orderly, accepted, and unremarkable' – for both a wife accustomed to rule and a husband accustomed to serve or obey.

Panek concludes her essay by suggesting provocatively that 'sometimes, the bedroom may be the only place where the man wants to be on top'.[13] But we cannot assume that he would want to be on top even there or that the woman being on top is any less acceptable at night than in the day. Panek's concluding remark evokes the bedtime banter between the Duchess and Antonio in which she calls him a 'Lord of Misrule', to which he responds that his 'rule is only in the night' (3.2.7–8). If he is a Lord of Misrule then he is both a ruler, at least at night, and he is stepping out of his usual subordinate role. This is the kind of inversion that draws attention to the hierarchy it reverses. Leonora Leet Brodwin, too, assumes that Antonio is on top at night. Brodwin resolves the conflict between the spirits of greatness and of woman in the Duchess by imagining that she manages to have it both ways through a kind of shift work: she 'saves herself by halves' (adapting Antonio's phrase at 5.3.48): 'She will be both sovereign by day and secret wife by night'.[14] Brodwin seems to accept an association of submissiveness with the categories woman and wife. In contrast, Linda Woodbridge celebrates the Duchess as a 'hero of desire' without trying to defend her against being on top; she suggests that the Duchess's sovereignty might be sexy.[15]

Other critics insist on 'sexy reciprocity' between the spouses. Barbara Correll argues that the class and gender disparities between husband and wife balance each other out because of 'the links between administrative hirelings and women, who are marginally but instrumentally positioned in the power hierarchy, who are essential but threatening to social power'. For Correll, the Duchess 'raises Antonio to reciprocity'. The play's utopian possibility, then, inheres in its positive depiction of the Duchess's desire for 'a realm of egalitarian reciprocity and power sharing'.[16] Judith Haber argues that the play goes even further: the Duchess 'effectively positions herself (and Antonio) both as subject and as object, both as penetrator and as penetrated'.[17]

So while critics agree that there is something sexy about the relationship between the Duchess and Antonio, their interpretations of the nature of that sexiness vary widely. Critics argue persuasively that Antonio is on top, that the Duchess is, or that they engage in sexy reciprocity. This indeterminacy is precisely the point. However compelling the erotic teasing among the Duchess, Antonio and Cariola, we cannot be sure what it means.

In this particular case, knowing that the wife is a Duchess and the husband a steward, even peering at them as they prepare for bed and talk about sex, does not enable us to know for sure how they interact. The class disparity between them is part of what helps them keep their marriage a secret; no one, not even Bosola, the 'politic dormouse' (1.1.199), guesses that the Duchess might have married Antonio until she finally reveals that secret herself, giddy with the pleasure of hearing Bosola praise Antonio. Antonio himself explains that no one knows how to read the situation. They say the Duchess is a 'strumpet', not imagining her to be married.

> They do observe I grow to infinite purchase
> The left-hand way, and all suppose the Duchess
> Would amend it if she could. [...]
> For other obligation
> Of love or marriage between her and me,
> They never dream of. (3.1.28–30; 35–7)

The class disparity between the Duchess and Antonio leads observers to posit a familiar story – a dishonest steward – and to ignore other possibilities that are equally conventional or at least imaginable, such as the lusty widow and the steward whose ambition leads him to marriage rather than theft. The Duchess plays to the popular disparagement of Antonio when she accuses him of theft as an excuse to get him out of her castle and away from her brothers (3.2).

The fact that observers never dream of love or marriage between the Duchess and Antonio protects their relationship. But secrecy grants them more than safety and sustainability; the Duchess suggests that the potential for danger adds savour and excitement to their relationship. Wondering if they should sleep apart while Ferdinand is in the castle, she suspects 'But you'll say / Love mixed with fear is sweetest' (3.2.64–5). Whatever Antonio and the Duchess feel for one another, whatever the nature of their intimacy, its secrecy and their consequent fear are constitutive of their love. In the wooing scene, the Duchess reassures Antonio that 'all discord without this circumference / Is only to be pitied and not feared' (1.2.378–9). By 'this circumference' she seems to mean the ring she has given him, or their embrace, or, more generally, their marriage. But, as her later remark about 'love mixed with fear' suggests, fear is *within* their relationship and not simply held at bay outside it. While Ferdinand fears and attempts to eradicate secrets, the Duchess, and she suggests, Antonio, have chosen and even enjoy secrecy, and the fear of discovery it entails. The only hint we get of why the Duchess keeps her secret as long as she does is that it pleases them both to do so. Even if love, sexuality and marriage are a consolation for the uncertainty and meaninglessness in Malfi, they are also themselves a ground of epistemological mystery.

Historical context cannot resolve this indeterminacy because all of the models of marriage and of conjugal sexuality critics find in the play were available in the period, widely represented, variously espoused or lamented. Nor can the play itself prove anything about contemporary attitudes – towards clandestine marriage, widows' remarriage, how and why one should marry or how spouses should interact. The play proves only that these were all contested issues and that the contestation itself made it difficult to read marriage from the outside. A remarrying widow might be viewed as self-indulgent, dutiful or irresponsible, depending on her circumstances, the perspective from which she was viewed, and the genre of the work in which she was discussed. The Duchess and Antonio's marriage might operate as a hierarchy determined by rank, a hierarchy determined by gender, or a partnership between companions made possible in part because the two hierarchies balance one another out. The spouses might toggle between different modes of relation. The play does not make it wholly clear. The one thing the Duchess tells us about their sexual relationship is that fear heightens it.

Even the play's arguably most famous line mystifies the Duchess's relation to her marriage. When she announces, movingly, that she is 'Duchess of Malfi still' (4.2.137), she insists not only that who she is cannot be scared out of her, stripped away or alienated by madness. She also proclaims that her status was never subsumed, diminished or transformed in marriage. One can take this as positive or negative intelligence about the marriage. The Duchess did not surrender power, status, title or name to her husband. Most wives changed their names at marriage – that is how the Duchess of Malfi became the Duchess of Malfi, after all. As a result of this convention, women sometimes disappear from the historical record when they marry. Yet the Duchess of Malfi refers to herself as she is defined by her first husband rather than her second. In her proclamation, the Duchess asserts that, in the midst of her eccentrically covert marriage, she remained herself uncovered, a *feme sole*, still known as she was as a widow, rather than a *feme covert*, defined by her second husband's name and status.

The Duchess's reproductive life is as secretive as her marriage. Bosola curses that her loose gowns prevent him from inspecting the big belly that, he suspects, encloses 'the young springal cutting a caper' (2.1.156). As Lynn Enterline reminds us, the body Bosola longs to see, and invites the audience to imagine, was, of course, played on stage by a boy actor. The truth of the maternal body constantly recedes from our grasp. 'If one could actually see the body hidden beneath the "rich tissew," the play asks its viewers, what would one know? Would seeing be knowing?'[18] The play suggests that it would not, even as it teases us with its constant emphasis on concealment. The Duchess gives birth to her first child by Antonio in the middle of the night, under the cover of the lie that she has been poisoned. She bears two more children between Acts II and III. Michelle Dowd argues that the Duchess has these children in a 'parallel universe'– and that, as a result, 'the audience is essentially put in the same position that Ferdinand and Bosola find themselves in earlier in the play, forced to follow a receding trail of evidence about the Duchess's reproductive life'. Dowd argues that the impossibility of proving that the Duchess is pregnant, or of pinning down who the father is, drives Bosola to give the Duchess apricots as a kind of test 'to provide empirical evidence of an otherwise inscrutable female condition'.[19] However unusual the clandestine births may be in *The Duchess of Malfi*, they point to the ways in which all pregnancies were inscrutable, all births might be viewed as uncanny disruptions rather than predictable consequences of doing what comes naturally.

As various historians point out, one could not prove pregnancy in the early modern period, let alone paternity. Although various symptoms were considered indicators, none was definitive. As Eve Keller puts this, 'the maternal body was understood to be opaque; given to ambiguous changes, it was ultimately uninterpretable'.[20] Even signs we might assume to be incontrovertible – quickening or fetal movement and growing 'great bellied' – could mislead, deceiving even the woman who had the symptoms. Take the phantom pregnancies of Queen Mary Tudor. Rumours circulated in September 1554 that her doctors had told her she was pregnant; she does not seem to have believed it herself until she felt quickening in November of 1554. By late May of 1555, there were rumours that she was not, in fact, pregnant; her doctors continued to insist she was – until she emerged from 'semi-seclusion' in July without having given birth. She claimed to be pregnant again, and seven months along, in January 1558. By April it was clear that, again, she had not been pregnant. Defending Mary against charges that she was 'delusional' or 'hysterical', her biographer, Judith Richards, reminds readers 'just how hard it could be in early modern times to determine whether a woman was indeed pregnant' – until she gave birth. If Mary was confused, so were her doctors. These pregnancies are evidence less of Mary's psychological state than of the secrecy of pregnancy itself.[21]

While women, especially married women, were sometimes assumed to have privileged access to the secrets of the gendered body, rooted in their own experience of sex, pregnancy and childbirth, they were also distrusted as authorities. When it came to the mystery of 'the opaque female body', according to Laura Gowing, 'female testimony was at once absolutely necessary, and fundamentally unreliable'. To the extent that women were assumed to have some knowledge it 'was always provisional and comparative'. Even women themselves could only speculate about pregnancy and the causes of and cures for illness. By the seventeenth century in England, 'it was less and less possible to represent, and treat, female bodies as women's secrets' because male physicians were asserting more ownership over knowledge of women's anatomy.[22] Katharine Park similarly argues that the meaning and ownership of the 'secrets of women' shifted dramatically in fifteenth- and sixteenth-century Italy from women as possessors of secret knowledge about the body, particularly sex and reproduction, to women as themselves secrets. As objects of arcane knowledge, women's bodies were as mysterious to them as to most men; only male medical experts were supposed to be able to decipher these enigmas, yet their knowledge, too, remained contingent and speculative.[23]

Mary Tudor's 'semi-seclusion' is a reminder that women's 'confinement' or 'lying in' might entail not just a cozy withdrawal into a world of women but, for privileged women, a kind of domestic imprisonment for a month or more. This is a parallel universe, as Dowd calls it, into which most elite pregnant women were compelled.[24] Paradoxically, in keeping her pregnancies secret, the Duchess remains in free circulation before and after the births. As Haber points out, the castle's officers are locked in rather than the Duchess during the birth of her first child. This reverses the usual practice of confining the mother, which is then re-asserted when the Duchess is imprisoned in her own castle.[25] Before that final confinement, the Duchess's dissimulation of her pregnancies allows her to circulate more freely than other elite pregnant women, who had to stage their pregnancies and births in the interests of documenting a legitimate succession.

For most early modern women, clandestine births were more suspicious, and more severely punished, than clandestine marriages. It was assumed that married women would have no cause to hide pregnancies or births. But since unmarried mothers could be punished for 'bastard bearing' or pressed to reveal the name of their child's father, they had incentives to conceal their pregnancies and births. Such concealment then might be taken as criminal in itself. About a decade after *The Duchess of Malfi* was first performed, a 1624 statute declared that, if an unmarried woman concealed her pregnancy and delivery, and her baby was born dead, she could be convicted of infanticide unless she could produce a witness to the birth who confirmed that the infant was stillborn. A widow and a Duchess could guard her body's secrets more successfully than could an unmarried woman, especially one who was a dependent in a household. For a vulnerable woman, such as a servant rather than a Duchess, female spies among her neighbours might be as menacing as Bosola, especially since they had freedoms he does not: they might squeeze a woman's breasts or search her body and bedclothes for evidence of delivery.[26] By disguising her pregnancies and deliveries, the Duchess places herself in the legally suspect position of single women giving birth to illegitimate children. Since one could not usually tell after the fact whether a child had been stillborn or if the mother had killed or criminally neglected the newborn, the law took the mother's status (married or unmarried) and the circumstances of the birth (secret or open) as sufficient proofs.[27] This statute, written to control unmarried women's reproduction, affords insight into the epistemological, ethical and legal complications uncertain marital status and clandestinity could entail.

In the play, the Duchess's unsuccessful attempt to keep her pregnancies a secret ultimately makes her family vulnerable by provoking suspicion and intervention. 'If women's secrets can be seen as a source of autonomy, authority or protection, they can seem, too, to be a weapon against women', as Gowing points out.[28] Celia R. Daileader argues that the opacity of the female body often worked as a provocation to male violence.[29] Here, that provocative, if quotidian, opacity is shrouded in extra layers of secrecy. When Bosola sends news that the Duchess has had a child, Ferdinand says 'rogues do not whisper't now, but seek to publish't' (2.5.5). By the time the Duchess has three children, Delio asks Antonio: 'What say the common people?' To which he replies: 'The common rabble do directly say / She is a strumpet' (3.1.24–6). The problem is no longer the fact that she is married but rather that her success in keeping her marriage a secret has helped to make the open secret of her pregnancies scandalous.

The Duchess's secrets are no longer hers to keep or to reveal. The Duchess invites 'private conference' with Ferdinand about 'a scandalous report' that is being spread 'touching [her] honour', attempting to defuse the scandal by introducing it herself. But this strategy requires her to go out of her way to deny her marriage and children. While Ferdinand dismisses these rumours as 'paper bullets, court calumny, / A pestilent air, which princes' palaces / Are seldom purged of', reassuring his sister to 'be safe in your own innocency', it is this gossip that seems to provoke him to solve the mystery, to violently plumb the Duchess's depths (3.1.46–51, 55). Threatened by Ferdinand in the next scene, the Duchess's first line of defense is 'I am married' (3.2.81). But how could he have known that? Nor does her candour make much difference at this point, after years of deception and denial.

Throughout, the play depicts its characters trying, and failing, to confide their own secrets – not just information but also emotions, commitments and values – as well as trying, and failing, to grasp what others hold inside them. Antonio, returning to the Duchess's bedchamber just after Ferdinand has left, conspicuously and conveniently late, wishes he could tell Ferdinand of his 'warrantable love' (3.2.147). Yet he and his wife lack a warrant that could mean anything to Ferdinand. Antonio cannot 'relate' his 'warrantable love' to Ferdinand precisely because his warrant resides in his heart. According to the Duchess, Antonio both holds her heart in his own bosom (1.2. 359) and has been 'entered into' her heart (3.2.60). If the heart is exchangeable, it is also a container for what one receives from a loved one. Secret devotion is to be worn 'on th'inside of [the] heart', as Bosola facetiously promises (3.2.305); to be intimate is to be 'a secret to your heart' as Julia has been to the Cardinal (5.2.223). Whereas the Duchess makes Antonio's bosom 'the treasury of all my secrets' (1.2.409), the Cardinal mocks the possibility that anyone can so serve another when he taunts Julia: 'Think you your bosom / Will be a grave dark and obscure enough / For such a secret?' (5.2.256–8). The bosom or, more specifically, the heart contains secrets but it cannot promise to hold them safe; it cannot produce them as a 'warrant' legible to Ferdinand. At parting from the Duchess, Antonio's heart is 'turned to a heavy lump of lead' (3.5.89) – a dead weight rather than a warrant or a sanctuary for another's secrets.

For Ferdinand, the heart's contents are at worst poisonous and at best unknowable. Ferdinand and the Cardinal's hearts are, as Bosola claims, 'hollow graves / Rotten and rotting others' (4.2.308–9). Ferdinand describes his own heart as wrapped in the lead from the coffin of the Duchess's first husband (3.2.111–13); he describes the Duchess's heart as 'a hollow bullet / Filled with unquenchable wildfire' (114–15). He earlier threatens to use the Duchess's bleeding heart as 'a sponge' to wipe his memory clean (2.5.15–16). Ultimately, Ferdinand claims his heart was injected with gall by the Duchess's marriage (4.2.276). His sister's illegibility leads him to proclaim that he 'will no longer study in the book / Of another's heart' (4.1.16–17). Whereas Cariola claims that her heart is an open book – advising a suspicious Antonio 'when / That you have cleft my heart, you shall read there / Mine innocence' (3.2.142–4) – Ferdinand does not think the heart is legible. Since, as the Duchess recognizes, 'false hearts speak fair / To those they intend most mischief' (3.5.25–6), she knows that he means it literally when he writes of Antonio, 'I had rather have his heart than his money' (3.5.35–6). He wants to rip out the heart in part because he despairs of deciphering it.

If the heart is a grave or an illegible book in this play, the conscience, too, is alternately described as self-evident and an enigma.[30] The Duchess asserts independence of conscience as well as a capacity to consecrate her choices without the sanction of clergy: 'What can the church force more?' (1.2.394); 'How can the church build faster?' (1.1.397). When she presumes to sanctify her marriage to Antonio herself, she preserves it from the hypocrisy the play associates with the church, its rituals and its leaders. Julia tells her husband she is visiting an old anchorite when she visits the Cardinal (2.4); Ferdinand advises the Duchess to keep Antonio in an anchorite's chamber so that his identity will not be found out (3.2); the Duchess refuses to be cased up like a holy relic (3.2); the Cardinal suggests that Bosola hunt down Antonio by bribing Delio's confessor (5.2); and the Cardinal poisons the 'book' which he requires Julia to kiss (5.2). The Church is associated with secrecy and with the inability to keep secrets even under the seal of confession. In such a context, the Duchess's claim that she and Antonio can 'force more' and 'build faster' than the church seems justified. But in administering an inviolable 'sacrament o'th' church', as she later calls her marriage (4.1.38), the Duchess also mires herself in the deception and intrigue the play associates with the church, long before she follows Bosola's advice and pretends to go on a pilgrimage to Our Lady of Loreto so as to justify leaving her country (and fleeing from her brothers). When Cariola balks at the idea – 'I do not like / This jesting with religion, this feigned pilgrimage' – the Duchess dismisses her as a 'superstitious fool' (3.2.319–21). In some ways a dismissal of superstition, and a willingness to use outward forms to suit her own purposes, corresponds to the Duchess's willingness to make her marriage sacred and secret at once. Yet the Duchess also refuses here to reflect on her own complicity in deception.

If anything, the Duchess becomes more enigmatic as she suffers, shoring up her boundaries rather than breaking open. She closes around her secrets and defines herself through them. In the process, the meaning of her secrets shifts so that, while they remain fundamentally unknowable, they also come to stand as the core of her identity, and the engine of her stoical endurance. As she faces her death, the Duchess's 'strange disdain' (4.1.12) ossifies her into the monument she first insisted she was not ('This is flesh and blood, sir: / 'Tis not the figure cut in alabaster / Kneels at my husband's tomb' (1.2.363–5). She imagines herself to be her own 'picture, fashioned out of wax' (4.1.62); according to Cariola, she becomes her own 'picture in the gallery' 'like some reverend monument / Whose ruins are even pitied' (4.2.30, 32–3). Standing her ground, she likens herself to a taunted bear: 'I am chained to endure all your tyranny' (4.2.59).[31] Critics have variously read the Duchess as 'a female Christ' and a figure for the virgin Mary.[32] But if the play associates the Duchess with the sacred, it also views her from an iconoclastic perspective, emphasizing the materiality of the idol, the 'picture' rather than the spirit it represents. Despite Ferdinand's and Bosola's combined efforts to make her 'fly in pieces' (3.5.104), she becomes hardened into a kind of statue, mute and mysterious.

One might argue that, in death, the Duchess does fly in pieces. Her voice survives her as an echo in the ruins of an ancient abbey (5.3). Cariola briefly survives her. She tries on the Duchess's roles of wife and mother, claiming to be engaged and to be pregnant as if either will save her from death. As the Duchess's story shows, marriage and pregnancy are vulnerabilities not protections. Perhaps something of the Duchess is split off into her echo or into Cariola's ill-advised protestations, but it is her brothers who seem to be fragmented by her death. Ferdinand attacks his shadow and robs graves (5.2); the Cardinal is menaced by his own reflection: 'when I look into the fishponds in my garden, / Methinks I see a thing armed with a rake / That seems to strike at me' (5.5.5–7); Bosola claims that 'the Duchess / Haunts me' (5.2.328–9).[33] All three are, then, divided against themselves by the Duchess's death. Knowledge of the Duchess's death, her final secret, proves fatal. Julia dies because she knows this secret; Antonio learns it as he dies.

What happens after death or what death means is the play's ultimate secret. In parting with Antonio, the Duchess says 'I know not which is best, / To see you dead, or part with you' (3.5.64–5). In these lines, she acknowledges that both death and parting entail equally wrenching losses of his company. She also acknowledges the great danger he is in – and the almost unbearable uncertainty that lies ahead for them both. To see him dead would at least mean that she knew what had happened to him, that she knew the worst. 'Dost thou think we shall know one another / In th'other world?' the Duchess later asks Cariola (4.2.17–18). Cariola insists that the answer is yes, but the Duchess and Antonio seem to share the conviction that the only certainty in life is the inevitability of suffering, loss and death. To her son at parting she says 'Thou art happy that thou hast not understanding / To know thy misery, for all our wit / And reading brings us to a truer sense / Of sorrow' (3.5.66–9). As Antonio says, 'Heaven fashioned us of nothing; and we strive / To bring ourselves to nothing' (80–1). 'Our value never can be truly known' until we are dead, as the Salmon advises the Dogfish in the Duchess's parable (3.5. 134–5).

As the play unfolds, other characters come to endorse this certainty that all is uncertain. The mayhem at the end of the play emphasizes the impossibility of having enough information to choose appropriate courses of action. Antonio says at the start that Ferdinand 'Dooms men to death by information, / Rewards by hearsay' (1.1.94–5). But everyone in this play makes ill-informed decisions. At the beginning of Act V, Antonio asks Delio 'What think you of my hope of reconcilement / To the Aragonian brethren?' to which Delio responds, sensibly, 'I misdoubt it' (5.1.1–2). For Antonio to imagine there is any hope at this point reveals how little he understands the situation. The Cardinal prepares listeners not to credit his own cries for help and thus not to intervene to help him (5.5). Bosola kills Antonio, the one person he hopes to save, 'in a mist; I know not how – / Such a mistake as I have often seen / In a play' (5.5.92–4). Bosola concludes 'We are only like dead walls or vaulted graves / That, ruined, yields no echo' (5.5.95–6). In the images of 'dead walls and vaulted graves', Bosola suggests that humans are not sanctuaries for secrets. They are empty. The secrecy that begins as the Duchess's strategy for outwitting her brothers' prohibition against her marriage is revealed at last to be the defining condition of human life, at least in the courts of princes. We are all mysteries to ourselves and one another. 'Contempt of pain – that we may call our own', Delio concludes (5.3.56).

One of the uneasy pleasures the play affords is that it includes us in secrets that elude even a professional spy; but, in doing so, it sometimes threatens to place the viewer in Ferdinand's anguished position of wanting to see but failing to understand, or in Bosola's position of grimly labouring to turn what we 'observe' into a 'parcel of intelligency' (2.1.69; 2.3.67). The Duchess hints at this uncomfortable identification when she confides 'I account this world a tedious theatre, / For I do play a part in't 'gainst my will' (4.1.81–2). Ferdinand is a negative avatar for the spectator who must expose and destroy what is kept secret from him. He is also a failure. On hearing from Ferdinand that the Duchess 'hath had most cunning bawds to serve her turn, / And more secure conveyances for lust / Than towns of garrison for service' (2.5.9–11), the Cardinal asks 'Can this be certain?' (2.5.12). Ferdinand does not really answer him. Of course, one cannot be certain of this rumour, which we in the audience know to be false, but neither can her brothers be certain that the Duchess is actually married or, more important, what that marriage means to her and her husband. When Ferdinand asks 'how thrives our intelligence?', Bosola must answer 'uncertainly' (3.1.58). Uncertainty fuels the play's plot; it also serves as the evasive 'answer answerless' to the various questions the play poses.[34] By refusing to resolve its own mysteries, and revealing that Ferdinand's curiosity leads to suffering and death rather than certainty, the play invites us to resist identifying with Ferdinand's bloody insistence on knowing. The Duchess and Antonio, revelling in the freedom and frisson of the secret, suggest that one might, instead, surrender one's self to *not* knowing: 'I am lost in amazement; I know not what to think on't' (2.1.177).

Notes

1. Dympna Callaghan, '*The Duchess of Malfi* and Early Modern Widows', in *Early Modern English Drama: A Critical Companion*, ed. by Garrett A. Sullivan, Jr., Patrick Cheney and Andrew Hadfield (New York: Oxford University Press, 2006), pp. 272–86, esp. 15; Theodore B. Leinwand, '*Conjugium Interruptum* in Shakespeare and Webster', *ELH*, 72 (2005), 239–57 (p. 252); Wendy Wall, 'Just a Spoonful of Sugar: Syrup and Domesticity in Early Modern England', *Modern Philology*, 104.2 (2006), 149–72 (pp. 164 and 155).
2. Wall, 'Just a Spoonful', 162.
3. Lena Cowen Orlin, *Locating Privacy in Tudor London* (Oxford: Oxford University Press, 2007), pp. 173, 192. While Lisa Hopkins argues that 'to the Duchess, interiors represent safety', work such as Orlin's suggests that the interior is not necessarily safe (Lisa Hopkins, *The Female Hero in English Renaissance Tragedy* [Houndmills, Basingstoke: Palgrave, 2002], pp. 122–3).
4. Huston Diehl, *Staging Reform, Reforming the Stage: Protestantism and Popular Theater in Early Modern England* (Ithaca: Cornell University Press, 1997), p. 195.
5. Martin Ingram, *Church Courts, Sex and Marriage in England, 1570–1640* (Cambridge: Cambridge University Press, 1987), pp. 189–218; David Cressy, *Birth, Marriage and Death: Ritual, Religion, and the Life-Cycle in Tudor and Stuart England* (Oxford: Oxford University Press, 1997), pp. 316–35; Dympna Callaghan, 'Introduction', *The Duchess of Malfi: Contemporary Critical Essays*, ed. by Callaghan (Houndmills: Macmillan, 2000), pp. 1–24; Subha Mukherji, *Law and Representation in Early Modern Drama* (Cambridge: Cambridge University Press, 2006), pp. 17–54. As Leah Marcus argues in her essay in this volume, clandestine marriage was legal in many Italian states.
6. Theodora A. Jankowski, 'Defining/Confining the Duchess: Negotiating the Female Body in John Webster's *The Duchess of Malfi*', in Callaghan, *Duchess of Malfi*, pp. 80–103; Christina Luckyj, *A Winter's Snake: Dramatic Form in the Tragedies of John Webster* (Athens and London: University of Georgia Press, 1989), pp. 46–9; Margaret Mikesell, 'Matrimony and Change in Webster's *Duchess of Malfi*', *Journal of the Rocky Mountain Medieval and Renaissance Association*, 2 (1981), 97–111; Mary Beth Rose, *The Expense of Spirit: Love and Sexuality in English Renaissance Drama* (Ithaca: Cornell University Press, 1988), esp. 155–77; Sara Jayne Steen, 'The Crime of Marriage: Arbella Stuart and *The Duchess of Malfi*', *Sixteenth Century Journal*, 22.1 (1991), 61–76; Linda Woodbridge, 'Queen of Apricots: The Duchess of Malfi, Hero of Desire', in *The Female Tragic Hero in English Renaissance Drama*, ed. by Naomi Conn Liebler (New York: Palgrave, 2002), pp. 161–84 (p. 178).
7. James L. Calderwood, '*The Duchess of Malfi*: Styles of Ceremony', in *Twentieth-Century Interpretations of The Duchess of Malfi*, ed. by Norman Rabkin (Edgewood Cliffs, NJ: Prentice-Hall, 1968), pp. 73–84 (p. 79); Lisa Jardine, *Still Harping on Daughters: Women and Drama in the Age of Shakespeare* (Sussex: Harvester,

1983), p. 90; Clifford Leech, *John Webster: A Critical Study* (London: Hogarth Press, 1951), p. 69; Joyce E. Petersen, *Curs'd Example: 'The Duchess of Malfi' and Commonweal Tragedy* (Columbia: University of Missouri Press, 1978), p. 74.

8. According to Frank Whigham, 'the duchess is a family pioneer who ruthlessly carves out for herself the privatized domestic realm of the future, based on personal rather than familial or class imperatives' ('Sexual and Social Mobility in *The Duchess of Malfi*', *PMLA*, 100.2 [March 1985], 167–86 [p. 171]). Whigham's important essay was revised and reprinted in his *Seizures of the Will in Early Modern English Drama* (Cambridge: Cambridge University Press, 1996). See also, among others, Catherine Belsey, *The Subject of Tragedy: Identity and Difference in Renaissance Drama* (London: Methuen, 1985), p. 197. For a particularly thoughtful challenge to arguments that depict the Duchess's end as 'a historical beginning', see Wall, 'Just a Spoonful of Sugar'.
9. Leinwand, '*Conjugium Interruptum*', 250; Whigham, 'Sexual and Social Mobility', 173 and 176. Katherine Rowe argues that the play depicts how the Duchess's wayward will dismembers the one flesh she and Antonio are supposed to form through marriage, with tragic results. See Katherine Rowe, *Dead Hands: Fictions of Agency, Renaissance to Modern* (Stanford: Stanford University Press, 1999), pp. 86–110.
10. See, for instance, Margaret Lael Mikesell, 'Catholic and Protestant Widows in *The Duchess of Malfi*', *Renaissance and Reformation*, n. s. 7.4 (1983), 265–79, who argues that the play places caricatures of 'Catholic' views on the remarrying widow in the mouths of its villains; see also Jennifer Panek, *Widows and Suitors in Early Modern English Comedy* (Cambridge: Cambridge University Press, 2004).
11. Lara Bovilsky, *Barbarous Play: Race on the English Renaissance Stage* (Minneapolis: University of Minnesota Press, 2008), pp. 103–33; G. K. Hunter, 'English Folly and Italian Vice', *Dramatic Identities and Cultural Tradition: Studies in Shakespeare and His Contemporaries* (New York: Barnes and Noble Books, 1978), pp. 103–21.
12. Linda Woodbridge, *Women and the English Renaissance: Literature and the Nature of Womankind, 1540–1620* (Urbana: University of Illinois Press, 1984), p. 260.
13. Jennifer Panek, 'Why Did Widows Remarry? Remarriage, Male Authority, and Feminist Criticism', in *The Impact of Feminism in English Renaissance Studies*, ed. by Dympna C. Callaghan (Houndmills: Palgrave, 2007), pp. 281–98, esp. 288, 286, 287, 294.
14. Leonora Leet Brodwin, *Elizabethan Love Tragedy: 1587–1625* (New York: New York University Press, 1971), p. 284.
15. Woodbridge, 'Queen of Apricots', p. 178.
16. Barbara Correll, 'Malvolio at Malfi: Managing Desire in Shakespeare and Webster', *Shakespeare Quarterly*, 58.1 (2007), 65–92, esp. 72, 81, 83, 86.
17. Judith Haber, '"My Body Bestow upon My Women": The Space of the Feminine in *The Duchess of Malfi*', *Renaissance Drama*, 28 (1997), 133–59, esp. 140.
18. Lynn Enterline, *The Tears of Narcissus: Melancholia and Masculinity in Early Modern Writing* (Stanford: Stanford University Press, 1995), pp. 248, 259. See also 279, 398n. 59.
19. Michelle M. Dowd, 'Delinquent Pedigrees: Revision, Lineage, and Spatial Rhetoric in *The Duchess of Malfi*', *English Literary Renaissance*, 39.3 (2009), 499–526, esp. 519–20 and 508. Enterline argues that, for Ferdinand, the Duchess's maternity causes a profound disturbance (*Tears of Narcissus*, pp. 244–45).
20. Eve Keller, *Generating Bodies and Gendered Selves: The Rhetoric of Reproduction in Early Modern England* (Seattle: University of Washington Press, 2007), p. 134; see also Laura Gowing, *Common Bodies: Women, Touch and Power in Seventeenth-Century England* (New Haven and London: Yale University Press, 2003), p. 45.

21. Judith M. Richards, *Mary Tudor* (London: Routledge, 2008), pp. 173–79, 223 (p. 173).
22. Gowing, *Common Bodies*, pp. 44, 46, 48.
23. Katharine Park, *Secrets of Women: Gender, Generation, and the Origins of Human Dissection* (New York: Zone, 2006), pp. 77–120. See also Patricia Parker, *Shakespeare from the Margins: Language, Culture, Context* (Chicago: University of Chicago Press, 1996), pp. 229–72.
24. At the same time, vagrant women routinely gave birth outside. See Paul Griffiths, *Lost Londons: Change, Crime, and Control in the Capital City, 1550–1660* (Cambridge: Cambridge University Press, 2008), pp. 55–60.
25. Haber, '"My Body Bestow upon My Women"', 143.
26. Laura Gowing, 'Secret Births and Infanticide in Seventeenth-Century England', *Past & Present*, 156 (August 1997), 87–115.
27. Frances E. Dolan, *Dangerous Familiars: Representations of Domestic Crime in England, 1550–1700* (Ithaca: Cornell University Press, 1994), pp. 127–39.
28. Gowing, *Common Bodies*, p. 51.
29. Celia Daileader, *Eroticism on the Renaissance Stage: Transcendence, Desire, and the Limits of the Visible* (Cambridge: Cambridge University Press, 1998), p. 84; see also Michael Neill, *Issues of Death: Mortality and Identity in English Renaissance Tragedy* (Oxford: Clarendon Press, 1998), pp. 180, 178.
30. On conscience and on forgetting as a strategic un-knowing in the play, see Garrett Sullivan, *Memory and Forgetting in English Renaissance Drama: Shakespeare, Marlowe, Webster* (Cambridge: Cambridge University Press, 205), pp. 109–31. See Katharine Eisaman Maus, *Inwardness and Theater in the English Renaissance* (Chicago: University of Chicago Press, 1995) on the perceived difficulty of knowing another person.
31. Macbeth similarly remarks: 'They have tied me to a stake. I cannot fly, / But bear-like I must fight the course' (5.7.1–2).
32. On the Duchess as 'a female Christ' see Daileader, *Eroticism*, p. 87; as a figure for the virgin Mary, see Dale B. J. Randall, 'The Rank and Earthy Background of Certain Physical Symbols in *The Duchess of Malfi*', *Renaissance Drama*, 18 (1987), 171–203; see also Diehl, *Staging Reform*, pp. 156–81 and Neill, *Issues of Death*, pp. 328–53.
33. As Correll argues, Bosola is not moved by the Duchess's death but by Ferdinand's refusal to pay him ('Malvolio in Malfi', p. 85). For an opposing view, see Diehl, *Staging Reform*, pp. 200–01 or Dympna Callaghan, '*The Duchess of Malfi* and Early Modern Widows', p. 283.
34. Replying to Parliamentary petitions urging her to execute Mary Stuart in November of 1586, Elizabeth I offered 'an answer without answer', asking Parliament to 'hold yourselves satisfied with this answer answerless' (*Elizabeth I: Collected Works*, ed. by Leah S. Marcus, Janel Mueller and Mary Beth Rose [Chicago: University of Chicago Press, 2000], pp. 199–200). Mary was executed 8 February 1587.

CHAPTER SEVEN

'Greek is Turned Turk': Catholic Nostalgia in *The Duchess of Malfi*

Todd Borlik

While serving as chaplain to the Venetian embassy in London, Orazio Busino attended a production of Webster's *Duchess of Malfi* and was mortified by the portrayal of the conniving, lascivious Cardinal. The chaplain took particular umbrage at the scene of the Cardinal's installation as a soldier at the shrine of Loreto, which he saw as a 'condemnation of the grandeur of the Church, which they despise and which in this kingdom they hate to the death'.[1] Due to his status as a foreign Catholic priest writing at a time of mounting anti-Catholic sentiment, is it not possible (as Leah Marcus suggests in her contribution to this volume) that an element of paranoia infects Busino's account? His remarks may be the best contemporary record of the play's reception, but only by virtue of the fact that no other comparable testimony survives. His observations are certainly noteworthy, but no more objective or representative than, say, the anti-theatrical diatribes of Puritans like Philip Stubbes. Nevertheless, much modern commentary on *The Duchess of Malfi* has blithely echoed Busino in characterizing it as a rococo fantasy of 'exaggerated Catholic depravity'.[2] In a classic essay, William Empson frames the play as a precursor of the Gothic novels of Radcliffe and 'Monk' Lewis, a sensationalized account of 'the wickedness of Roman Catholic southern Europeans'. Similarly, Alison Shell has taken critics to task for finding modern agnosticism where Webster's contemporaries would recognize anti-Catholic polemic. Huston Diehl, meanwhile, draws parallels between the horrified audience witnessing the onstage bloodbaths and the Protestant community forged via readings of Foxe's *Acts and Monuments*. Swelling the chorus of critical orthodoxy, David Gunby and Dominic Baker-Smith have implicated the playwright's grim view of mortality with Calvinist doctrine.[3]

While there is certainly abundant evidence linking Webster with the committed Protestantism of the urban middling classes, many members of those classes, it turns out, retained a complex or even half-wistful regard for the old dispensation. In the wake of Eamon Duffy's *Stripping of the Altars* (1992) and Christopher Haigh's *English Reformations* (1993), the historical gash between a Catholic medieval era and a Protestant Renaissance no longer appears so surgically neat and clean. Like the whitewash over the Catholic icons, assumptions regarding the Reformation's swift and decisive triumph in sixteenth-century England are gradually being peeled away to reveal a colourful and jumbled spectrum of religious beliefs. Pluralism, as opposed to fundamentalism, is beginning to look like the rule rather than the exception. In the past decade a flurry of studies – including Stephen Greenblatt's *Hamlet in Purgatory* (2001), Arthur Marotti's *Religious Ideology and Cultural Fantasy* (2005) and the essay collection on *Marian Moments in Early Modern British Drama* (2007), to name a few – have detected a spectre of recusancy stalking the English Renaissance, whose authors were generally viewed in retrospect as participating in the formation of a Protestant national identity. Webster, perhaps due to his pronounced anti-Catholic slant, has so far remained outside the arc of the new 'religious turn' in early modern studies. But even Webster may be brought into the fold of those with fractured religious allegiances. Building upon the growing appreciation of the peculiar synergy between theatre and Catholic ritual, this discussion reappraises Webster's complex response to the old faith, focusing on three momentous scenes in his famed tragedy: the pilgrimage to Loreto, Antonio's meditation among the ruins and the Duchess's death.

Marian Moments in *Malfi*

Suspecting that her brothers have placed her under surveillance, the Duchess decides to rendezvous with her husband Antonio at the shrine of Our Lady of Loreto. An absolutely pivotal moment in the play thus unfolds at the most sacred site of the Marian cult in early modern Europe. For a Jacobean audience, the name of this shrine would likely call to mind its domestic counter-part, Our Lady of Walsingham in Norfolk. An historian of the English shrine observes that the two are so similar – both consecrated to the Virgin Mary, both located near the sea, both founded through angelic interventions – that 'it is impossible to study the one without the other'.[4] Remarkably, Webster scholars have neglected to comment on the English sister shrine despite the fact that Walsingham, known as 'England's Nazareth', was second only to Canterbury as a pilgrimage destination in the late middle ages.[5] Its wealth and opulent décor were legendary. References to Walsingham crop up in the Paston Letters, as well as countless state documents; virtually every king between Henry III and Henry VIII paid it a visit and contributed to it lavishly. Around 1433 the eccentric mystic Margery Kempe made the trek from King's Lynn. Roughly a century later, the Palmer in John Heywood's play *The Four PP* includes 'Walsyngham' on his itinerary encompassing the holiest sites in Christendom.[6]

As early as the fourteenth century, however, Walsingham was already becoming notorious as a destination for what we would now call a 'dirty weekend' – a reputation that the Duchess's scheme appears to confirm. In *Piers Plowman*, Langland grumbles, 'Hermytes on an heep with hoked staves / Wenten to Walsyngam – and hire wenches after'.[7] But the most scathing exposé on the shrine is Erasmus's *A Pilgrimage for Religion's Sake* (1526). Based on the Dutch scholar's visits to Walsingham in 1512 and 1514, the colloquy is a comic indictment of the shrine as a shameless tourist trap run by greedy monks, promoting superficial displays of piety. Although the newly crowned Henry VIII had walked barefoot to the shrine and prostrated himself before the Madonna, he would eventually come to embrace the Reformers' viewpoint. In 1536 the Anglican Church issued its first formal proscription on shrines and two years later Cromwell published Injunctions forbidding the worship of 'feigned images'. Among the first images seized by Cromwell's henchmen was the 'Sybil' at Walsingham. At the urging of Bishop Latimer the statue was carted to London and tossed on a bonfire of vanities in July 1538. The following month the Walsingham Priory was officially dissolved and its wealth confiscated by the state.[8]

But the new moratorium on pilgrimage did not find unanimous support among Henry's subjects. Besides destroying a venerable religious tradition, the policy dealt a crippling blow to the local economy. The resentment was such that authorities feared an uprising like the Pilgrimage of Grace in the North. While Cromwell managed to quash Catholic demonstrations in Norfolk, other pilgrimage sites remained centres of recusant activity. One of the most notorious was the well of St. Winifred in Wales, which became a rallying-point for defiant pilgrimages throughout the late sixteenth and early seventeenth centuries.[9] Given the ongoing controversy surrounding this shrine, the fact that the Spanish-born Duchess swears by Saint Winifred merits some scrutiny. In the following scene, which hinges on a running pun on the word 'will', the Duchess plans to dispose of her worldly goods, while her steward Antonio urges her to remarry.

ANTONIO I'd have you first provide for a good husband:
Give him all.
DUCHESS All?
ANTONIO Yes, your excellent self.
DUCHESS In a winding sheet?
ANTONIO In a couple.
DUCHESS St. Winfred! That were a strange will!
(1.2.302–4)

As St. Winifred was beheaded for resisting the advances of a lecherous knight, the Duchess's oath might be taken as a kind of protective charm against Antonio's lewd suggestion. Her reply may also hint that Antonio's advice weirdly verges on necrophilia, as the Duchess would have to be resuscitated like the saint in order to 'couple' with a second husband. More importantly for my purposes, just as Hamlet's oath to St. Patrick implies a residual belief in Catholic purgatory,[10] the Duchess's invocation of St. Winifred associates her with English recusants who ventured to her shrine in Wales. For early audiences, it would, moreover, foreshadow her upcoming voyage to Loreto.

By using the journey to Loreto as a cover for a romantic tryst the play appears to vindicate the concerns of Reform-minded writers like Langland and Chaucer who associated pilgrimage with erotic holiday. But, significantly, it is Bosola, not the Duchess, who proposes the ruse. Furthermore, the maid Cariola reminds the audience of the scheme's impiety: 'I do not like / This jesting with religion, this feigned pilgrimage' (3.1.319–20). The Duchess promptly dismisses her as a 'superstitious fool' (3.1.321). Nevertheless, as Thomas Rist observes, Cariola's respect for 'the Virgin Mary's emphatically Catholic reliquary presents an alternative and so ambiguous view of the matter'.[11] The Cardinal, too, comments on the irreverence of the plan: 'Doth she make religion her riding hood / To keep her from the sun and tempest?' In response, Ferdinand fumes: 'That! / That damns her' (3.3.58–60). To be sure, the Cardinal comes across as a hypocritical Machiavellian rather than an agent of divine retribution. Yet insofar as we sympathize with the Duchess's attempt to flee from under the patriarchal thumb of her brothers, her pilgrimage to Loreto supports an idea gaining currency among feminist-inflected studies of the Reformation: namely, that 'women's religious, personal, and political empowerment could be facilitated, rather than impeded, by the "old religion" and the functioning in it of the figure of Mary and the practices of Marian devotion'.[12]

Although the Duchess makes no explicit reference to Walsingham as she does to Winifred, the scene at Loreto is both shaped by and reflects upon the legacy of the English shrine. If it was no longer a mecca for pilgrims in the early seventeenth century, Walsingham was kept alive in the collective memory of Jacobean England by a celebrated ballad:

> As you came from the holy land
> Of blessed Walsingham
> O met you not with my true love
> By the way as ye came?[13]

The mad Ophelia sings some snippets of the song, and the famous opening stanza also appears in Beaumont's comedy *Knight of the Burning Pestle*, which premiered at Blackfriars a few years before *Malfi*.[14] In the Walsingham ballad, a jilted lover bewails inconstancy and insists that true love resembles 'the lasting fire' of a votary candle set before a sacred image. Just as the ballad embraces sacred love as a metaphor for profane love, Webster's drama – through its delight in extravagant spectacle – appropriates the illicit worship of images to create a kind of dramaturgical idolatry.

Critics have frequently commented on Webster's flair for spectacle.[15] Prior studies, however, have failed to fully register the theological charge of these moments. Similar to Protestant Reformers who equated the mass with a 'dumb show', Webster often evinces discomfort with the emotive power of spectacle to shock and awe viewers. The dubious status of spectacle in Webster is underscored by the fact that he consistently inserts pantomimes to dramatize scenes of violence and deception. In *The White Devil* idolatry literally becomes fatal when Isabella dies after kissing a poisoned painting. But, paradoxically, Webster undercuts our ability to draw an iconoclastic moral from this event by couching it in the form of a dumb show, in effect transforming the stage itself into a tableau vivant, a living icon. Perhaps the most stunning example of Webster's ambiguous treatment of the theatricality of Catholic worship occurs at the shrine of Loreto.

The scene opens with the First Pilgrim commending the shrine's beauty: 'I have not seen a goodlier shrine than this, / Yet I have visited many' (3.4.1–2). Just prior to the dumb show, the Second Pilgrim cues viewers to 'expect / A noble ceremony' (3.4.5–6), a phrase Puritans would regard as highly suspect. Since the pilgrims function as choric figures, their expectations could plausibly reflect those of some audience members. If Webster merely wanted to telescope the action (as Berry suggests), he could have omitted the shrine scene altogether and reported it second-hand, as Shakespeare does with the ambassadors' visit to Delphi in *The Winter's Tale*. Instead, Webster confronts us with one of the most extravagant stage spectacles in early modern English drama:

> *Here the ceremony of the* CARDINAL*'s instalment [sic] in the habit of a soldier, performed in delivering up his cross, hat, robes and ring at the shrine, and investing him with sword, helmet, shield, and spurs. Then* ANTONIO, *the* DUCHESS *and their Children, having presented themselves at the shrine, are, by a form of banishment in dumb-show expressed towards them by the Cardinal and the state of Ancona, banished.* (s.d. 3.4.7)

Paradoxically, a great deal of the dramatic energy in Webster's tragedy is generated by a religious ceremonialism it ostensibly abhors.[16]

While Busino's indignation at the depiction of the Cardinal here is certainly understandable, it is also, I think, significant that he fails to mention the Duchess or the Madonna. Part of the confusion surrounding this scene stems from the fact that the stage direction really contains three separate actions that should not be conflated: the installment, the Duchess and her family 'present[ing] themselves', and the banishment. Critics who posit that Webster sought to create an 'elaborate imitation' of the Loreto shrine and the Cardinal's Catholic rites are, I think, correct about the latter but not the former.[17] The middle stage direction is not elaborate at all, but conspicuously brief. Perhaps the laconic phrasing implies that the Duchess's devotions are disingenuous. However, the effect arguably could be to juxtapose her humble piety with the Cardinal's worldly militarism. The scene's layered spectatorship further destabilizes the anti-Catholic satire; by having us watch the pilgrims watching the ceremonies, Webster's staging invites the audience to view Marian worship through more sympathetic eyes. The pilgrims' reaction to the banishment supports such a reading. They berate the Cardinal for 'bear[ing] himself too cruel' (3.4.26) and the Pope for seizing the Dukedom, but – although they question the propriety of the Duchess's marriage – do not criticize her devotions. Moreover, since Counter-Reformation apologists found a scriptural precedent for pilgrimage in the Holy Family's Flight into Egypt, the Duchess's pilgrimage to escape her brothers would link them with the tyrannical baby-killer Herod and draw a subtle connection between the Duchess and Mary.[18] From these perspectives, the real quarry of Webster's invective appears to be the agents of a corrupt Roman Catholicism and ostentatious ceremonialism, not ceremonialism per se.

Webster's ambiguous representation of the Marian cult finds a striking counter-point in Caravaggio's painting, *The Madonna of Loreto* (ca. 1605). Rejecting the traditional iconography of the Virgin as a quasi-angelic being, Caravaggio depicts her as eminently human, a stately but ordinary Roman matron (the painter often found his models among the city's demimonde), shockingly barefoot, with only the wispiest of halos. Just as Bosola rails against the 'painting' (i.e. cosmetics) that obscures 'the deep ruts and foul sloughs' (2.1.29) in the Old Lady's face, and the 'rich tissue' (2.1.64) that conceals the aging body, Caravaggio rebels against excessively decorative style of Catholic painting, portraying the pilgrims with soiled feet, shabby clothes and grotesquely wizened skin.[19] Even the paint on the wall of the shrine is chipped away, exposing plain brick beneath. Although the artists' religious loyalties differ, their aims are broadly similar. Influenced by the Counter-Reformation, Caravaggio's altarpiece shuns the gaudy opulence and overly exuberant piety that irked Protestant iconoclasts. Likewise, the minimalism of the stage-direction in which the Duchess presents herself constitutes a simple act of piety, shorn of the trappings of Marian idolatry, in stark contrast to the extravagance of the Cardinal's arming.

The peculiar mixture of fascination and repugnance with which Webster regarded the theatricality of Catholic worship resurfaces during the Duchess's imprisonment. Curiously, one aspect of pilgrimage often lambasted by Protestants was what Grace Tiffany terms the 'stage management of shrines'.[20] In his famous colloquy on Walsingham, Erasmus reports that his guide accosted him with a series of grisly relics, including skulls, jaws, fingers and a severed arm 'brought forth with the blood-stained flesh still on it'.[21] The anecdote is uncannily reminiscent of the macabre scene in Webster's tragedy in which Ferdinand torments the Duchess with a wax arm she is led to believe belonged to her husband. He dupes the Duchess into kissing the hand just as the cleric in Erasmus's tale invites the pilgrims to kiss the bones, skulls and decomposing arms on display in the crypt. Webster knew *The Colloquies*, a text featured on well over half the surviving Tudor grammar school syllabi, including Merchant Taylors, which the playwright most likely attended.[22]

Erasmus can, I believe, provide something of a barometer for gauging how early modern audiences might have responded to such scenes in Webster's plays. The Dutch scholar was recognized as inveighing against ecclesiastical abuses and naïve, literal-minded piety sanctioned by a corrupt clergy, but he was very far from endorsing a radical split with Catholic tradition. In other words, even faithful Catholics could be critical of the crude histrionics of some Catholic worship. That Webster's sensibility aligns with those advocating moderate reform can be further deduced from his citing Richard Hooker, the spokesperson for the Elizabethan compromise, in *The Devil's Law Case*.[23] At the very least, Webster's admiration for Erasmus and Hooker raises questions about Baker-Smith's reading of *Malfi* as expounding Calvinist theology. This take on the play's religious bent falls under further strain when it is recalled that Ferdinand's masque of lunatics includes a Puritan, who bellows: 'Greek is turned Turk – we are only to be saved by the Helvetian translation' (4.2.90–1).[24] Jacobean spectators and readers would have instantly identified this 'Third Mad Man' as a hard-line Calvinist, denouncing the recently published Authorized Version, or King James Bible, in favour of the Genevan edition. In this satire on the Puritan zealotry, Webster sounds more like Ben Jonson, who wavered between Catholic and Anglican beliefs, than the Protestant firebrand he is sometimes regarded to be.

'Webster and the "Curse of the Dissolution"'

If Webster uses theatre to expose the theatricality of Catholic ritual, he also at times voices nostalgia for the Catholic past, as evident from his tacit critique of the dissolution. In *The Devil's Law Case*, the widow Leonora rebukes nobles who stoop to 'begging Churchland', and oddly refers to it as 'a ruine / Worth all mens pitie' (1.1.198–9). The metaphor of pitiful ruins (which also occurs, as we shall see, in *Malfi*) was a freighted one in post-Reformation England. For many of Webster's contemporaries, it would aggravate a nagging remorse for the destruction of the Catholic monasteries. In her study of shifting attitudes towards the dissolution in post-Reformation England, Margaret Aston detects a recurring cycle of 'new zeal, new desolation, new nostalgia' in the management of old monastic ruins.[25] A wave of nostalgia struck the 1590s around the time Shakespeare penned his sonnet commemorating the 'bare ruined choirs where late the sweet birds sang', and a Lincolnshire cleric noted, 'many do lament the pulling down of abbayes. They say it was never a merry world since'.[26] Even the destruction of Walsingham was bemoaned in a little-known Elizabethan protest elegy:

> Bitter, bitter O, to behold
> The grass to grow
> Where the walls of Walsingam
> So stately did show.
> … … … … … … … … … … ….
> Level, level with the ground
> The towers do lie,
> Which with their golden, glittering tops
> Pierced once to the sky.[27]

Preservationist feeling waned in the aftermath of the Gunpowder plot, but the years in which Webster wrote his great tragedies were, I believe, also marked by the renewed nostalgia described by Aston. King James himself had expressed regret about the destruction of the nation's architectural heritage, wishing he could have preserved the buildings for some godly purposes. Now that a Tudor no longer occupied the throne, grievances with Henry VIII's handling of the dissolution could be aired more openly. This cultural background is absolutely vital to understanding Antonio's meditation among the ruins.

When the Duchess inquires how her imprisonment has affected her, Cariola compares her to 'some reverend monument / Whose ruins are even pitied' (4.2.32–3). Webster undoubtedly had this line in mind when we actually witness a character pitying ruins just a few scenes later. In 5.3 Antonio visits the Cardinal's residence built alongside 'the ruins of an ancient abbey' (5.3.2), where he hears an echo with an eerie resemblance to the voice of his dead wife. Surveying the crumbling 'piece of a cloister' (5.3.4), Antonio virtually echoes the critics of the dissolution:

> I do love these ancient ruins.
> We never tread upon them but we set
> Our foot upon some reverend history.
> And questionless, here in this open court,
> Which now lies naked to the injuries
> Of stormy weather, some men lie interred
> Loved the church so well, and gave so largely to't,
> They thought it should have canopied their bones
> Till doomsday. (5.3.9–17)

Huston Diehl duly observes that the speech concludes by insinuating that the collapse of Roman Catholicism was inevitable. Yet as contemporary sermons reveal, this understanding of religion as a mortal, organic entity that 'must have like death we have' was entirely compatible with an abhorrence of the dissolution.[28] Antonio's speech, which has no analogue in Webster's source, stands as an elegiac meditation on the decay of the old faith.

Despite the play's impatience with Catholic superstition, *Malfi* even goes so far to perpetuate a belief that families who benefited from the dissolution were cursed. In 1613, the same year Webster wrote his celebrated tragedy, an antiquarian by the name of Henry Spelman began compiling his *History and Fate of Sacrilege*, which sets out to illustrate 'the infelicity of meddling with consecrated places' by chronicling, with unabashed schadenfreude, all the 'strange misfortunes' that afflicted families who purchased Church land.[29] In *Malfi*, the Cardinal acquires

Antonio's forfeited estate containing the old 'citadel of St Bennet' (5.1.19). The narrative in effect reverses the events of the English Reformation. But rather than restore the sacred ground to godly uses, the Cardinal bestows the estate on his mistress. Shortly afterwards, we learn that the Cardinal's own estate occupies the remains of an ancient abbey, which he has transformed into a 'fortification', an act that mirrors his perverse swapping of liturgical robes for armour in Act III. With the exception of the Marquis, every character entangled with confiscated church property suffers a violent death. For the play's early audience, the implications were clear: the curse had claimed another string of victims. More than a curious piece of historical trivia, the curse holds considerable implications for our understanding of Webster's philosophy. The fatalism scholars have often noted in Webster's tragedy and associated with Calvinist predestination derives in part from a superstition conjured by the Reformation's guilty conscience.

As a Protestant antiquarian (who happens to have been educated at Walsingham) with an avid interest in Catholic culture, Spelman provides a useful touchstone for assessing the theological nuances of Webster's Italian tragedy. Whereas the Catholic author of 'The Wracks of Walsingham' laments the shrine's desecration, Antonio's speech participates in Spelman's project to re-consecrate monastic ruins as monuments of 'reverend history'. Rather than a defiantly pro-Catholic moment, then, the ruins scene in *Malfi* smacks of an early modern antiquarianism through which, according to Jennifer Summit, 'the formerly sacred artifacts of the medieval church were recuperated into new uses as objects of secularized historical interest'. Yet as Summit remarks, wary Puritans often tended to regard antiquarianism as 'a kind of Catholicism *manqué*'.[30] From the vantage point of 1613, the line between medieval relic and historical artefact was often gossamer-thin.

Websterian Tragedy and the *Ars Moriendi*

Webster is intrigued not only by commemoration of the dead, but also by their rites of passage. In the final portion of this essay, I would like to glance at the under-appreciated affinity between Websterian tragedy and the *Ars moriendi* tradition.[31] In the late middle ages, a number of treatises proffered advice for the dying and soon-to-be bereaved. The name of the genre derives from an early fifteenth-century Latin manuscript, first printed in English as the *Arte and Crafte to Knowe Well to Dye*.[32] The text asks readers to meditate on the inevitability of death and schools them on how to deflect the temptations that may assail them in final moments of bodily agony by comparing their pains with those of Christ on the cross. As the everyman's condition worsens, the manual turns its attention to the clergy, family and friends gathered round the bed, coaching them on how to ease the soul's passage to the afterlife.

With the advent of the Reformation, the Catholic protocol for the Last Rites had to be revised. A transitional text in this regard is the 1534 *Treatise of Dying Well*. The author, Thomas Lupset, was a disciple of Colet and Erasmus, and he infuses the genre with the spirit of humanism. In addition to the usual Christian litany of consoling thoughts, he appeals to Seneca and the grim tenets of classical stoicism. The text has been seen as heralding 'the emergence of the individual thinker and philosopher as the proper religious authority rather than the Christian *traditio*'.[33] The onus of spiritual preparation for death falls even harder on the individual in the explicitly Protestant contributions to the genre such as Thomas Becon's *The Syckmans Salue* and William Perkins' *A Salue for Sicke man*. Becon overhauls the *Ars moriendi* to fortify anxious readers and depict for them what a properly Protestant death will look like shorn of the old ceremonies. Instead of being passively coddled by the ministrations of the clergy, the dying protagonist plays an active role in the narrative of his death. He participates in the scriptural recitations and theological debates with exceptional verve for someone allegedly in hospice care, railing against the 'superstitious masse-mongers' and their naive faith in the power of the sacraments to guarantee entrance into heaven.

When Bosola, dressed as a tomb-maker, first accosts the Duchess, she replies: 'Thou speakst as if I lay upon my deathbed / Gasping for breath' (4.2.116). The line frames the scene that follows as a stand-off between Catholic and Protestant versions of the *Ars moriendi*, a point that becomes more apparent when Bosola poses as 'the common bellman / That usually is sent to condemned persons / The night before they suffer' (4.2.166–8). Among the few reliable details known about Webster's life is that he attended St. Selpuchre's in Smithfield, near Newgate prison. This piece of biographical trivia is notorious for a single reason: in 1605 a parishioner named Robert Dove (or Dowe) bequeathed the Church fifty pounds to pay for ringing a great bell at midnight outside the cell of prisoners condemned to die. The playwright likely knew of this macabre ritual given that his father served on the Common Council of the Merchant Taylors, which witnessed the deed of gift. Critics have been quick to point out that Dove's homily may have inspired Bosola's dirge.[34] What has escaped notice is that, on a doctrinal level, the two are in fact quite distinct. A plaque on the walls of St. Sepulchre's provides the closest thing to a transcription of the bellman's speech:

> All you that in the condemned hole do lie
> Prepare you for tomorrow you shall die
> Watch all, and pray: the hour is drawing near

> That you before the Almighty must appear.
> *Examine well yourselves*, in time repent.
> That you may not to eternal flames be sent;
> And when St. Sepulchre's bell in the morning tolls
> The Lord Above have mercy on your souls.

The imperative 'Examine well yourselves' corresponds with the inward-directed nature of Protestant *Ars moriendi*. Bosola's dirge, in contrast, conforms to the Catholic protocol, which encourages the invocation of saints and the devotional use of religious paraphernalia like perfumes and relics. Following the invocation of 'Our Dame' (another allusion to the Virgin Mary), the song culminates with the advice: 'Strew your hair with powders sweet, / Don clean linen, bathe your feet, / And, the foul fiend more to check, / A crucifix let bless your neck' (4.2.183–6). The first two lines invoke the Catholic ministrations involving the washing and anointing of the terminally ill, the unction that Perkins dubs 'the greasie sacrament of the Papists'. The final line, meanwhile, sanctions the Catholic's use of the crucifix in deathbed devotions. This is consistent with Bosola's request in the previous scene that Ferdinand furnish her with a 'penitential garment [and] [...] beads and prayer books' (4.1.116–18). Meanwhile, Bosola's insistence that he will only return to the Duchess when 'the business shall be comfort' (4.2.133) anticipates his transformation from ruthless hitman to tormented avenger.

Brachiano's death-bed scene in *The White Devil* even more explicitly dramatizes a Catholic rendition of the *Ars moriendi*, complete with 'Crucifix' and a 'Hollowed taper'. Although the play casts the ritual in a lurid light given that the monks turn out to be assassins, Vittoria pointedly remarks that the crucifix 'settles his wild spirits' (5.3.131). The ceremonial ministrations of Catholicism, in other words, appear to be astonishingly efficacious.[35] *The White Devil* thus seems haunted by the same 'maimed rites' that Shakespearean commentators have detected in *Hamlet*. Cornelia sings a mad song in the vein of Ophelia, bewailing that her son Marcello has been denied a proper, ceremonious burial, and later performs an act of ritual grieving that, as the allusion to 'granddames' betrays, recalls pre-Reformation mourning customs.

> And there is such a solemn melodie
> 'Tweene dolefull songes, teares, and sad elegies
> Such, as old granddames watching by the dead,
> Were wont t'out-wear the nights with. (5.4.50–3)

Francisco reports that the scene brought tears to his eyes, but Flamineo sniffs at such 'superstitious howling' (5.4.59). Nevertheless, when he pulls back the discovery curtain, Flamineo is undeniably moved by the spectacle of his mother's grief: 'I have a strange thing in mee, to th'which / I cannot give a name, without it bee / Compassion' (5.4.107–9). The unmooring of Protestant scepticism becomes further evident when Flamineo sees Brachiano's ghost shortly after this incident and immediately asks: 'what religions best / For a man to die in?' (5.4.122–3). The question speaks to contemporary anxieties about the inadequacy of the Protestant *Ars moriendi*. Although the ending of the play is ambiguous, as Flamineo requests 'no harsh flattering Bels resound [his] knell' (5.4.269), and assassins exploit the Catholic Last Rites as a cloak for villainy, yet it could be argued that, in staging and emptying out these rites, Webster's plays aggravate a need for these taboo ceremonies.

Unlike Brachiano, the Duchess does not seem to accept the traditional ministrations offered by Bosola. She initially bristles at his 'dismal preparation, / This talk, fit for a charnel' (4.2.157–8), whereas Bosola insists he has come to offer 'last benefit' (4.2.161). Significantly, in contrast to Cariola, who make a series of desperate excuses to defer her execution, the Duchess dies with supreme composure and grace. Despite her Protestant fortitude and self-reliance, she reverts to a more Catholic-tinged humility in her final moments, asking the executioners for assistance, as if they have taken on the role of priests easing her passage to the afterlife.

> Pull and pull strongly; for your able strength
> Must pull down heaven upon me.
> Yet stay – heaven gates are not so highly arched
> As princes palaces; they that enter there
> Must go upon their knees. [*Kneels*] (4.2.222–6)

Her sudden decision to kneel signifies a turn towards a more accommodating sensibility. As John Russell Brown observes, 'when the Duchess stops her executioners so that she may kneel before her death [...] she is repeating the ritual posture that she had taken before at the shrine of Our Lady'.[36] Rather than simply wave a banner for the Anglican compromise, Webster's tragedies voice both Protestant distrust of Catholic ritual and poignant defenses of the old faith's ceremonialism. It would, therefore, be reductive to treat *Malfi* as programmatically endorsing a particular religious ideology. In glorifying the heroic resolve of characters that confront their mortality with magnanimous poise, Webster's Senecan-inflected tragedy itself becomes a secular *Ars moriendi*.

The aim of this discussion has *not* been to imply that Webster wanted to revive pilgrimage or the worship of images: far from it. But beneath the recurrent Catholic-baiting in his Italian tragedies, I would argue that the playwright caters to contemporary nostalgia for these outlawed rituals, and sought to appease that sentiment in part by devising elaborate theatrical spectacles. This transition from ritual to theatre is underscored by the fact that Blackfriars was itself a former monastic property now converted for commercial uses in the manner decried by critics of the dissolution like Spelman. Blackfriars even boasted a chapel dedicated to the Virgin Mary where scenes of adoration like that depicted by Webster would have taken place on a regular basis.[37] By 1613 many Anglicans had begun to harbour conflicted feelings towards the Catholic faith; respect for its grandeur and 'reverend history', as Antonio puts it, was tempered with suspicion of its alleged venality and outward-oriented piety. This ambivalence is reflected in the Duchess herself, and helps imbue the character with greater psychological complexity and tragic subjectivity. Although in the opening act the Duchess performs a Protestant, clandestine marriage that denies the need for clerical intercession, she later defends its sacramental character, rebuking her brother for 'violating a sacrament o'th' church' (4.1.38). She adamantly declines to play the part of the mourning Catholic widow – 'the figure cut in alabaster / Kneel[ing] at my husband's tomb' (1.2.364–5), yet the most heinous curse she flings at the stars is to 'Let all the zealous prayers of mortified churchmen / Forget them' (4.1.103–4). When Cariola likens the Duchess to a 'reverend monument / Whose ruins are even pitied', Webster draws on an aesthetic regard for monastic ruins to shape the audience's reaction to his heroine. Flawed yet unflappable, imprudent but tenaciously dignified, the Duchess elicits the same moral ambivalence as the collapse of the old faith 80 years after Henry's split with Rome.

In a brief meditation on the echoing ruins scene, the renowned art historian Edgar Wind observed 'what the ruin is to the sense of sight, the echo is to the sense of hearing: a faint reflection of the past. A ruin "lives" as long as it yields an echo'.[38] With Wind's quotation in mind, we might begin to perceive *The Duchess of Malfi* itself, metonymically speaking, as an uncanny and eloquent echo through which the medieval Catholic past continues to speak to Webster's sceptical present.

Notes

An early version of this research was presented at the Renaissance Society of America conference in Chicago in April 2008. I would like to thank Horacio Sierra for organizing the panel, Arthur Kinney for shuffling his plans that day to come hear it, and Christina Luckyj for her incisive feedback on an early draft.

1. Cited from the translation of Busino's letter in *John Webster: A Critical Anthology*, ed. by G. K. and S. K. Hunter (Harmondsworth: Penguin, 1969), p. 32.

2. Charles Forker, 'Webster and Barnes: The Source of the Ceremony of the Cardinal's Arming in *The Duchess of Malfi* Once More', *Anglia*, 106: 3–4 (1988), 420.
3. William Empson, 'Mine Eyes Dazzle', *Essays in Criticism*, 14 (1964), 80–86. Alison Shell, *Catholicism, Controversy, and the English Literary Imagination, 1558–1660* (Cambridge: Cambridge University Press, 1999), p. 54. Huston Diehl, *Staging Reform, Reforming the Stage* (Ithaca: Cornell University Press, 1997), pp. 182–212. David Gunby, 'The Duchess of Malfi: A Theological Approach', in *John Webster*, ed. by Brian Morris (London: Ernest Benn 1970), pp. 181–204. Dominic Baker-Smith, 'Religion and John Webster', in *John Webster*, pp. 207–28.
4. H. M. Gillett, *Walsingham: The History of a Famous Shrine* (London: Burns Oates & Washbourne, 1946), p. 3.
5. Lisa Hopkins is the sole exception. In an essay published after the first draft of this chapter was already written, Hopkins notes the affinity between Loreto and Walsingham, remarking that 'though [*The Duchess of Malfi*] generally has little time for Catholicism, [Webster] presents the shrine at Loreto as something which is indeed holy, and should not be jested with'. See '"Black but Beautiful": Othello and the Cult of the Black Madonna', in *Marian Moments in Early Modern British Drama*, ed. by Regina Buccola and Lisa Hopkins (Aldershot: Ashgate, 2007), pp. 75–86, 77.
6. My account of the history of the shrine is indebted to J. C. Dickinson, *The Shrine of Our Lady of Walsingham* (Cambridge: Cambridge University Press, 1956).
7. William Langland, *The Vision of Piers Plowman*, ed. by A. V. C. Schmidt (London: Dent, 1978), I, 53–5.
8. Latimer's letter is reprinted in Gillet, *Walsingham*, p. 64.
9. For more on the background of the Welsh shrine, see Andrew Breeze, 'St. Winifred of Wales and *The Duchess of Malfi*', *Notes and Queries*, 45:1 (March 1998), 33–4.
10. Stephen Greenblatt, *Hamlet in Purgatory* (Princeton: Princeton University Press, 2001), pp. 233–4.
11. Thomas Rist, *Revenge Tragedy and the Drama of Commemoration* (Aldershot: Ashgate, 2008), p. 137.
12. Arthur Marotti characterizes this viewpoint as typical of revisionist accounts of the Reformation in his Foreword to *Marian Moments*, p. xx.
13. The Walsingham ballad exists in several different versions. The one cited in this article is reprinted in Bishop Percy's *Reliques of Ancient English Poetry*, ed. by Henry B. Wheatley (London: George Allen & Unwin, 1885), II, 102–3.
14. For more on Ophelia's song, see Philip Edwards, *Pilgrimage and Literary Tradition* (Cambridge: Cambridge University Press, 2005), pp. 24–44. Strains from the ballad Walsingham can also be heard in Nashe's *Have with you to Saffron Walden* (1596) and Daubridge-court Belchier's *Hans Beer-pot* (1618).
15. Although he avoids speculating about Webster's religious inclinations, Ralph Berry compares Webster's tragedies to Baroque art, a genre 'imbued with the immediate and latent power of the Counter-Reformation'. See *The Art of John Webster* (Oxford: Clarendon Press, 1972), p. 8, and 'Masques and Dumb Shows in Webster's Plays', in *Elizabethan Theatre VII*, ed. by G. R. Hibbard (Hamden, CT: Archon Books, 1977), p. 132. Samuel Schuman dubs Webster 'an essentially visual artist', influenced by the genre of still life and woodcuts in Renaissance emblem books in '*The Theatre of Fine Devices*': *The Visual Drama of John Webster* (Salzburg: Institut fur Anglistik und Amerikanistik, 1982), I, 48–63.
16. See Leah Marcus's incisive comparison of the moral ambivalence of spectacle in Webster with the ambivalence aroused and internalized by Bosola in her edition of *The Duchess of Malfi* (London: Methuen, 2009), pp. 40–2.
17. Brian Gibbons, ed., *The Duchess of Malfi* (New York: Norton, 2001), p. 76; Rist, p. 137.

18. While Protestants no longer regarded Mary as an intercessor, more restrained adoration of the Virgin still continued under Anglicanism. See Marotti's Foreword and Buccola and Hopkins's Introduction in *Marian Moments*, pp. xiii–xx, 2–4, and Jennifer Summit, *Lost Property: The Woman Writer and English Literary History 1380–1589* (Chicago: University of Chicago Press, 2000), pp. 124–5.
19. Ralph Berry comments on some of the compelling affinities between Webster and Caravaggio, but fails to mention the *Madonna of Loreto*, the one Caravaggio painting that actually corresponds to a scene in Webster's plays. A discussion of the theological and political sub-text of the painting can be found in Pamela Jones, *Altarpieces and their Viewers in the Churches of Rome from Caravaggio to Guido Reni* (Aldershot: Ashgate, 2008), pp. 75–136.
20. Grace Tiffany, *Love's Pilgrimage: The Holy Journey in English Renaissance Literature* (Newark: University of Delaware Press, 2006), p. 85.
21. *The Colloquies of Erasmus*, ed. by Craig R. Thompson (Chicago: University of Chicago Press, 1965), p. 305. For references to the statues at Walsingham, see Dickinson, *The Shrine of Our Lady*, pp. 8, 35–36, 42. For more on the prevalence of images at shrines prior to the Reformation, see Eamon Duffy, *The Stripping of the Altars* (New Haven: Yale University Press, 1992), pp. 155–60. Albert H. Tricomi has nominated *Exècrable des Sorciers* as another potential influence on the wax-works scene in "The Severed Hand in Webster's *Duchess of Malfi*" *SEL*, 44:2 (Spring 2004), 347–8.
22. R. W. Dent detects no less than six different echoes from various colloquies, although he fails to mention the thematic parallels between *Malfi* and 'The Pilgrimage for Religion's Sake'. See *John Webster's Borrowings* (Berkeley: University of California Press, 1960), pp. 44, 151–2.
23. The line, 'We observe / Obedience of creatures to the Law of Nature / Is the stay of the whole world' (4.2.250), paraphrases Hooker's famous adage almost verbatim.
24. To be fair, Baker-Smith does acknowledge some problems with seeing Webster as Calvinist, which he accounts for on the grounds that it would be misguided to expect 'conscious theological precision in the drama' (p. 215). Rather than dismissed as artistic license, this inconsistency could be understood as reflecting the theological hybridity of Jacobean Anglicanism.
25. Margaret Aston, 'English Ruins and English History: The Dissolution and the Sense of the Past', *Journal of Warburg-Courtauld Institutes*, 36 (1973), 236.
26. *Tudor Treatises*, ed. by A. G. Dickens (Yorkshire Archaeological Society Record Series, 1959), p. 38.
27. The poem is preserved in manuscript now at the Bodleian Library in Oxford: Rawlinson MSS. 219, f.16r–v. The piece is transcribed and analysed in Edwards, *Pilgrimage and Literary Tradition*, pp. 26–7.
28. In 1613, a Cambridge preacher named Foulke Robartes posed the following question: of those 'enriched by the spoil of Church, how few of so great estates are not already ruinated? It is true that there is an interchange of things in this world, and that it is a vain thing for men to think their names, lands and houses shall continue for ever; but yet that in so short a space so great a change should be of so many families [...] must needs make men see [...] that the fact was displeasing unto almighty God.' Qtd. in Keith Thomas, *Religion and the Decline of Magic* (New York: Oxford University Press, 1971), p. 98.
29. Henry Spelman, *History and Fate of Sacrilege* (1698; London: John Hodges, 1895), p. 146.
30. Summit, *Lost Property*, p. 143.
31. Some of my insights here have been anticipated by Bettie Anne Doebler in 'Continuity in the Art of Dying: *The Duchess of Malfi*', *Comparative Drama*, 14 (1980), 203–15. Doebler, however, does not properly distinguish between Catholic and

Protestant variations of the rite. Jill Philips Ingram also briefly alludes to a link between Websterian tragedy and *Ars moriendi* in her essay, '"Noble Lie": Casuistry and Machiavellianism in *The Duchess of Malfi*', *Explorations in Renaissance Culture*, 31:1 (Summer 2005), 135–60.

32. My summary of the *Ars moriendi* tradition draws from the work of Mary Catharine O'Connor, *The Art of Dying Well: The Development of the Ars Moriendi* (New York: Columbia University Press, 1942), and Nancy Lee Beaty, *The Craft of Dying: A Study in the Literary Tradition of the Ars Moriendi in England* (New Haven: Yale University Press, 1970).
33. Beaty, *The Craft of Dying*, p. 65
34. Charles Forker, *The Skull Beneath the Skin: The Achievement of John Webster* (Carbondale: Southern Illinois University Press, 1986), pp. 21–4; *The Works of John Webster*, ed. by Gunby *et al.* (Cambridge: Cambridge University Press, 2007), p. 650.
35. Susan McLeod remarks on the scene's recreation of the Roman rite, *Commendatio Animae* in *Dramatic Imagery in the Plays of John Webster* (Salzburg: University of Salzburg, 1977), pp. 65–6.
36. John Russell Brown, ed., *The Duchess of Malfi* (Manchester: Manchester University Press, 1997), p. 15.
37. Joseph Quincy Adams, *Shakespearean Playhouses* (Boston: Houghton Mifflin, 1917), p. 81.
38. Edgar Wind, 'Ruins and Echoes', *Journal of the Warburg Institute*, 1:3 (1938), 259. Michael Neill comments on Webster's awareness of the commemorative powers of literature in his elegy for Prince Henry entitled *A Monumental Column*, 'Monuments and Ruins as Symbols in *The Duchess of Malfi*', in *Themes in Drama 4*, ed. by James Richmond (Cambridge: Cambridge University Press, 1982), p. 84.

CHAPTER EIGHT

A Survey of Resources

Christy Desmet

A teacher looking for a representative Renaissance tragedy, complete with riveting action, accessible characters and dramatic poetry that will stand up under sustained close reading would probably think first of *Hamlet*. But what recommends *Hamlet* for classroom use can also be found in *The Duchess of Malfi*, which offers as well a sense of novelty (being less canonized than Shakespeare's plays), a complex emphasis on social institutions and gender roles, and the shivery pleasure of gothic horror. In Volume 1 of the eighth edition of *The Norton Anthology of English Literature*, furthermore, Webster's *Duchess of Malfi* is packaged with *Twelfth Night* (which also deals with gender issues) and *King Lear* (which also can be read as a bleak representation of the human condition). This introduction to current pedagogical approaches to *Duchess* is divided into three principal sections. The first discusses suitable texts for student and teacher use, plus audio-visual supplements, online resources and appropriations; the second surveys approaches to teaching the play; the third offers an annotated bibliography of useful criticism.

Part 1. Texts

Unless *Duchess* is part of a larger anthology of Renaissance drama or literature, a single-play edition or compact edition of several Webster plays will be needed. Among the multiple-play editions, the best balance between apparatus and cost is probably achieved by the Oxford World's

Classics edition (edited by René Weis), which includes sufficiently generous glosses in notes at the back of the volume. Brian Gibbons's New Mermaid edition contains excellent glosses, an extensive scholarly introduction, information about past productions with some production photographs and suggestions for further reading. Jackie Moore's edition in the Oxford Student Texts series includes contextual information about Webster, an extensive discussion of different methods for interpreting the play and sample essay questions. The cheapest editions generally include no notes, but offer a clean text at low prices (e.g. Casey, Griffiths). Among scholarly texts, Leah S. Marcus's authoritative edition for the Arden Early Modern Drama series should be consulted by teachers. The extensive Introduction offers excellent discussions of such topics as humours psychology and lycanthropy, the play's use of *sententiae* and the emblem tradition. A succinct account of key theatrical productions includes photographs, and two appendices are devoted to the play's sources. A library copy of John Russell Brown's scholarly Revels edition would also be helpful to the teacher and includes an excerpt of Webster's source from William Painter's *Palace of Pleasure*. While the Gunby, Carnegie, Hammond and DelVecchio Old-Spelling Critical Edition would never be used as a course text, teachers might want to consult the Critical Introduction and especially the extensive Theatrical Introduction, which offers invaluable remarks about dramaturgy (including such topics as costumes, casting and staging) and a detailed stage history. Among the most useful online texts are the University of Oregon's Renascence edition, which is available in both HTML and PDF formats; and Larry A. Brown's HTML online edition. In the latter, the play can be accessed as a single document, which makes it superior for word and word-string searches. However, both online editions use texts from the public domain, which must be checked carefully against a reputable scholarly text.

Print editions

Webster, John, *The Duchess of Malfi*, ed. by John Russell Brown, Revels Plays (Cambridge, Mass.: Harvard University Press, 1964).

—, *The Duchess of Malfi*, ed. by John Russell Brown, Revels Student Editions (Manchester: Manchester University Press, 1997).

—, *The Duchess of Malfi*, ed. by Kathy Casey, Dover Thrift Edition (Mineola, NY: Dover, 1999) (paperback).

—, *The Duchess of Malfi*, ed. by Brian Gibbons, New Mermaids (London: A&C Black; New York: W.W. Norton, 2001) (paperback).

—, *The Duchess of Malfi*, in *The Works of John Webster: An Old-Spelling Critical Edition*, I, ed. by David Gunby, David Carnegie, Antony Hammond and Doreen DelVecchio (Cambridge: Cambridge University Press, 1995).

—, *The Duchess of Malfi*, ed. by Trevor R. Griffiths (London: Hern Books, 1999) (paperback).
—, *The Duchess of Malfi*, ed. by Leah S. Marcus, Arden Early Modern Drama (London: A&C Black Publishers, 2009).
—, *The Duchess of Malfi*, ed. by Jackie Moore, Oxford Student Texts (Oxford: Oxford University Press, 2007) (paperback).
—, *The Duchess of Malfi and Other Plays*, ed. by René Weis, Oxford World's Classics (Oxford: Oxford University Press, 1996) (paperback).

Online editions

Webster, John, *The Duchess of Malfi: The Complete Text, with Notes and Commentary*, ed. by Larry A. Brown <http://laryavisbrown.homestead.com/files/Malfi/malfi_home.htm> [accessed 24 October 2009].
—, *The Duchess of Malfi*, ed. by Risa Stephanie Bear, Renascence Editions <http://www.luminarium.org/renascence-editions/webster1.html> [accessed 24 October 2009].

Part 2. Approaches to Teaching *The Duchess of Malfi*

A. Webster-Shakespeare and other dramatic comparisons

For classroom purposes, *The Duchess* may be compared with a number of Shakespeare's plays, although it is worth keeping in mind Christopher Ricks's cynical observation that critics often invoke comparisons with Shakespeare whenever the analogy will enhance the reputation of the lesser-known dramatist.[1] Webster himself, however, was aware of Shakespeare as a fellow dramatist and referred to him in the Address to the Reader that prefaces *The White Devil*. One obvious companion piece for *Duchess* is *Hamlet*. Coddon suggests that the conclusion of *Duchess* confirms Horatio's summary of *Hamlet*'s events as 'accidental judgements and casual slaughters'.[2] *Duchess* also shares with *Hamlet* a study of melancholy, painted women, the conflict between public and private, a consideration of the place of human beings in a theological universe and the art of dying. A more direct connection is between *Duchess* and *Othello*. The Duchess's death is directly indebted to Desdemona's in that both are strangled and revive briefly before finally expiring. *Duchess* 3.2, furthermore, borrows its intimate staging and abrupt juxtapositions from 4.3 and Act V of *Othello*. As Rose observes, however, the Duchess's death more clearly reflects female heroism. (See Bartels, Calderwood, Callaghan, Kerwin, Leinwand and K. Peterson for other connections between the plays.) Correll makes a persuasive argument for *Duchess* as a response to *Twelfth Night* and its figure of the household steward. Other plays compared by critics to *The Duchess of Malfi* are: Shakespeare's *Measure for Measure*, as a play that uses and critiques Renaissance stereotypes of femininity (Desmet); *Antony and Cleopatra*, as a play about disrupted marital consummation (Leinwand); Elizabeth Carey's *Tragedy of Mariam*, which also celebrates an unconventional wife (Luckyj, 'Historicizing Gender'); Thomas Heywood's *A Woman Killed with Kindness* and Ben Jonson's *Bartholomew Fair*, which focus on the female sexual, maternal body (Haslem); John Ford's *'Tis Pity She's a Whore*, as taking its preoccupation with incest from *Duchess* (Bradbrook, Wymer), Thomas Middleton and John Rowley's *The Changeling* (Jardine, '*The Duchess of Malfi*'); and Middleton's *The Revenger's Tragedy* (Finke, Zimmerman). A substantial body of criticism also discusses *The Duchess of Malfi* in relation to Webster's earlier play, *The White Devil* (see Aughterson, *Webster*, Jardine, '*The Duchess of Malfi*', Price, Ranald and others).

B. Structure and imagery

Critics of *Duchess* see the play as structured either by antithesis (Belsey, Best) or repetition (Bliss, Luckyj, *A Winter's Snake*, '"Great Women of Pleasure"'). Another notable structural feature is the fact that the play's titular character dies at the end of Act IV, which leads to discussion of whether or not a true tragic hero can meet her end in the middle of the play. Finally, Webster likes to work with paired scenes (see Aughterson, *Webster*, Part 1).

Students familiar with Shakespeare will find Webster's imagery approachable, yet complex. Among the words appearing frequently in the play are 'love' and its antithesis, 'death'. ('Hate' appears infrequently, but has emotional power.) Other common words are 'nothing' and 'thing', both of which contribute to a pessimistic ethos and dehumanize the play's characters. Imagistic patterns of 'white' and 'black' also link *Duchess* to *Othello*. Among the larger networks of imagery relevant to the play's exploration of identity are animal images. While references to animals, here as in *Othello*, can chart the characters' descent in the moral and cosmological hierarchy, Woodbridge ('Apricots') sees the play's characters as prey rather than predators. Duer ('Landscape of Imagination') sees the webs of imagery, spread as they are among speakers, as cohering in a surreal landscape. Words such as 'storm', 'fury', 'thunder', 'devil', 'hell', 'lightning', 'thunder' and 'whirlwind' give this landscape a theological scope (see also Bogard, chapter 5).

Duchess's imagery also intersects with the cultural concerns of other Jacobean plays. The complex of metaphors used to describe Fortune (a whore), the court as a fountain that takes its character from the sovereign, and the pervasive imagery of poison and disease are good starting points. Bosola has an entire constellation of dark metaphors of his own: for instance, the image of Ferdinand and the Cardinal as plum trees eaten up by caterpillars and crows; political sycophants as horse leeches; and Tantalus as the symbol of the political petitioner's hopeless state. The Duchess, by contrast, tends to use images and metaphors derived from religion. Other important terms come from politics. The word 'merit', although it appears only a few times, is crucial to the play's consideration of 'merit' and 'degree' (Selzer). Finally, an emphasis on 'eyes' reflects not only the play's preoccupation with spying, but also the importance of visual spectacle to knowledge (Feinberg). Stage props can also become symbols: rings, the dagger, jewels and the apricots are prominent examples (Tricomi, 'Severed Hand' and 'Historicizing Imagery of the Demonic', Price, Randall, Schuman). Finally, there are embedded emblems (such as the fountain, Tantalus and the Cardinal's rake) that should be read according to the moral tradition of Reformation emblems (Belsey, Duer, 'Painter and Poet', Marcus, ed.).

C. Reading *Duchess* through the lens of gender

Approaching *Duchess* through the lens of gender involves investigation of selfhood, marriage and politics. First, there is the question of the Duchess's public body (as a ruler) versus her private body (as a widow, and then wife and mother). The public-private divide in the play is discussed by many critics (e.g. Bliss, Calbi, Goldberg, Haber, Ray, Rist, Wall, Whigham). More specifically, the public body of the female ruler can be seen generally in terms of contemporary debates over the legitimacy of female rule (Jankowski, J. Peterson). The relation of public and private in the case of the Duchess can also be explored through marriage and conduct literature (Haslem, Luckyj, 'Historicizing Gender', Mikesell), through anti-feminist polemic and manuals on such topics as face-painting (Dolan, Finke, Garner); or the Woman Controversy (Desmet). While Luckyj ('Historicizing Gender') discusses classroom uses for print versions of primary sources on these topics (either through microfiche or Early English Books Online), modern edited texts also exist (see 'Background' in Bibliography).

More generally, criticism on *Duchess* addresses the question of its heroine's moral status, which is often linked to her play-acting. Earlier critics generally accepted that the play condemned the Duchess's violation of social norms (Calderwood, Leech, J. Peterson). Some feminists also consider *Duchess* ideologically conservative; Whigham and Jardine see the Duchess's choice of private desire over public responsibility as destructive, making the play a cautionary tale about female willfulness, while McLuskie sees *Duchess* as celebrating its heroine as a strong-willed woman while still supporting a conservative gender politics.

Some recent criticism, however, examines how the Duchess achieves agency within the confines of early modern gender ideologies (Bartels; see also Haber, Lord).

Part of what sets *Duchess* apart from other plays dealing with stereotypes about (sexual) women is the heroine's maternal streak (Haber, Wall). The Duchess dies instructing Antonio to give her boy 'syrup for his cold' and to make sure the girl says her prayers. But a woman's pregnant body, especially when she is also a ruler, is problematic. Critics are unsure whether the play shares Ferdinand's revulsion against the feminine body (Haslem) or whether the figure of the pregnant monarch suggests a new, feminine politics based on matrilineal descent and merit (Ray). Finally, not all critics even accept the premise of a public-private split in *Duchess*. Wendy Wall, for instance, uses domestic literature to show that household matters informed an aristocratic woman's public self.

Exploring the intersection of public and private spheres in *Duchess* raises issues of genre – specifically, of the Duchess's status as a tragic hero. While Callaghan denies that there can be a Renaissance female tragic hero, Susan Baker places the Duchess within a tradition of static heroes, who have found something about which they must inexorably take a stand. Woodbridge ('Queen of Apricots') argues that the Duchess is specifically a 'hero of desire' defending ordinary appetites in a world governed by asceticism. Other characters who have been offered up as the play's tragic hero are Bosola (Pearson, Whigham), Antonio (Belton, Lewis) and even Ferdinand (Whigham).

D. *Duchess* and early modern culture

A historical approach to *The Duchess of Malfi* need not be the least bit dull, for the play's references to early modern culture help to create its gothic atmosphere. Critics have discussed the play in terms of the period's attitudes towards madness (Jackson) and as depicting more broadly the relationship between madness and politics as forms of acting (Coddon). Not surprisingly, given its obsession with corruption and bodily decay, *Duchess* refers to contemporary medical debates about the relative efficacy of homeopathic cures and curing by opposites (Hunt) and touches on early modern struggles to define legitimate medicine (Kerwin; see also Calbi). Finally, there is the case of Ferdinand's lycanthropy, which has been discussed in terms of demonic possession (Tricomi, 'Historicizing Imagery of the Demonic'), as a symptom of political and social disease (Enterline), and as a screen for cultural anxieties about masculinity, foreigners and Catholicism (Hirsch).

One further social dimension touched on by *The Duchess of Malfi* is its representation of death. Rist offers an overview of Catholic versus Protestant attitudes towards proper mourning. In terms of the play's staging, furthermore, the scenes of death dramatize a nearly medieval struggle between Despair and God's Mercy for the human soul (Doebler). On the other hand, the play also depicts death as a form of social performance (Barker). Susan Zimmerman discusses the play's copious display of corpses. Finally, Kaara Peterson addresses the play's representation of 'revivification', the early modern belief that a wandering womb could cause a false death, as when the Duchess momentarily returns to life.

E. *The Duchess of Malfi* and the visual arts

Given the lack of available photos and films, it is difficult to imagine how the characters and events of this play might look, in either an early modern or contemporary production. One way of approaching *Duchess* is through Renaissance art forms such as portraiture, the masque, sculpture, and architecture.

Roy Eriksen suggests treating the play through the lens of Mannerist art. Analyzing portraits such as Bronzino's *Portrait of Laura Battiferri* or Parmigianino's *Portrait of a Young Woman* not only acquaints students with images of aristocratic Italian women from the period, but also illustrates how in these portraits, elegant, elongated hands functioned symbolically. Representative Renaissance portraits are easily available for pedagogical fair use through Google Image. Teachers can also consult Philippa Sheppard's list of books with relevant images. Inga-Stina Ewbank (formerly Ekeblad) and Laurie Finke also discuss the play's relation to Renaissance perspective paintings and formal portraits of women.

Another form of art important to *Duchess* is the masque. Ekeblad sees the dance of the madmen as charting the Duchess's fate by turning the marriage masque into a masque of death. Coddon argues that the three spectacles inflicted on the Duchess embody the corrupt political power of Ferdinand by enacting feminine stereotypes. Pearson offers a good analysis of the masque of the madmen as a distortion of the play world, equating specific madmen with the main characters (see also Kiefer for the symbolism of the Dance of the World); Doebler links the Duchess's torments generally to the visual iconography of the *ars moriendi*, or tradition of dying well. David Bergeron discusses the power of the tableau of wax figures by tracing the play's references to funerary art (see also Zimmerman). Wymer, Bergeron and Neill analyse the significance that the image of the ruined abbey might hold for a theatre audience of 1613.

F. *Duchess* in performance and through appropriation

Webster is performed much less frequently than Shakespeare, making live performance difficult to come by as a classroom enhancement.

Nevertheless, teachers can access a number of resources for studying the play in performance. The Actors' Shakespeare Project website offers high quality production photographs that would be suitable for discussing staging, costuming and other performance options. Christina Luckyj's *A Winter's Snake* discusses landmark productions throughout the twentieth century, and the Old-Spelling Critical Edition of Gunby, Carnegie, Hammond and DelVecchio offers an extensive performance history and discussion of performance choices. Leah Marcus's edition provides a vivid account of key productions, complete with photographs. McLuskie and Uglow's volume in the Plays in Performance series takes the reader through *Duchess* scene by scene, noting particular production choices; Kate Aughterson (*Webster*) also provides analysis of key performances. Some photos can be found in Aughterson and in McLuskie and Uglow (see individual entries in Bibliography).

The Duchess of Malfi also lacks the rich cache of audio and filmed performances available for teaching Shakespeare. The 1968 Howard Sackler audiobook, which reproduces the complete text and offers high-quality performances, is a good resource. Used copies are available, although unfortunately at exorbitant prices. Cedric Messina's television production, only available through libraries, cuts the text, but is generally faithful to it and offers period sets and costumes. On the Web is Benjamin Capps's production of Act III, Scene Two, shot in 16 mm., and set in the International Museum of Surgical Science's 'Hall of Immortals'. There are also production photos and brief audio clips. *A Question About Hell*, a 1964 film adaptation with a script by Kingsley Amis, is set in post-colonial Caribbean. Angela (the Duchess) is engaged secretly to her 'colored' chauffeur; her brothers are rich white landowners. There are a few dramatic appropriations of the play as well. Bertolt Brecht's English adaptation of *Duchess* adds a Prologue in which Ferdinand confesses to a Friar an incestuous desire to marry his own sister; shrinks the cast of characters and eliminates figures such as Julia; cuts many of the Duchess's 'tortures', including the masque of madmen; and concludes the play with the Duchess's death, which is achieved by Bosola's offer of a poisoned book for the Duchess to kiss instead of strangulation. Lewis Theobald's eighteenth-century adaptation, *The Fatal Secret*, attempts to regularize *Duchess's* plot and tacks on a happy ending, which might help with discussion of tragic structure. The latter two are available only as printed texts in scholarly editions.

The cheapest and most widely available DVD of a performance/appropriation is Mike Figgis's *Hotel*, a loose adaptation that chronicles the production of a Dogme 95-style version of *Duchess*, whose rehearsals are simultaneously being recorded by an obnoxious documentary filmmaker. *Hotel* may be taught as an appropriation of *Duchess* or as a comment on the Shakespeare film industry generally and, more specifically, on *Shakespeare in Love*'s satiric view of Webster as dramatist (see Aebischer). (*Shakespeare in Love* depicts Shakespeare as a handsome romantic, Webster as a perverted child who tortures small animals.) *Hotel* includes cannibalism, nudity, severed body parts and explicit sexual behaviours, and so would be appropriate only for mature audiences. Finally, *The Duchess of Malfi* is developing a small presence on YouTube. In 2010, videos of *Duchess* ran the gamut from snippets of professional and college productions to home-grown teen parodies and English Literature projects.

Many of the techniques used for teaching Shakespeare through performance would also work for *Duchess*. The Performance Promptbook exercise, as described by the Folger Shakespeare Library's *Shakespeare Set Free* series, would help students imagine their own production. The comparative film exercises also could spark discussion of particular scenes, especially if the Cedric Messina video were being studied in conjunction with one of the *Hamlet* or *Othello* films. For instance, the closet scene of *Hamlet* could be compared with the confrontation between the Duchess and Ferdinand, or the Duchess's death scene compared with that of Desdemona. Theatre trailers on YouTube, which are short, also work well for this purpose. Given *Duchess*'s affinity with Renaissance art, visual resources could be used to help articulate not only costumes and props, but even blocking. In the absence of full-scale performance, tableaux vivants of a scene work well as a pedagogical exercise and could also draw on the vocabulary of visual arts from the period.[3] (YouTube provides a handy venue for publishing student films and drama.) Analysis of production and publicity photos or of playbills available in online collections can also help students think in concrete ways about the play. Finally, although critics have not discussed their connections substantively, a number of popular novels have titles that refer to *Duchess*. The list includes: *Sleeping Murder*, by Agatha Christie; *Cover Her Face* and *The Skull Beneath the Skin*, by P. D. James; *Queen of the Damned*, by Anne Rice; and *The Stars' Tennis Balls*, by Stephen Fry. The Introduction to Leah Marcus's edition (pp. 112–13) notes several poems that refer to *Duchess* and could be used to spark class discussion.

Resources for teaching *Duchess* through performance and appropriation

Actors' Shakespeare Project. Available online: <http://www.actorsshakespeare-project.org/press/images.html> [cited 12 January 2010].

Brecht, Bertolt, *The Duchess of Malfi*, in Volume 7 of *Collected Plays*, ed. by Ralph Manheim and John Willett (New York: Random House, 1974), pp. 331–50.

Theobald, Lewis, *The Fatal Secret* (London: Printed for J. Watts, 1735). Available in *Nahum Tate's Injur'd Love, or, The Cruel Husband, and Lewis Theobald's The Fatal Secret*, ed. by James Hogg (Salzburg and Portland, Oregon: University of Salzburg; distributed in the U.S. by International Specialised Book Services Inc., 1998). The text is also available through the Chadwyck-Healy database, Literature Online (LION).

The Duchess of Malfi, dir. by James McTaggert, prod. by Cedric Messina, perf. by Eileen Atkins, Michael Bryant, Charles Kay, Gary Bond. British Broadcasting System, 1971. Distributed by Films for the Humanities and Sciences.

The Duchess of Malfi, dir. by Howard Sackler, read by Barbara Jefford, Robert Stephens, Alec McCowen (HarperCollins Audio Books, 1968) (2 audiocassettes).

Hotel, dir. by Mike Figgis, perf. by Max Beeseley, Saffron Burrows, Heathcote Williams, Moonstone Entertainment and Innovation Film Group (IFG), 2001; DVD, Innovation Film Group, 2005.

John Webster's The Duchess of Malfi, dir. by Benjamin Capps. Available online: <http://www.benjamincapps.com/duchess.html> [cited 21 January 2010].

A Question About Hell, dir. by Claude Whatham, written by Kingsley Amis, perf. by Richard Johnson, Patrick Wymark, Caroline Mortimer, Granada Television Productions, 1964.

Part 3. Bibliography

The Bibliography of critical resources is organized into four sections: Background Materials, General Studies of Webster, Essay Collections and Essays and Articles. Critical works were chosen for their intelligence, clarity, availability and focus on key issues.

A. Background materials

Aughterson, Kate, ed., *Renaissance Woman, A Sourcebook: Constructions of Femininity in England* (London: Routledge, 1995).

Of particular interest to Duchess are the sections on physiology (including medicine, pregnancy and midwifery), conduct books, sexuality and motherhood.

Axton, Marie, *The Queen's Two Bodies: Drama and the Elizabethan Succession* (London: Royal Historical Society, 1977).

While divine right theories of kingship advanced the concept of the king's two bodies – a political body that is infallible and a natural body that is not – the concept of a female monarch was complicated by a general social and medical ideology suggesting that women's bodies were weaker and more corruptible than men's.

Dolan, Frances E., 'Taking the Pencil out of God's Hand: Art, Nature, and the Face-Painting Debate in Early Modern England', *PMLA*, 108, 2 (1993), 224–39.

When women paint their faces, they usurp God's creative power, and much literature against face-painting emphasizes the corrupted mortal body beneath the cosmetics. Although the essay does not discuss *Duchess*, it provides a useful context for Bosola's rant against painting to the old woman. (See also Garner, below.)

Henderson, Katherine Usher and Barbara McManus, eds., *Half Humankind: Contexts and Texts of the Controversy about Women in England, 1540–1640* (Urbana: University of Illinois Press, 1985).

This book gives an overview of the Woman Controversy and offers well-edited texts in modern print.

Klein, Joan Larsen, ed., *Daughters, Wives, and Widows: Writings by Men about Women and Marriage in England, 1500–1640* (Urbana: University of Illinois Press, 1992).

As the title suggests, this anthology provides examples of the orthodox masculine version concerning women's social place and familial roles.

Mann, J. G., 'English Church Monuments, 1536–1625', *Walpole Society*, 21 (1932–33), 1–22.

Bergeron suggests this source for useful examples of English funerary art from the period. See note 15 in his essay.

Orlin, Lena Cowen, *Private Matters and Public Culture in Post-Reformation England* (Ithaca: Cornell University Press, 1994).

Although it does not discuss *Duchess* or Webster directly, this book provides important background on the concepts of 'privacy' and the 'household'. Chapter 2 deals with patriarchy and chapter 3 with the literature on domestic economies.

Ornstein, Robert, *The Moral Vision of Jacobean Tragedy* (Madison: University of Wisconsin Press, 1960).

Argues that Jacobean tragedy reflects not the decline of humanism or a general loss of religious belief, but an epistemological conflict between old and new ways of determining moral values. The plays often foreground a Machiavellian politics.

Sheppard, Philippa, 'Fair Counterfeits: A Bibliography of Visual Aids for Renaissance Drama', in *Approaches to Teaching English Renaissance Drama*, ed. by Karen Bamford and Alexander Leggatt (New York: Modern Language Association, 2002), pp. 43–50.

This resource catalogues print sources for images that illuminate *Duchess*'s cultural context or staging possibilities. Topics include art and architecture, family life, clothing, food and drink and death.

Woodbridge, Linda, *Women and the English Renaissance: Literature and the Nature of Womankind, 1540–1620* (Urbana: University of Illinois Press, 1984).

Although only a few pages focus directly on *Duchess*, this book is essential reading for background on ideologies of gender and the Woman Controversy.

B. General studies of Webster

Aughterson, Kate, *Webster: The Tragedies* (Houndsmill, Basingstoke, Hampshire: Palgrave, 2001).

Aimed primarily at students, this book offers close readings of scenes and speeches from *Duchess* and *The White Devil* and concludes with analysis of different stage productions.

Berry, Ralph, *The Art of John Webster* (Oxford: Clarendon, 1972).

Analysing Webster as a baroque artist, Berry discusses his technique, including such topics as: sensationalism and movement, irony, parody, character and caricature and multiplicity and unity.

Bliss, Lee, *The World's Perspective: John Webster and the Jacobean Drama* (New Brunswick, NJ: Rutgers University Press, 1983).

Focusing on Webster as an experimental dramatist, this major study focuses on Webster's 'art of distance' that reflects in part, the individual's alienation from society. This is achieved through contrasting perspectives and patterns of opposition. The chapter on *Duchess* examines the play as a romantic tragedy, with the Duchess as a strong-willed, but courageous and royal figure.

Bogard, Travis, *The Tragic Satire of John Webster* (Berkeley: University of California Press, 1955).

This older monograph studies the way in which tragedy and satire combine to create a morally ambiguous world. Chapter 5 discusses the rhetoric of satire.

Boklund, Gunnar, *The Duchess of Malfi: Sources, Themes, Characters* (Cambridge, Mass.: Harvard University Press, 1962).

The section on sources is exhaustive and weighs the relevance of possible influences and analogues for *Duchess*.

Bradbrook, M. C., *John Webster: Citizen and Dramatist* (New York: Columbia University Press, 1980).

Places Webster within the context of London dramatic life and the Middle Temple as a literary centre. Offers a good extended discussion of Bosola.

Callaghan, Dympna, *Woman and Gender in Renaissance Tragedy: A Study of King Lear, Othello, The Duchess of Malfi, and The White Devil* (Atlantic Highlands, NJ: Humanities Press International, 1989).

Callaghan argues that Woman, as a logical and social category, disrupts tragic paradigms, be they classical, Renaissance or modern. Woman becomes polarized into the figure that instigates the tragedy and its consecrated victim.

Forker, Charles R., *Skull Beneath the Skin: The Achievement of John Webster* (Carbondale and Edwardsville: Southern Illinois University Press, 1986).

Forker's chapter on *Duchess* in this monumental work surveys prominent themes (identity, death, fame and reputation), characterization, staging, patterns of opposition and convergence and important imagery patterns.

Goldberg, Dena, *Between Worlds: A Study of the Plays of John Webster* (Waterloo: Wilfrid Laurier University Press, 1987).

Duchess is 'the tragedy of the irreconcilable contradiction between public life and personal desire' (p. 9).

Leech, Clifford, *John Webster: A Critical Study* (London: Hogarth Press, 1951).

In this early study, the chapter on *Duchess of Malfi* includes an extended comparison with *The White Devil* that emphasizes the Duchess's guilt.

Luckyj, Christina, *A Winter's Snake: Dramatic Form in the Tragedies of John Webster* (Athens: University of Georgia Press, 1989).

This study of 'repetitive form' in Webster's drama discusses how dramatic structure in *Duchess* arouses tension without ever dispelling it. Contains helpful analysis of opening scenes and subplots and of *Duchess* in performance.

McLuskie, Kathleen and Jennifer Uglow, *The Duchess of Malfi, by John Webster*, Plays in Performance (Bristol: Bristol Classical Press, 1989).

Takes the reader through the play scene by scene, discussing particular performance choices.

Pearson, Jacqueline, *Tragedy and Tragicomedy in the Plays of John Webster* (Manchester: Manchester University Press, 1980).

Discusses generally the development of tragicomedy as a genre and argues that the play is a tragedy eliciting 'pity' until the Duchess's death, when the tragic ethos is distorted into comedy, satire and tragicomedy.

Peterson, Joyce, *Curs'd Example: 'The Duchess of Malfi' and Commonweal Tragedy* (Columbia: University of Missouri Press, 1978).

Comparing the Duchess to Mary Stuart, this monograph argues that the Duchess, who puts 'private desires' before 'public responsibility', loses decorum, reputation and finally freedom.

Ranald, Margaret Loftus, *John Webster*, Twayne's English Authors Series (Boston: Twayne Publishers, 1989).

This substantive, yet compact introduction to Webster contains a succinct biography and chapters on the plays, providing information about the text, date, stage history, sources and critical comments.

Wymer, Rowland, *Webster and Ford*, English Dramatists (New York: St. Martin's 1995).

This introduction to Webster's plays in the theatre not only attends to specific features of important productions, but also suggests how the author thinks the play works in performance.

C. Essay collections

John Webster, ed. by Brian Morris, Mermaid Critical Commentaries (London: Ernest Benn Limited, 1970).

Offers theatrical, theological and generic perspectives on Webster's play; includes Ewbank's 'Webster's Realistic Art'.

Approaches to Teaching English Renaissance Drama, ed. by Karen Bamford and Alexander Leggatt (New York: Modern Language Association, 2002).

Part 1, 'Practices and Materials', contains valuable information for teachers. The essays by Leggatt, Bamford, Berry and Luckyj are particularly relevant.

The Duchess of Malfi: Contemporary Critical Essays, ed. by Dympna Callaghan, New Casebooks (Houndsmill, Basingstoke, Hampshire: Macmillan, 2000).

The Casebook considers politics, gender, morality and artistic form and includes the essays listed here by Coddon, Desmet, Henderson, Jankowski, McLuskie, Rose and Whigham.

John Webster, ed. by G. K. and S. K. Hunter (Harmondsworth: Penguin, 1969).

The best of the older essay collections, this offers a range of commentary from sources in the nineteenth to mid-twentieth centuries and describes modern productions and adaptations.

John Webster's The Duchess of Malfi, ed. by Harold Bloom, Modern Critical Interpretations (New York: Chelsea House, 1987).

A brief collection of relevant essays that unfortunately does not include the original footnotes. Includes essays by Best, Duer ('Landscape of Imagination'), Selzer, Belsey and Jardine ('*The Duchess of Malfi*; A Case Study').

Twentieth Century Interpretations of The Duchess of Malfi, ed. by Norman Rabkin (Englewood Cliffs, NJ: Prentice Hall, 1968).

A good collection of older pieces focusing on structural, ethical and symbolic interpretations.

D. Essays and articles

Aebischer, Pascale, 'Shakespearean Heritage and the Preposterous "Contemporary Jacobean" Film: Mike Figgis's *Hotel*', *Shakespeare Quarterly*, 60, 3 (October 2009), 279–303.

This essay sees Figgis as commenting on the heritage Shakespeare film industry and *Shakespeare in Love* in particular. The film is concerned with man's control of woman's sexuality, but the Duchess's desiring gaze, for which she is punished, is also the solution to her oppression.

Baker, Susan C., 'The Static Protagonist in *The Duchess of Malfi*', *Texas Studies in Literature and Language*, 22.3 (1980), 343–57.

This essay argues that the Duchess should be understood in the tradition of 'static protagonists', who never change, grow or reach new truths. Rather, they identify a value worth taking a stand on – in the Duchess's case, resisting the irrational demands of her male relatives – and defend that position even to death.

Barker, Roberta, '"Another Voyage": Death as Social Performance in the Major Tragedies of John Webster', *Early Theatre*, 8.2 (2005), 35–56.

Duchess associates acting not only with social mobility, but also with the anti-theatrical trope of self-destructive hypocrisy.

Barranger, Milly S., 'The Shape of Brecht's *Duchess of Malfi*', *Comparative Drama*, 12 (1978), 61–74.

Discusses differences between Brecht's adaptation and *Duchess* in relation to Brecht's Marxism. Brecht is influenced by his Hollywood experience, and the text shows the influence of cinematic technique and of Brecht's characteristic 'epic staging'.

Bartels, Emily, 'Strategies of Submission: Desdemona, the Duchess, and the Assertion of Desire', *Studies in English Literature*, 36 (1996), 417–33.

Examines how postures of obedience are used as strategies for female agency and self-expression.

Belsey, Catherine, 'Emblem and Antithesis in *The Duchess of Malfi*', *Renaissance Drama*, n.s. 11 (1980), 115–34.

Duchess is poised between the emblematic medieval stage and the realism of post-Restoration theatre. The play defines good and evil by antithesis (e.g. the fountain versus poison, or nature and artifice, the Old Lady versus the Duchess).

Belton, Ellen R., 'The Function of Antonio in *The Duchess of Malfi*', *Texas Studies in Literature and Language*, 18 (1976), 474–85.

Analyses Antonio as a Christian stoic whose ability to endure suffering is transferred to the Duchess herself at point of death.

Bergeron, David, 'The Wax Figures in *The Duchess of Malfi*', *Studies in English Literature*, 18 (1978), 331–39.

Reviewing possible sources for the wax figures in *Duchess,* Bergeron discusses the tableau's indebtedness to funerary sculpture.

Best, Michael, 'A Precarious Balance: Structure in *The Duchess of Malfi*', in *Shakespeare and Some Others: Essays on Shakespeare and Some of His Contemporaries*, ed. by Alan Brissenden (Adelaide: University of Adelaide Press, 1976), pp. 159–77.

Discusses the Duchess, Cardinal and Ferdinand as a triangle whose tensions structure the play; Best sees Bosola as succeeding the Duchess as the play's focus in the last two acts.

Calbi, Maurizio, '"That body of hers": The Secret, the Specular, the Spectacular in *The Duchess of Malfi* and Anatomical Discourses', in *Approximate Bodies: Gender and Power in Early Modern Drama and Anatomy* (London and New York: Routledge, 2005), pp. 1–31.

The Duchess's body – sexual, pregnant, and even subject to aging – is nevertheless engaged with discourses of state, family and society and becomes a site that Ferdinand and Bosola struggle to control.

Calderwood, James L., '*The Duchess of Malfi*: Some Styles of Ceremony', *Essays in Criticism*, 12 (1962), 133–47.

Explores the theme of the individual versus social norms, arguing that *Duchess* uses ceremony and ritual to assess private actions; the essay includes a good close reading of the Duchess's wooing of Antonio.

Coddon, Karin S., '*The Duchess of Malfi*: Tyranny and Spectacle in the Jacobean Drama', in *Madness in Drama*, ed. by James Redmond (Cambridge: Cambridge University Press, 1993), pp. 1–17.

This essay suggests that madness, like political power, is a product of acting. The Duchess offers an alternative to this dialectic between performance and madness. But the equation of theatricality and madness raises the question of whether drama itself is relegated to the realm of unreason.

Correll, Barbara, 'Malvolio and Malfi: Managing Desire in Shakespeare and Webster', *Shakespeare Quarterly*, 58, 1 (Spring 2007), 65–92.

In *Duchess*, Webster responds to Shakespeare's *Twelfth Night* by dividing the figure of Malvolio, as steward, into those of Antonio and Bosola. The two steward figures exist with the Duchess in a cross-class triangle that balances the aristocratic triangle involving the Duchess and her brothers. Comparing also the erotic banter between Olivia and Viola in *Twelfth Night* with that between the Duchess and Antonio, Correll argues that the Duchess demystifies the language of the market to imagine erotic desire as a radically new space of 'egalitarian reciprocity and power sharing' (p. 83).

Desmet, Christy, '"Neither Maid, Widow, nor Wife": Rhetoric of the Woman Controversy in *The Duchess of Malfi*', in *In Another Country: Feminist Perspectives on Renaissance Drama*, ed. by Dorothea Kehler and Susan Baker (Metuchen, NJ and London: Scarecrow, 1991), pp. 71–92.

Defining the Duchess as a woman rather than a prince is the rhetorical aim of her opponents, and the rhetoric by which she is confined and excoriated is familiar from the Renaissance Woman Controversy.

Doebler, Bettie Ann, 'Continuity in the Art of Dying: *The Duchess of Malfi*', *Comparative Drama*, 14 (1980), 203–15.

Argues for the centrality to *Duchess* of the *ars moriendi*, or art of dying well. The death-bed scene becomes a battle between Despair and God's Mercy for the Duchess's soul. Bosola tempts the Duchess to despair by stressing the mortality of the flesh, but the Duchess is humble (going down on her knees) and assured of heaven.

Duer, Leslie, 'The Landscape of Imagination in *The Duchess of Malfi*', *Modern Language Studies*, 10, 1 (1979–80), 3–9.

An excellent introduction to the imagery of *Duchess*, this essay discusses how the play, like the unstable pictures of perspectivist painting, creates a disorienting, surrealist landscape.

Duer, Leslie, 'The Painter and the Poet: Visual Design in *The Duchess of Malfi*', *Emblematica*, 1, 2 (1986), 293–316.

Discusses post-Reformation imagery as emblematic rather than realistic and discusses several emblems in Duchess (e.g. the fountain, Tantalus and the Cardinal's rake).

Ekeblad, Inga-Stina, 'The "Impure Art" of John Webster', *Review of English Studies*, 9 (1958), 253–67.

Sees the masque of the madmen as mirroring the play's structure and the disunity of the Duchess's world.

Enterline, Lynn, '"Hairy on the in-side": "The Duchess of Malfi" and the Body of Lycanthropy', in *The Tears of Narcissus: Melancholia and Masculinity in Early Modern Writing* (Stanford: Stanford University Press, 1995), pp. 242–303.

Examining the dissolution of masculine identity through melancholia, this essay sees the Duchess as a mirror that disrupts her twin Ferdinand's reality and alienates him from his body. Ferdinand's dismemberment of corpses externalizes his own self-division.

Eriksen, Roy, 'Framing the Duchess; Webster and the Resources of Renaissance Art', *Nordlit*, 2 (1977), 3–22.

Recommends teaching the play through its visual and symbolic connections to Mannerist art, a style in which paintings combine crowded surfaces with 'unbalanced' frames to create sudden shifts in perspective. Through comparison with concrete examples, we see how the Duchess is 'framed' by her brothers.

Ewbank, Inga-Stina, 'Webster's Realism, or "A cunning piece wrought perspective"', in *John Webster*, ed. by Brian Morris (London: Ernest Benn, 1970), pp. 157–78.

Discusses how techniques of reading perspective pictures can be applied to interpreting *Duchess*. The reader approaches the play from different points of view; most will prove jumbled and confused, but one will click into place and make sense to create a kind of realism.

Feinberg, Anat, 'Observation and Theatricality in Webster's *The Duchess of Malfi*', *Theatre Research International*, 5, 1 (1980–81), 36–44.

This essay analyses the imagery of eyes and flawed vision; observation is both a means for spying and a source of knowledge.

Finke, Laurie, 'Painting Women: Images of Femininity in Jacobean Tragedy', *Theatre Journal*, 36, 3 (1984), 357–70.

Discusses the 'painted woman' as both a symbol of male fears about female sexuality and a strategy for preserving an idealized version of woman by 'killing them into art'. The Duchess becomes both a lifeless 'monument' and a version of her own portrait.

Garner, Shirley, '"Let her paint an inch thick": Painted Ladies in Renaissance Drama and Society', *Renaissance Drama*, 20 (1989), 123–39.

In addition to providing background on literature about face-painting and social uses of makeup, the essay compares Bosola's attitude towards cosmetics with Hamlet's.

Haber, Judith, '"My body bestow upon my women": The Space of the Feminine in *The Duchess of Malfi*', in *Desire and Dramatic Form in Early Modern England* (Cambridge: Cambridge University Press, 2009), pp. 71–86.

The Duchess, through her marriage and pregnancies, seeks to combat Ferdinand's phallic assault by creating a circular feminine space free from such invasions.

Haslem, Lori Schroeder, '"Troubled with the Mother": Longings, Purgings, and the Maternal Body in *Bartholomew Fair* and *The Duchess of Malfi*', *Modern Philology*, 92, 4 (1995), 438–59.

This essay considers the Duchess's pregnant body in light of early modern associations between pregnancy and digestive superfluity, excretion and disease. The play celebrates maternity, but is ambivalent towards the Duchess's pregnant body.

Henderson, Andrea, 'Death on Stage, Death of the Stage: The Antitheatricality of *The Duchess of Malfi*', *Theatre Journal*, 42 (1990), 194–207.

This essay argues that *Duchess* reflects a growing sense of the theatrical nature of personal identity, exacerbated by the growth of a market economy.

Hirsch, Brett D., 'An Italian Werewolf in London: Lycanthropy and *The Duchess of Malfi*', *Early Modern Literary Studies*, 11, 2 (2005), 43 paragraphs. Available online: <http://extra.shu.ac.uk/emls/11-2/hirswere.htm> [cited 21 January 2010].

For early modern audiences, the term lycanthropy referred both to a reality achieved by witchcraft and the delusion of such a transformation, whether caused by madness, drugs or other causes. The werewolf also became a site for cultural anxieties about masculinity, foreigners, Catholicism and the Irish.

Hunt, Maurice, 'Webster and Jacobean Medicine: The Case of *The Duchess of Malfi*', *Essays in Literature*, 16, 1 (1989), 33–49.

Analyses two approaches to medicine referred to in the play: the homeopathic cure (where madness is cured by similar humours) and the cure by contraries. While Ferdinand's doctor unsuccessfully tries a homeopathic cure for his melancholy, Bosola as physician restores the Duchess to sanity with the comic masque of the madmen.

Jackson, Ken, S., '"Twin" Shows of Madness: John Webster's Stage Management of Bethlem in *The Duchess of Malfi*', in *Separate Theaters: Bethlem ('Bedlam') Hospital and the Shakespearean Stage* (Newark: University of Delaware Press, 2005), pp. 183–203.

In the early modern period, the spectacle of madness is designed to elicit pity and charitable donations more than ridicule or revulsion. Antonio and the Duchess are objects of pity, but Ferdinand's mad show of lycanthropy elicits ridicule.

Jankowski, Theodora, 'Defining/Confining the Duchess: Negotiating the Female Body in John Webster's *The Duchess of Malfi*', *Studies in Philology*, 87 (1990), 221–45.

Arguing against those who see the Duchess as uniting her public and private bodies, this essay argues that the Duchess divorces the political from the natural body. But despite the Duchess's inability to rule successfully as a female sovereign, she subverts patriarchal norms by keeping the marriage private and by ruling her husband.

Jardine, Lisa, '*The Duchess of Malfi*: A Case Study in the Literary Representation of Women', in *Teaching the Text*, ed. by Susanne Kappler and Norman Bryson (London: Routledge & Kegan Paul, 1983), pp. 203–17.

This essay considers the Duchess as a strong woman, but concludes that this literary representation ultimately underwrites a cautionary tale against female will and autonomy.

Kerwin, William, '"Physicians are like kings": Medical Politics and *The Duchess of Malfi*', *English Literary Renaissance*, 28 (1998), 95–117.

Discusses the 'nightmarish' medicine of *Duchess* in relation to the Jacobean debate about legitimate and illegitimate medicine. The Cardinal, Ferdinand, Bosola and the doctor of Act V are physicians whose actions show that medicine in Malfi serves the ends of a corrupt aristocracy.

Kiefer, Frederick, 'The Dance of the Madmen in *The Duchess of Malfi*', *Journal of Medieval and Renaissance Studies*, 17, 2 (1987), 211–33.

Analyses the dance of the madmen in relation to a visual tradition in which the World (as Woman) stands aloof in a dance of mad figures. The essay contains a number of black-and-white illustrations.

Leinwand, Theodore B., '*Coniugium Interruptum* in Shakespeare and Webster', *ELH*, 72, 1 (2005), 239–57.

Analyses *Duchess* in relation to *Macbeth*, *Othello* and *Antony and Cleopatra* as plays that dramatize '*coniugium interruptum*', the interruption of marital relations by the public world that plagues the private bedroom behaviour of couples in an emerging structure of affective relationships.

Lewis, Cynthia, "'Wise Men, Folly-Fall'n": Characters Named Antonio in English Renaissance Drama', *Renaissance Drama*, 20 (1989), 197–236.

Analysing a range of 'Antonios', the essay links the character type as the wise fool, struggling against his own demons and both nobly and foolishly sacrificing himself, to the figure of St. Anthony.

Lord, Joan M., '*The Duchess of Malfi*: "The Spirit of Greatness" and "of Woman"', *Studies in English Literature*, 16, 2 (1976), 305–17.

This essay focuses on the ability of role-playing to produce moral character. As she faces death, the Duchess achieves tragic status through a fusion of acting and true emotion.

Luckyj, Christina, '"Great women of pleasure": Main Plot and Subplot in *The Duchess of Malfi*', *Studies in English Literature*, 27 (1987), 267–83.

A useful, condensed discussion of plot and subplot in *Duchess*.

—, 'Historicizing Gender: Mapping Cultural Space in Webster's *The Duchess of Malfi* and Cary's *The Tragedy of Mariam*', in *Approaches to Teaching English Renaissance Drama*, ed. by Karen Bamford and Alexander Leggatt (New York: Modern Language Association, 2002), pp. 134–41.

Offers a helpful approach to gender issues in these paired plays through primary documents on gender and marriage.

McLuskie, Kathleen, 'Drama and Sexual Politics', in *Drama, Sex, and Politics*, ed. by James Redmond (Cambridge: Cambridge University Press, 1985), pp. 77–91.

Webster offers an unusually sympathetic portrayal of a strong-willed, sexual woman, but that appeal masks the play's conservative sexual politics.

Mikesell, Margaret Lael, 'Catholic and Protestant Widows in *The Duchess of Malfi*', *Renaissance and Reformation*, 7 (1983), 265–79.

The play reflects contradictory opinions from the early modern debate about women's remarriage. Catholic writers argue that women should not remarry, but instead devote themselves to Christ. Protestant reformers suggest that second marriages are sanctioned by God. In *Duchess*, the 'lusty widow' of Catholic polemic is a fantasy of the Duchess's brothers, who also attempt to mold the Duchess as a virtuous widow devoted to God.

Neill, Michael, 'Monuments and Ruins as Symbols in *The Duchess of Malfi*', in *Drama and Symbolism*, ed. by James Redmond (Cambridge: Cambridge University Press, 1982), pp. 71–87.

This rich essay discusses the funerary monument as an ambivalent symbol of death and enduring fame. Discusses the Duchess's tomb and the ruined abbey as a symbolic pair.

Peterson, Kaara L., 'Shakespearean Revivification: Early Modern Undead', *Shakespeare Studies*, 32 (2004), 240–66.

This essay discusses revivification, a phenomenon by which women can experience a false hysterical death caused by a wandering womb and frustrated sexual desire.

Price, Hereward, 'The Function of Imagery in Webster', *PMLA*, 70, 4 (1955), 717–39.

Price's much-cited essay discusses imagery of poison, the devil, disease and leprosy and whiteness and blackness. Every image pattern has its response, swiftly delivered.

Randall, Dale B. J., 'The Rank and Earthy Background of Certain Physical Symbols in *The Duchess of Malfi*', *Renaissance Drama*, n.s. 18 (1987), 171–203.

This useful essay discusses the dead man's hand as part of a group of phallic references, but also, ironically, as a symbol of marriage; and the apricots, as related not only to fecundity, but also to sexuality and sin.

Ray, Sid, '"So troubled with the mother": The Politics of Pregnancy in *The Duchess of Malfi*', in *Performing Maternity in Early Modern England*, ed. by Kathryn M. Moncrief and Kathryn R. McPherson (Aldershot: Ashgate, 2007), pp. 17–28.

While early modern political discourse uses the head-body analogy to legitimate (male) monarchy, in the figure of the pregnant monarch, the notion of the king's two bodies is altered. Paradoxically, the Duchess is both head and body of her political realm. The succession of the duchy to her son by Antonio offers a new concept of rule based on (Antonio's) merit and matrilineal descent.

Rist, Thomas, *Revenge Tragedy and the Drama of Commemoration in Reforming England* (Aldershot, England: Ashgate, 2008).

Chapter 1 discusses Reformed versus Catholic approaches to mourning and commemorating the dead; Chapter 3 analyses *Duchess*. Ferdinand, in seeking to keep the Duchess a widow, sees her role as a Catholic one, commemorating in perpetuity her dead husband. Antonio and the Duchess have Reformist attitudes towards mourning and support the concept of remarriage.

Rose, Mary Beth, 'The Heroics of Marriage in Renaissance Tragedy', in '*The Expense of Spirit*': *Love and Sexuality in English Renaissance Drama* (Ithaca and London: Cornell University Press, 1988), pp. 155–77.

Duchess dramatizes an emerging Protestant emphasis on the private life. Both Antonio's worship of the Duchess's chastity and the brothers' obsession with controlling her place them in an earlier ideological frame that ultimately destroys her. Bosola the malcontent feels trapped between the old aristocracy and a new order based on merit. Includes a comparison between the deaths of the Duchess and Desdemona.

Schuman, Samuel, 'The Ring and the Jewel in Webster's Tragedies', *Texas Studies in Literature and Language*, 14 (1972), 253–68.

Both the ring and jewel, as prominent symbols in *Duchess*, have double meanings – as sentimental and even religious symbols of love and honour and as sexual symbols for male and female genitalia. These antithetical meanings come together in marriage, which defines people's place as between the angels and animals.

Selzer, John L., 'Merit and Degree in Webster's *The Duchess of Malfi*', *English Literary Renaissance*, 11 (1981), 70–80.

While her corrupt brothers stand for a social order based solely on degree, in marrying Antonio the Duchess follows the French King's example in seeking to create a court where advancement is based on merit.

Tricomi, Albert H., 'Historicizing the Imagery of the Demonic in *The Duchess of Malfi*', *Journal of Medieval and Early Modern Studies*, 34, 2 (2004), 345–72.

Hell and the devil play a strong role in the characters', especially Bosola's and Ferdinand's, emotional lives. These two are acutely aware of hell as a real place that awaits them in the afterlife. The essay discusses superstition, demonism and lycanthropy as demonic possession.

Tricomi, Albert H., 'The Severed Hand in Webster's *The Duchess of Malfi*', *Studies in English Literature*, 44 (2004), 347–58.

Traces the severed hand that Ferdinand offers the Duchess to Henry Boguet's *Discours exécrable des sorciers* (1590), which tells the story of a wife turned wolf whose secret is revealed by her wedding ring. This tale connects the symbol that Ferdinand uses to 'dismember' the Duchess's marriage with his own subsequent lycanthropy.

Wall, Wendy, 'Just a Spoonful of Sugar: Syrup and Domesticity in Early Modern England', *Modern Philology*, 104, 2 (2006), 149–72.

The symbol of 'syrup' stands at once for the Duchess's maternal care, her erotic desires (she characterizes her first kiss with Antonio as a dessert 'sweet'), and general human mortality. The symbol is therefore complex rather than merely sentimental.

Whigham, Frank, 'Sexual and Social Mobility in *The Duchess of Malfi*', *PMLA*, 100, 2 (1985), 167–86.

Sees *Duchess* as being concerned less with sexual than with social mobility. Ferdinand, as a 'threatened aristocrat', is consumed with a fear of class contamination. The Duchess colonizes 'a new realm of privacy', but her retreat to that private world becomes claustrophobic and, eventually, deadly. Bosola, the most deeply alienated character, is an unsuccessful employee in a new world governed purely by economic relations. Whigham's argument is challenged by Woodbridge, 'Queen of Apricots'.

Woodbridge, Linda, 'Queen of Apricots: The Duchess of Malfi, Hero of Desire', in *The Female Tragic Hero in English Renaissance Drama*, ed. by Naomi Conn Liebler (New York: Palgrave Macmillan, 2002), pp.161–84.

Arguing against critics who see sexuality as a screen for class anxieties, Woodbridge argues that the Duchess is a 'hero of desire', championing sexual desire by defending its wholesomeness and importance to living a complete human life.

Zimmerman, Susan, 'Invading the Grave: Shadow Lives in *The Revenger's Tragedy* and *The Duchess of Malfi*', in *The Early Modern Corpse and Shakespeare's Theatre* (Edinburgh: Edinburgh University Press, 2005), pp. 128–71.

The corpse of the Duchess not only signifies the widespread decay of the human mind and body politic, but is also a disturbing object in its own right. The early modern corpse, not fully dead until the body had become a skeleton, occupied a middle position between death and life. The spectacle of wax figures also disturbs the boundary between the (live) bodies of actors, the (dead) bodies of the Duchess's family and the (artfully inanimate) wax figures of Ferdinand's tableau.

Notes

1. Christopher Ricks, 'The Tragedies of Webster, Tourneur, and Middleton: Symbols, Imagery, and Conventions', in *English Drama to 1710*, ed. by Christopher Ricks (New York: Peter Bedrick Books, 1987), pp. 315–61.
2. Coddon, Karin S., '*The Duchess of Malfi*: Tyranny and Spectacle in the Jacobean Drama', in *Madness in Drama*, ed. by James Redmond (Cambridge: Cambridge University Press, 1993), p. 41.
3. For the comparative film-clip exercise, see *Shakespeare Set Free: Teaching A Midsummer Night's Dream, Romeo and Juliet, and Macbeth,* ed. by Peggy O'Brien et al. (New York: Washington Square Press, 2006), pp. 154–5; for the Promptbook exercise, p. 147 ff., and for Tableaux Vivants, p. 163 ff.

Bibliography

Abarbanel, Jonathan, Rev. of *The Duchess of Malfi*, dir. by Michael Halberstam, *Theatremania*, 25 May 2006. 8 August 2009 <http://www.theatermania.com/new-york/reviews/05-2006/the-duchess-of-malfi_8325.html>

Actors' Shakespeare Project <http://www.actorsshakespeareproject.org/press/images.html> [accessed 12 January 2010]

Adams, John Quincy, *Shakespearean Playhouses* (Boston: Houghton Mifflin, 1917)

Adams, Thomas, *The Works of Thomas Adams* (London, 1630)

Aebischer, Pascale, 'Shakespearean Heritage and the Preposterous "Contemporary Jacobean" Film: Mike Figgis's *Hotel*', *Shakespeare Quarterly*, 60, 3 (October 2009), 279–303

Agate, James, 'Words, Words, Words', in *The Contemporary Theatre 1944–45* (London: George G. Harrap and Co., 1946)

Allen Cave, Richard, *The White Devil and The Duchess of Malfi* (Basingstoke: Macmillan, 1988)

Allison, Alexander, 'Ethical Themes in *The Duchess of Malfi*', *Studies in English Literature*, 4 (1964), 263–73

Allman, Eileen, *Jacobean Revenge Tragedy and the Politics of Virtue* (Newark and London: Associated University Presses, 1999)

Amussen, Susan D., 'Gender, Family and the Social Order, 1560–1725', in *Order and Disorder in Early Modern England*, ed. by Anthony Fletcher and John Stevenson (Cambridge: Cambridge University Press, 1985)

Anderson, Thomas, 'The Art of Playing Dead in Revenge Tragedy', in *Performing Early Modern Trauma from Shakespeare to Milton* (Burlington, VT: Ashgate, 2006)

Approaches to Teaching English Renaissance Drama, ed. by Karen Bamford and Alexander Leggatt (New York: Modern Language Association, 2002)

Archer, William, 'Webster, Lamb and Swinburne', *New Review*, 8 (January 1893), 96–106

Archer, William, *The Old Drama and the New* (London: Heinemann, 1923)

Armstrong, Katherine A., 'Possets, Pills and Poisons: Physicking the Female Body in Early Seventeenth-Century Drama', *Cahiers Elisabethains*, 61 (2002), 43–56

Aston, Margaret, 'English Ruins and English History: The Dissolution and the Sense of the Past', *Journal of Warburg-Courtauld Institutes*, 36 (1973), 231–55

Aughterson, Kate, ed., *Renaissance Woman, A Sourcebook: Constructions of Femininity in England* (London: Routledge, 1995)

—, *Webster: The Tragedies* (Houndsmill: Palgrave, 2001)

Axton, Marie, *The Queen's Two Bodies: Drama and the Elizabethan Succession* (London: Royal Historical Society, 1977)

Baker, Susan C., 'The Static Protagonist in *The Duchess of Malfi*', *Texas Studies in Literature and Language*, 22.3 (1980), 343–57

Baker-Smith, Dominic, 'Religion and John Webster', in *John Webster*, ed. by Brian Morris (London: Ernest Benn, 1970), 207–28

Barber, John, 'Sinister Tricks', *Daily Telegraph*, 8 July 1985

Barker, Roberta, 'An Actor in the Main of All: Individual and Relational Selves in *The Duchess of Malfi*', *Early Modern Tragedy, Gender, and Performance, 1984–2000: The Destined Livery* (New York: Palgrave, 2007)

—' "Another Voyage": Death as Social Performance in the Major Tragedies of John Webster', *Early Theatre*, 8.2 (2005), 35–56

—*Early Modern Tragedy, Gender and Performance, 1984–2000: The Destined Livery* (Basingstoke: Palgrave Macmillan, 2007)

Barranger, Milly S., 'The Shape of Brecht's *Duchess of Malfi*', *Comparative Drama*, 12 (1978), 61–74

Bartels, Emily, 'Strategies of Submission: Desdemona, the Duchess, and the Assertion of Desire', *Studies in English Literature*, 36 (1996), 417–33

Bassett, Kate, Rev. of *The Duchess of Malfi*, dir. by Gale Edwards, *Independent*, 12 November 2000

Beaty, Nancy, *The Craft of Dying: A Study in the Literary Tradition of the Ars Moriendi in England* (New Haven: Yale University Press, 1970)

Bellany, Alastair, *The Politics of Court Scandal in Early Modern England: News Culture and the Overbury Affair, 1603–1660* (Cambridge: Cambridge University Press, 2002)

Belsey, Catherine, 'Emblem and Antithesis in *The Duchess of Malfi*', *Renaissance Drama*, n.s. 11 (1980), 115–34

—*The Subject of Tragedy: Identity and Difference in Renaissance Drama* (1985; rpt London: Routledge, 1991)

Belton, Ellen R., 'The Function of Antonio in *The Duchess of Malfi*', *Texas Studies in Literature and Language*, 18 (1976), 474–85

Benjamin, Walter, 'The Work of Art in the Age of Mechanical Reproduction', *Illuminations*, trans. by Hannah Arendt (New York: Harcourt Brace, 1968), 217–52

Bennett, Susan, *Performing Nostalgia: Shifting Shakespeare and the Contemporary Past* (London: Routledge, 1996)

Bentley, G. E., *The Jacobean and Caroline Stage*, 7 vols (Oxford: Clarendon Press, 1941)

Bergeron, David, 'The Wax Figures in *The Duchess of Malfi*', *Studies in English Literature*, 18 (1978), 331–9

Berry, Kevin, Rev. of *The Duchess of Malfi*, dir. by Philip Franks, *The Stage*, 27 October 2006. 8 August 2009 <http://www.thestage.co.uk/reviews/review.php/ 14687/the-duchess-of-malfi>

Berry, Ralph, *The Art of John Webster* (Oxford: Clarendon, 1972)

—'Masques and Dumb Shows in Webster's Plays', in *Elizabethan Theatre VII*, ed. by G. R. Hibbard (Hamden, CT: Archon, 1977)

Berstein, Mashey, '"Fiction": A Modern Jacobean Drama', *Los Angeles Times* 23 January 1993. 1 August 2009 <http://articles.latimes.com/1995-01-23/entertainment/ca-23287_1_pulp-fiction>

Best, Michael, 'A Precarious Balance: Structure in *The Duchess of Malfi*', in *Shakespeare and Some Others: Essays on Shakespeare and Some of His Contemporaries*, ed. by Alan Brissenden (Adelaide: University of Adelaide Press, 1976), 159–77

Billington, Michael, Rev. of *The Duchess of Malfi*, dir. by Phyllida Lloyd, *Guardian*, 29 January 2003

—'The Taming of the Duchess of Malfi', *Guardian*, 13 November 2000

Bliss, Lee, *The World's Perspective: John Webster and the Jacobean Drama* (New Brunswick, NJ: Rutgers University Press, 1983)

Bogard, Travis, *The Tragic Satire of John Webster* (Berkeley: University of California Press, 1955)

Boklund, Gunnar, *The Duchess of Malfi: Sources, Themes, Characters* (Cambridge, Mass: Harvard University Press, 1962)

Botelho, Keith, '"Into Russian Winter": Russian Extremes in *The Duchess of Malfi*', *English Language Notes*, 42, 3 (2005), 14–18

Bovilsky, Lara (2008), *Barbarous Play: Race on the English Renaissance Stage* (Minneapolis: University of Minnesota Press)

Boyer, C. V., *The Villain as Hero in Elizabethan Tragedy* (London: Routledge, 1914)

Bradbrook, M. C., *John Webster: Citizen and Dramatist* (New York: Columbia University Press, 1980)

—*Themes and Conventions of Elizabethan Tragedy* (Cambridge: Cambridge University Press, 1935)

—'Webster's Power Game' in *The Artist and Society in Shakespeare's England* (Sussex: Harvester, 1982)

Brantley, Ben, 'A "Duchess" Returns, Engulfed by Depravity', *New York Times*, 11 December 1995

Brecht, Bertolt, 'Attempted Broadway Production of *The Duchess of Malfi*', in *Brecht: Collected Plays 7*, ed. by Ralph Manheim and John Willett (New York: Vintage Books, 1975)

—*The Duchess of Malfi*, in *Collected Plays*, ed. by Ralph Manheim and John Willett (New York: Random House, 1974) VII, 331–50

Breeze, Andrew, 'St. Winifred of Wales and *The Duchess of Malfi*', *Notes and Queries*, 45:1 (1998), 33–4

Brodwin, Leonora Leet, *Elizabethan Love Tragedy: 1587–1625* (New York: New York University Press, 1971)

Brooke, Rupert, *John Webster and the Elizabethan Drama* (London: Sidgwick & Jackson, 1916)
Brooks, Peter, *The Melodramatic Imagination: Balzac, Henry James, Melodrama, and the Mode of Excess* (1976; Yale University Press, 1995)
Brown, John Russell, 'Introduction', *The Duchess of Malfi* by John Webster, ed. by John Russell Brown (London: Revels Plays, 1964; Manchester: Manchester University Press, 1997)
Busino, Horatio, in *The Journals of Two Travellers in Elizabethan and Early Stuart England: Thomas Platter and Horatio Busino*, ed. by Peter Razzell (London: Caliban, 1995)
Calbi, Maurizio, '"That Body of Hers": The Secret, the Specular, the Spectacular in *The Duchess of Malfi* and Anatomical Discourses', *Approximate Bodies: Gender and Power in Early Modern Drama and Anatomy* (New York: Routledge, 2005), 1–31
Calderwood, James L., '*The Duchess of Malfi*: Some Styles of Ceremony', *Essays in Criticism*, 12 (1962), 133–47; rpt. in *Twentieth-Century Interpretations of The Duchess of Malfi*, ed. by Norman Rabkin (Edgewood Cliffs, NJ: Prentice-Hall, 1968), 73–84
Caldwell, Ellen, 'Invasive Procedures in Webster's *The Duchess of Malfi*', in *Women, Violence, and English Renaissance Literature: Essays Honoring Paul Jorgensen*, ed. by Linda Woodbridge and Sharon Beehler (Tempe: University of Arizona Press, 2003), 149–86
Callaghan, Dympna, 'Introduction', in *The Duchess of Malfi: Contemporary Critical Essays*, ed. by Callaghan (Houndmills: Macmillan, 2000), 1–24
—'*The Duchess of Malfi* and Early Modern Widows', in *Early Modern English Drama: A Critical Companion*, ed. by Garrett A. Sullivan, Jr., Patrick Cheney and Andrew Hadfield (New York: Oxford University Press, 2006), 272–86
—*Woman and Gender in Renaissance Tragedy: A Study of 'King Lear,' 'Othello,' 'The Duchess of Malfi,' and 'The White Devil'* (Brighton: Harvester, 1989)
—ed., *New Casebooks: 'The Duchess of Malfi'* (New York: St. Martin's Press, 2000)
Carnegie, David, 'Theatrical Introduction to *The Duchess of Malfi*', in *The Works of John Webster*, ed. by David Gunby, David Carnegie and Antony Hammond, 3 vols (Cambridge: Cambridge University Press, 1995), I
Cavendish, Dominic, 'A Marvellous, Malignant Malfi', *Daily Telegraph*, 30 October 2006
Cecil, David, 'John Webster', in *Poets and Story-Tellers* (London: Constable, 1949)
Chambers, E. K., *The Elizabethan Stage*, 4 vols (Oxford: Clarendon Press, 1923)
Clifford, Anne, *The Diary of Anne Clifford 1616–1619: A Critical Edition*, ed. by Katherine O. Acheson (New York and London: Garland, 1995)
Clucas, Stephen and Rosalind Davies, ed., *The Crisis of 1614 and the Addled Parliament: Literary and Historical Perspectives* (Aldershot: Ashgate, 2003)
Coddon, Karin S., '*The Duchess of Malfi*: Tyranny and Spectacle in the Jacobean Drama', in *Madness in Drama*, ed. by James Redmond (Cambridge: Cambridge University Press, 1993), 1–17
Cogswell, Thomas, *The Blessed Revolution: English Politics and the Coming of War, 1621–1624* (Cambridge: Cambridge University Press, 1989)

Cole, David W., 'Webster's *The Duchess of Malfi*', *The Explicator*, 59, 1 (2000), 7–8

Collington, Philip D., 'Pent-up Emotions: Pity and the Imprisonment of Women in Renaissance Drama', *Medieval and Renaissance Drama in England*, 16 (2003), 162–91

Correll, Barbara, 'Malvolio at Malfi: Managing Desire in Shakespeare and Webster', *Shakespeare Quarterly*, 58, 1 (Spring 2007), 65–92

Cosin, Richard, *An Apologie for Sundrie Proceedings by Jurisdiction Ecclesiasticall* (London, 1593)

Cressy, David, *Birth, Marriage and Death: Ritual, Religion, and the Life-Cycle in Tudor and Stuart England* (Oxford: Oxford University Press, 1997)

Cunliffe, John W., *Early English Classical Tragedies* (Oxford: Clarendon Press, 1912)

—'*Gismond of Salerne*', *PMLA*, 21 (1906), 435–61

Daileader, Celia, *Eroticism on the Renaissance Stage: Transcendence, Desire, and the Limits of the Visible* (Cambridge: Cambridge University Press, 1998)

Dent, R. W., *John Webster's Borrowing* (Berkeley: University of California Press, 1960)

Desens, Marliss, 'Marrying Down: Negotiating a More Equal Marriage on the English Renaissance Stage', *Medieval and Renaissance Drama in England*, 14 (2001), 227–55

Desmet, Christy, '"Neither Maid, Widow, nor Wife": Rhetoric of the Woman Controversy in *The Duchess of Malfi*', in *In Another Country: Feminist Perspectives on Renaissance Drama*, ed. by Dorothea Kehler and Susan Baker (London: Scarecrow, 1991), 71–92

Dickens, A. G., ed., *Tudor Treatises* (Yorkshire Archaeological Society Record Series, 1959)

Dickinson, J. C., *The Shrine of Our Lady of Walsingham* (Cambridge: Cambridge University Press, 1956)

Diehl, Huston, *Staging Reform, Reforming the Stage: Protestantism and Popular Theater in Early Modern England* (Ithaca: Cornell University Press, 1997)

Doebler, Bettie Anne, 'Continuity in the Art of Dying: *The Duchess of Malfi*', *Comparative Drama*, 14 (1980), 203–15

Dolan, Frances E., *Dangerous Familiars: Representations of Domestic Crime in England, 1550–1700* (Ithaca: Cornell University Press, 1994)

—, 'Taking the Pencil out of God's Hand: Art, Nature, and the Face-Painting Debate in Early Modern England', *PMLA*, 108, 2 (1993), 224–39

Dowd, Michelle M., 'Delinquent Pedigrees: Revision, Lineage, and Spatial Rhetoric in *The Duchess of Malfi*', *English Literary Renaissance*, 39.3 (2009), 499–526

Downes, John, *Roscius Anglicanus (1708)*, ed. by Montague Summers (London: Fortune Press, 1928)

Ducassé-Turner, Milagro, 'Gods on Earth: Usurping Kingly and Godly Authority in Shakespeare's *Macbeth* and Webster's *The Duchess of Malfi*', *Anglophonia*, 17 (2005), 35–49

The Duchess of Malfi, dir. by Howard Sackler, read by Barbara Jefford, Robert Stephens, Alec McCowen (HarperCollins Audio Books, 1968)

The Duchess of Malfi, dir. by James McTaggert, prod. by Cedric Messina, perf. by Eileen Atkins, Michael Bryant, Charles Kay, Gary Bond (British Broadcasting System, 1971; Distributed by Films for the Humanities and Sciences)

The Duchess of Malfi: Contemporary Critical Essays, ed. by Dympna Callaghan, New Casebooks (Houndsmill, Basingstoke, Hampshire: Macmillan, 2000)

Duer, Leslie, 'The Landscape of Imagination in *The Duchess of Malfi*', *Modern Language Studies*, 10, 1 (1979–1980), 3–9

—, 'The Painter and the Poet: Visual Design in *The Duchess of Malfi*', *Emblematica*, 1, 2 (1986), 293–316

Duffy, Eamon, *The Stripping of the Altars: Traditional Religion in England c.1400–1580* (New Haven: Yale University Press, 1992)

'E. G.', 'What will be the Impact on London of "Malfi"'?, *Stratford-upon-Avon Herald* 2, December 1960

Edwardes, Jane, '*The Duchess of Malfi*', *Time Out* 14 December 1989

Edwards, Philip, *Pilgrimage and Literary Tradition* (Cambridge: Cambridge University Press, 2005)

Edwards, W. A., 'John Webster', *Scrutiny*, 2 (1933), 12–23

Ekeblad, Inga-Stina, 'The "Impure Art" of John Webster', *Review of English Studies*, 9 (1958), 253–67

Eliot, T. S., 'The Duchess of Malfi at the Lyric, and Poetic Drama', *Arts and Letters*, 3.1 (1920), 36–9

—'Whispers of Immortality', in *Complete Poems and Plays, 1909–1950* (New York: Harcourt Brace, 1980)

—*Selected Essays* (London: Faber and Faber, 1932)

Ellis-Fermor, Una, *The Jacobean Drama: An Interpretation* (London: Methuen, 1936)

Empson, William, 'Mine Eyes Dazzle', *Essays in Criticism*, 14 (1964), 80–6; rpt. in *Twentieth Century Interpretations of The Duchess of Malfi: A Collection of Critical Essays*, ed. by Norman Rabkin (Englewood Cliffs, N J: Prentice-Hall, 1968), 90–5

Enterline, Lynn, *The Tears of Narcissus: Melancholia and Masculinity in Early Modern Writing* (Stanford: Stanford University Press, 1995)

Erasmus, Desiderius, *The Colloquies of Erasmus*, ed. by C. R. Thompson (Chicago: University of Chicago Press, 1965)

Eriksen, Roy, 'Framing the Duchess; Webster and the Resources of Renaissance Art', *Nordlit*, 2 (1977), 3–22

Ewbank, Inga-Stina, 'Webster's Realism, or "A cunning piece wrought perspective"', in *John Webster*, ed. by Brian Morris (London: Ernest Benn, 1970), 157–78

Feinberg, Anat, 'Observation and Theatricality in Webster's *The Duchess of Malfi*', *Theatre Research International*, 5, 1 (1980–81), 36–44

Fielitz, Sonja, 'Testing the Woman's Body: Subtle Forms of Violence in Jacobean Drama', *The Aesthetics and Pragmatics of Violence: Proceedings of the Conference at Passau University*, 15–17 March 2001

Filmer, A. E., 'Sunday Shows', *Drama* 3–4 (1925–26)

Finke, Laurie, 'Painting Women: Images of Femininity in Jacobean Tragedy', *Theatre Journal*, 36, 3 (1984), 357–70

Forker, Charles R., *Skull Beneath the Skin: The Achievement of John Webster* (Carbondale and Edwardsville: Southern Illinois University Press, 1986)

—'Webster and Barnes: The Source of the Ceremony of the Cardinal's Arming in *The Duchess of Malfi* Once More', *Anglia*, 106, 3–4 (1988), 415–20

Gardner, Lyn, Rev. of *The Duchess of Malfi*, dir. by Philip Franks, *Guardian* 30 October 2006

Garner, Shirley, '"Let her paint an inch thick": Painted Ladies in Renaissance Drama and Society', *Renaissance Drama*, 20 (1989), 123–39

Gibbons, Brian, ed., *The Duchess of Malfi* (New York: Norton, 2001)

Gillett, H. M., *Walsingham: The History of a Famous Shrine* (London: Burns Oates, and Washbourne, 1946)

Goldberg, Dena, *Between Worlds: A Study of the Plays of John Webster* (Waterloo: Wilfrid Laurier University Press, 1987)

Gowing, Laura, *Common Bodies: Women, Touch and Power in Seventeenth-Century England* (New Haven and London: Yale University Press, 2003)

—'Secret Births and Infanticide in Seventeenth-century England', *Past & Present*, 156 (1997), 87–115.

Graves, R. B, '*The Duchess of Malfi* at the Globe and Blackfriars', *Renaissance Drama*, n.s. 9 (1978), 193–209

Green, Reina, '"Ears Prejudicate" in *Mariam* and *The Duchess of Malfi*', *Studies in English Literature*, 43, 2 (Spring 2003), 459–74

Greenblatt, Stephen, *Hamlet in Purgatory* (Princeton: Princeton University Press, 2001)

Griffiths, Paul, *Lost Londons: Change, Crime, and Control in the Capital City, 1550–1660* (Cambridge: Cambridge University Press, 2008)

Grote, David, *The Best Actors in the World: Shakespeare and His Acting Company* (Westport and London: Greenwood Press, 2002)

Gunby, D. C., '*The Duchess of Malfi*: A Theological Approach', in *John Webster*, ed. by Brian Morris (London: Ernest Benn, 1970), 181–204

—'"Strong Commanding Art": The Structure of *The White Devil, The Duchess of Malfi*, and *The Devil's Law-Case*', *Words that Count: Essays in Early Modern Authorship in Honor of MacDonald P. Jackson*, ed. by Brian Boyd (Newark: University of Delaware Press, 2004), 209–21

—, David Carnegie, Antony Hammond and MacDonald P. Jackson, eds., *The Works of John Webster* 3 vols (Cambridge: Cambridge University Press, 1996–2007)

Gurr, Andrew, *Playgoing in Shakespeare's London*, 3rd edn (Cambridge: Cambridge University Press, 2004)

Haber, Judith, '"My Body Bestow upon My Women": The Space of the Feminine in *The Duchess of Malfi*', *Renaissance Drama*, n.s. 28 (1999), 133–59; rpt. in *Desire and Dramatic Form in Early Modern England* (Cambridge: Cambridge University Press, 2009), 71–86

Habermann, Ina, '"She Has That in Her Belly Will Dry Up Your Ink": Femininity as Challenge in the "Equitable Drama" of John Webster', *Literature, Politics and Law in Renaissance England*, ed. by Erica Sheen and Lorna Hutson (New York: Palgrave, 2005), 100–20

Haigh, Christopher, *English Reformations: Religion, Society, and Politics Under the Tudors* (Oxford: Oxford University Press, 1993)

Haslem, Lori Schroeder, '"Troubled with the Mother": Longings, Purgings, and the Maternal Body in *Bartholomew Fair* and *The Duchess of Malfi*', *Modern Philology*, 92, 4 (1995), 438–59

Hay, Natasha, 'If You Want Blood', Rev. of *The Duchess of Malfi*, dir. by Colin McColl, *New Zealand Listener*, 30 July –4 August 2005

Helmholz, R. H., *Roman Canon Law in Reformation England* (Cambridge and New York: Cambridge University Press, 1990)

Henderson, Andrea, 'Death on Stage, Death of the Stage: The Antitheatricality of *The Duchess of Malfi*', *Theatre Journal*, 42 (1990), 194–207

Henderson, Katherine Usher and Barbara McManus, eds., *Half Humankind: Contexts and Texts of the Controversy about Women in England, 1540–1640* (Urbana: University of Illinois Press, 1985)

Heywood, John, 'The Playe Called the Foure PP', in *The Plays of John Heywood*, ed. by R. Axton and P. Happé (Cambridge: D.S. Brewer, 1991)

Hirsch, Brett D., 'An Italian Werewolf in London: Lycanthropy and *The Duchess of Malfi*', *Early Modern Literary Studies* 11, 2 (2005), 43 paragraphs. <http://extra.shu.ac.uk/emls/11-2/hirswere.htm> [cited 21 January 2010]

—'Werewolves and Severed Hands: Webster's *The Duchess of Malfi* and Heywood and Brome's *The Witches of Lancashire*', *Notes and Queries*, 53, 1 (2006), 92–4

Hirst, Derek, *England in Conflict 1603–1660: Kingdom, Community, Commonwealth* (London: Arnold, 1991)

Hopkins, Lisa, '"Black but Beautiful": Othello and the Cult of the Black Madonna', in *Marian Moments in Early Modern British Drama*, ed. by Regina Buccola and Lisa Hopkins (Aldershot: Ashgate, 2007), 75–86

—'With the Skin Side Inside: The Interiors of *The Duchess of Malfi*', in *Privacy, Domesticity, and Women in Early Modern England*, ed. by Corinne S. Abate (Aldershot: Ashgate, 2003), 21–30

—'Women's Souls: *The Duchess of Malfi* and *'Tis Pity She's a Whore*', in *The Female Hero in English Renaissance Tragedy* (New York: Palgrave, 2002)

Hotel, dir. by Mike Figgis, perf. by Max Beeseley, Saffron Burrows, Heathcote Williams (Moonstone Entertainment and Innovation Film Group (IFG), 2001; DVD, Innovation Film Group, 2005)

Hunt, Maurice, 'Webster and Jacobean Medicine: The Case of *The Duchess of Malfi*', *Essays in Literature*, 16, 1 (1989), 33–49

Hunter, G. K., 'English Folly and Italian Vice', in *Dramatic Identities and Cultural Tradition: Studies in Shakespeare and His Contemporaries* (New York: Barnes and Noble Books, 1978), 103–21

Hunter, G. K. and S. K., eds, *John Webster: A Critical Anthology* (Harmondsworth: Penguin, 1969)

Ingram, Jill Philips, '"Noble Lie": Casuistry and Machiavellianism in *The Duchess of Malfi*', *Explorations in Renaissance Culture*, 31, 1 (2005), 135–60

Ingram, Martin, *Church Courts, Sex and Marriage in England, 1570–1640* (Cambridge: Cambridge University Press, 1987)

Jack, Ian, 'The Case of John Webster', *Scrutiny*, 16 (1949), 38–43

Jackson, Ken, S., '"Twin" Shows of Madness: John Webster's Stage Management of Bethlem in *The Duchess of Malfi*', in *Separate Theaters: Bethlem ('Bedlam') Hospital and the Shakespearean Stage* (Newark: University of Delaware Press, 2005), 183–203

Jankowski, Theodora, 'Defining/Confining the Duchess: Negotiating the Female Body in John Webster's *The Duchess of Malfi*', *Studies in Philology* 87 (1990), 221–45; rpt. in *The Duchess of Malfi: Contemporary Critical Essays*, ed. by Dympna Callaghan (Houndmills: Macmillan, 2000), 80–103

—*Women in Power in the Early Modern Drama* (Urbana: University of Illinois Press, 1992)

Jardine, Lisa, '*The Duchess of Malfi*: A Case Study in the Literary Representation of Women', in *Teaching the Text*, ed. by Susanne Kappler and Norman Bryson (London: Routledge, 1983), 203–17

—*Still Harping on Daughters* (Brighton: The Harvester Press, 1983)

Jenkins, Harold, 'The Tragedy of Revenge in Shakespeare and Webster', *Shakespeare Survey*, 14 (1961), 45–55

John Webster, ed. by Brian Morris, *Mermaid Critical Commentaries* (London: Ernest Benn, 1970)

John Webster, ed. by G. K. and S. K. Hunter (Harmondsworth: Penguin, 1969)

John Webster's The Duchess of Malfi, dir. by Benjamin Capps <http://www.benjamincapps.com/duchess.html> [cited 21 January 2010]

John Webster's The Duchess of Malfi, ed. by Harold Bloom, *Modern Critical Interpretations* (New York: Chelsea House, 1987)

Jones, Emrys, 'Irregular Passions', *TLS*, 22 December 1989

Jones, Pamela, *Altarpieces and their Viewers in the Churches of Rome from Caravaggio to Guido Reni* (Aldershot: Ashgate, 2008), 75–136

Jonson, Ben, *The diuell is an asse: a comedie acted in the yeare, 1616, by His Maiesties seruants* (London, 1631)

Kathman, David, 'How Old Were Shakespeare's Boy Actresses?', *Shakespeare Survey*, 58 (2005), 220–46

Keller, Eve, *Generating Bodies and Gendered Selves: The Rhetoric of Reproduction in Early Modern England* (Seattle: University of Washington Press, 2007)

Kempe, Margery, *The Book of Margery Kempe*, ed. by W. Butler Bowdon (London: J. Cape, 1940)

Kerrigan, John C., 'Action and Confession, Fate and Despair in the Violent Conclusion of *The Duchess of Malfi*', *Ben Jonson Journal*, 8 (2001), 249–51

Kerwin, William, '"Physicians are like kings": Medical Politics and *The Duchess of Malfi*', *English Literary Renaissance*, 28 (1998), 95–117

Kiefer, Frederick, 'The Dance of the Madmen in *The Duchess of Malfi*', *Journal of Medieval and Renaissance Studies*, 17, 2 (1987), 211–33

King James VI and I, *Political Writings*, ed. by Johann P. Somerville (Cambridge: Cambridge University Press, 1995)

Klapisch-Zuber, Christiane, *Women, Family, and Ritual in Renaissance Italy*, trans. by Lydia G. Cochrane (Chicago: University of Chicago Press, 1985)

Klein, Joan Larsen, ed., *Daughters, Wives, and Widows: Writings by Men about Women and Marriage in England, 1500–1640* (Urbana: University of Illinois Press, 1992)

Lake, Peter, 'Feminine Piety and Personal Potency: The "Emancipation" of Mrs. Jane Ratcliffe', *The Seventeenth Century* 2 (1987)

Langland, William, *The Vision of Piers Plowman*, ed. by A .V. C. Schmidt (London: Dent, 1978)

Larque, Thomas, Rev. of *The Duchess of Malfi* dir. by Mark Edel-Hunt, *Early Modern Literary Studies* 11.3 (January 2005) 8 August 2009 <http://extra.shu.ac.uk/emls/11-3/revlarq.htm>

Leavis, F. R., *Determinations* (London: Chatto and Windus, 1934)

Leech, Clifford, *John Webster* (London: Hogarth Press, 1961)

—*John Webster: A Critical Study* (London: Hogarth Press, 1951)

—*Webster: The Duchess of Malfi* Studies in English Literature 8 (London: Edward Arnold, 1963)

Lees-Jeffries, Hester, *England's Helicon: Fountains in Early Modern Literature and Culture* (New York: Oxford University Press, 2007)

Lehmann, Courtney and Bryan Reynolds, 'Awakening the Werewolf Within: Self-Help, Vanishing Mediation, and Transversality in *The Duchess of Malfi*', *Transversal Enterprises in the Drama of Shakespeare and his Contemporaries*, ed. by Bryan Reynolds (New York: Palgrave, 2006)

Leinwand, Theodore B., '*Coniugium Interruptum* in Shakespeare and Webster', *ELH*, 72, 1 (2005), 239–57

Lesser, Zachary, *Renaissance Drama and the Politics of Publication: Readings in the English Book Trade* (Cambridge: Cambridge University Press, 2004)

Levack, Brian P., *The Civil Lawyers in England, 1603–1641* (Oxford: Clarendon, 1973)

Levin, Richard A., '*The Duchess of Malfi*: "What's to Come is Still Unsure,"' *Shakespeare's Secret Schemes: The Study of an Early Modern Dramatic Device* (Newark: University of Delaware Press, 2001)

Lewes, G. H., Rev. of *The Duchess of Malfi* at Sadler's Wells, *The Leader*, 30 November 1850

Lewis, Cynthia, '"Wise Men, Folly-Fall'n": Characters Named Antonio in English Renaissance Drama', *Renaissance Drama*, 20 (1989), 197–236

Lewson, Charles, Rev. of *The Duchess of Malfi* dir. by Clifford Williams, *Listener*, 22 July 1971

Limon, Jerzy, *Dangerous Matter: English Drama and Politics in 1623/24* (Cambridge: Cambridge University Press, 1986)

Lindley, Arthur, 'Uncrowning Carnival: The Laughter of Subversion and the Subversion of Laughter in *The Duchess of Malfi*', *Journal of the Australasian Universities Modern Language Association*, 106 (2006), 105–21

Lopez, Jeremy, 'Managing Asides', *Theatrical Convention and Audience Response in Early Modern Drama* (Cambridge: Cambridge University Press, 2003)

Lord, Joan M., '*The Duchess of Malfi*: "The Spirit of Greatness" and "of Woman"', *Studies in English Literature*, 16, 2 (1976), 305–17

Loveridge, Lizzie, Rev. of *The Duchess of Malfi* dir. by Gale Edwards, *Curtain Up*, November 2000. 9 August 2009 <http://www.curtainup.com/duchessofmalfi.html>

Luckyj, Christina, '"Great women of pleasure": Main Plot and Subplot in *The Duchess of Malfi*', *Studies in English Literature*, 27 (1987), 267–83

—*A Winter's Snake: Dramatic Form in the Tragedies of John Webster* (Athens: University of Georgia Press, 1989)

Macaulay, Alastair, Rev. of *The Duchess of Malfi*, dir. by Declan Donnellan, *Financial Times* 4 January 1996

Machiavelli, Nico, *The Prince and Selected Discourses*, trans. by Daniel Donno (New York and London: Bantam Books, 1966; rpt. 1971)

Madelain, Richard, '"The dark and vicious place": The Location of Sexual Transgression and its Punishment on the Early Modern English Stage', *Parergon*, 22, 1 (2005), 159–83

Mann, J. G., 'English Church Monuments, 1536–1625', *Walpole Society*, 21 (1932–33), 1–22

Marcus, Leah S., Janel Mueller, and Mary Beth Rose, eds., *Elizabeth I: Collected Works* (Chicago: University of Chicago Press, 2000)

Marcus, Leah S., *Puzzling Shakespeare: Local Reading and Its Discontents* (Berkeley and London: University of California Press, 1988)

Marotti, Arthur, 'Foreword', in *Marian Moments in Early Modern British Drama*, ed. by Regina Buccola and Lisa Hopkins (Aldershot: Ashgate, 2007), i–xxi

Marrapodi, Michele, 'Retaliation as an Italian Vice in English Renaissance Drama: Narratives and Theatrical Exchanges', in *The Italian World of English Renaissance Drama: Cultural Exchange and Intertextuality*, ed. by Marrapodi and A. J. Hoenselaars (Newark: University of Delaware Press, 1998), 190–207

Maus, Katharine Eisaman, *Inwardness and Theater in the English Renaissance* (Chicago: University of Chicago Press, 1995)

McCarthy, Mary, 'Five Curios', in *Sights and Spectacles, 1937–58* (London: Heinemann, 1959)

McLeod, Susan, *Dramatic Imagery in the Plays of John Webster* (Salzburg: University of Salzburg, 1977)

McLuskie, Kathleen, 'Drama and Sexual Politics', in *Drama, Sex, and Politics*, ed. by James Redmond (Cambridge: Cambridge University Press, 1985), 77–91

—, and Jennifer Uglow, *Plays in Performance: The Duchess of Malfi* (Bristol: Bristol Classical Press, 1989)

McMullan, Gordon, '"Plenty of Blood. That's the Only Writing": (Mis)Representing Jacobean Tragedy in Turn-of-the-Century Cinema', *La Licorne*, 2 (2008). 8 August 2009 http://edel.univ-poitiers.fr/licorne/document.php?id=4274

Mendelson, Sara and Patricia Crawford, *Women in Early Modern England 1550–1720* (Oxford: Oxford University Press, 1998)

Middleton, Thomas, *A Game at Chess*, in *Thomas Middleton: The Collected Works*, ed. by Gary Taylor and John Lavagnino (Oxford: Clarendon, 2007), 1773–1885

Mikesell, Margaret, 'Matrimony and Change in Webster's *Duchess of Malfi*', *Journal of the Rocky Mountain Medieval and Renaissance Association*, 2 (1981), 97–111

—, 'Catholic and Protestant Widows in *The Duchess of Malfi*', *Renaissance and Reformation*, 7.4 (1983), 265–79

Moore, Don D., *Webster: The Critical Heritage* (London: Routledge & Kegan Paul, 1981)

Moore Smith, G. C., ed., *William Heminges's Elegy on Randolph's Finger* (Oxford: Blackwell, 1923)

Morice, James, *A briefe treatise of oathes exacted by ordinaries and ecclesiasticall judges* (Middelburg, 1590)

Mukherji, Subha, *Law and Representation in Early Modern Drama* (Cambridge: Cambridge University Press, 2006)

Mulryne, J. R., 'Webster and the Uses of Tragicomedy', in *John Webster*, ed. by Brian Morris (London: Ernest Benn, 1970), 131–55

Murray, John, '*Tancred and Gismund*', *The Review of English Studies*, o.s. 14 (1938), 385–95

Murray, Peter B., *A Study of John Webster* (The Hague: Mouton, 1969)

Neill, Michael, *Issues of Death: Mortality and Identity in English Renaissance Tragedy* (Oxford: Clarendon Press, 1998)

—'Monuments and Ruins as Symbols in *The Duchess of Malfi*', in *Drama and Symbolism*, ed. by James Redmond (Cambridge: Cambridge University Press, 1982), 71–87

—' "What Strange Riddle's This?": Deciphering *'Tis Pity She's a Whore*', in *John Ford: Critical Re-Visions*, ed. by Michael Neill (Cambridge: Cambridge University Press, 1988), 153–79

Nightingale, Benedict, Rev. of *The Duchess of Malfi*, dir. by Declan Donnellan, *The Times*, 24 October 1995

O'Connor, Mary C., *The Art of Dying Well: The Development of the Ars Moriendi* (New York: Columbia University Press, 1942)

Orlin, Lena Cowan, *Locating Privacy in Tudor London* (Oxford: Oxford University Press, 2007)

—*Private Matters and Public Culture in Post-Reformation England* (Ithaca: Cornell University Press, 1994)

Ornstein, Robert, *The Moral Vision of Jacobean Tragedy* (Madison: University of Wisconsin Press, 1960)

Outhwaite, R. B., *Clandestine Marriage in England, 1500–1850* (London: Hambledon, 1995)

Painter, William, *Palace of Pleasure*, ed. by Joseph Jacobs, 3 vols (1890; rpt. Honolulu: University Press of the Pacific, 2002)

Palter, Robert, *The Duchess of Malfi's Apricots and Other Literary Fruits* (Columbia, SC: University of South Carolina Press, 2002)

Panek, Jennifer, *Widows and Suitors in Early Modern English Comedy* (Cambridge: Cambridge University Press, 2004)

—, 'Why did Widows Remarry? Remarriage, Male Authority, and Feminist Criticism', *The Impact of Feminism in English Renaissance Studies*, ed. by Dympna C. Callaghan (Houndmills: Palgrave, 2007), 281–98

—, ' "My Naked Weapon": Male Anxiety and the Violent Courtship of the Jacobean Stage Widow', *Comparative Drama*, 34, 3 (2000), 321–44

Park, Katharine, *Secrets of Women: Gender, Generation, and the Origins of Human Dissection* (New York: Zone Books, 2006), 121–59

Parker, Patricia, *Shakespeare from the Margins: Language, Culture, Context* (Chicago: University of Chicago Press, 1996), 229–72

Pearson, Jacqueline, *Tragedy and Tragicomedy in the Plays of John Webster* (Manchester: Manchester University Press, 1980)

Pepys, Samuel, *The Diary of Samuel Pepys: Volume Three: 1662*, ed. by Robert Latham and William Matthews, 11 vols (Berkeley: University of California Press, 1970–83)

Perry, Curtis, '*Gismond of Salern* and the Elizabethan Politics of Senecan Drama', in *Gender Matters*, ed. by Mara R. Wade (Amsterdam: Rodopi, forthcoming)

Peter, John, Rev. of *The Duchess of Malfi*, dir. by Declan Donnellan, *Sunday Times* 7 January 1996

Peters, Belinda Roberts, *Marriage in Seventeenth-Century English Political Thought* (Houndmills: Palgrave Macmillan, 2004)

Peterson, Joyce, *Curs'd Example: 'The Duchess of Malfi' and Commonweal Tragedy* (Columbia: University of Missouri Press, 1978)

Philips, Jill Ingram, 'The "Noble Lie": Casuistry and Machiavellianism in *The Duchess of Malfi*', *Explorations in Renaissance Culture*, 31, 5 (2005), 135–60

Poel, William, 'A New Criticism of Webster's *Duchess of Malfi*', *Library Review*, 2 (1893), 21–4

Potter, Lois, 'Realism versus Nightmare: Problems of Staging *The Duchess of Malfi*', in *The Triple Bond: Plays, Mainly Shakespearean, in Performance*, ed. by Joseph G. Price (University Park: Pennsylvania State University Press, 1975), 170–89

Price, Hereward T., 'The Function of Imagery in Webster', *PMLA*, 70 (1955), 717–39

Proceedings in Parliament 1610, ed. by Elizabeth Read Foster (New Haven and London: Yale University Press, 1966)

A Question About Hell, dir. by Claude Whatham, written by Kingley Amis, perf. by Richard Johnson, Patrick Wymark, Caroline Mortimer (Granada Television Productions, 1964)

Ranald, Margaret Loftus, *John Webster*, Twayne's English Authors Series (Boston: Twayne, 1989)

Randall, Dale B. J., 'The Rank and Earthy Background of Certain Physical Symbols in *The Duchess of Malfi*', *Renaissance Drama*, n.s. 18 (1987), 171–203

Ray, Sid, '"So troubled with the mother": The Politics of Pregnancy in *The Duchess of Malfi*', in *Performing Maternity in Early Modern England*, ed. by Kathryn M. Moncrief and Kathryn R. McPherson (Aldershot: Ashgate, 2007), 17–28

Rev. of *The Duchess of Malfi* at Sadler's Wells, *The Times*, 21 November 1850

Rev. of *The Duchess of Malfi*, dir. by George Rylands, *The Times*, 19 April 1945

Rev. of *The Duchess of Malfi*, *The Athenaeum*, 31 March 1855

Richards, Judith M., *Mary Tudor* (London: Routledge, 2008)

Ricks, Christopher, 'The Tragedies of Webster, Tourneur, and Middleton: Symbols, Imagery, and Conventions', in *English Drama to 1710*, ed. by Christopher Ricks (New York: Peter Bedrick, 1987), 315–61

Rist, Thomas, 'Melodrama and Parody: Remembering the Dead in *The Revenger's Tragedy, The Atheist's Tragedy, The White Devil* and *The Duchess of Malfi*', *Revenge Tragedy and the Drama of Commemoration in Reforming England* (Burlington, VT: Ashgate, 2008), 97–144

—, *Revenge Tragedy and the Drama of Commemoration* (Aldershot: Ashgate, 2008)

Roberts, Philip, *The Royal Court Theatre and the Modern Stage* (Cambridge: Cambridge University Press, 1999)

Rose, Mary Beth, *The Expense of Spirit: Love and Sexuality in English Renaissance Drama* (Ithaca: Cornell University Press, 1988)

Rowe, Katherine, *Dead Hands: Fictions of Agency, Renaissance to Modern* (Stanford, CA: Stanford University Press, 1999)

'S. E. W.', 'Stratford "Malfi" Ends in Bathos', *The Stage*, 22 July 1971

Salingar, L. G., 'Tourneur and the Tragedy of Revenge', in *The Age of Shakespeare*, ed. by Boris Ford (Harmondsworth: Penguin, 1955), 334–54

Sato, Yumi, '*The Duchess of Malfi* at Stratford' (unpublished MPhil thesis, Shakespeare Institute, University of Birmingham, 1991)

Schmitt, Julia, 'Sisterly Transgression: An Examination of Evadne from *The Maid's Tragedy* and the Duchess from *The Duchess of Malfi*', *Selected Papers from the West Virginia Shakespeare and Renaissance Association*, 25 (2002), 58–69

Schuman, Samuel, 'The Ring and the Jewel in Webster's Tragedies', *Texas Studies in Literature and Language*, 14 (1972), 253–68

—, *'The Theatre of Fine Devices': The Visual Drama of John Webster* (Salzburg: Institut fur Anglistik und Amerikanistik,1982)

Selzer, John L., 'Merit and Degree in Webster's *The Duchess of Malfi*', *English Literary Renaissance*, 11 (1981), 70–80

Seneca, Lucius Annaeus, *Tragedies*, ed. and trans. by John G. Fitch, 2 vols (Cambridge: Harvard University Press, 2002–04), II, 286

Shakespeare, William, *The Riverside Shakespeare*, ed. by G. Blakemore Evans, 2nd edn (Boston and New York: Houghton Mifflin, 1997)

Shakespeare in Love, dir. by John Madden, perf. by Joseph Fiennes, Gwyneth Paltrow, Judi Dench (Universal, 1998)

Shakespeare Set Free: Teaching A Midsummer Night's Dream, Romeo and Juliet, and Macbeth, ed. by Peggy O'Brien et al. (New York: Washington Square Press, 2006)

Shaw, George Bernard, *Our Theatre in the Nineties*, 3 vols (London: Constable, 1932)

Shell, Allison, *Catholicism, Controversy, and the English Literary Imagination, 1558–1660* (Cambridge: Cambridge University Press, 1999)

Sheppard, Philippa, 'Fair Counterfeits: A Bibliography of Visual Aids for Renaissance Drama', in *Approaches to Teaching English Renaissance Drama*, ed. by Karen Bamford and Alexander Leggatt (New York: Modern Language Association, 2002), 43–50

Shorter, Eric, 'Serious Malfi', *Daily Telegraph*, 17 September 1980

Shulman, Milton, Rev. of *The Duchess of Malfi*, dir. by Clifford Williams, *Evening Standard*, 16 July 1971

Shuttleworth, Ian, Rev. of *The Duchess of Malfi*, dir. by Philip Franks, *Financial Times*, 27 April 1995

Simkin, Stevie, ed., *New Casebooks, Revenge Tragedy* (Basingstoke: Palgrave, 2001)

Smith, Mona Z., *Becoming Someone: The Story of Canada Lee* (New York: Faber and Faber, 2005)

Smith, Peter J., 'Two Views of Malfi', *Cahiers Elisabéthains* 49 (April 1996), 77–81

Solga, Kim, *Violence Against Women in Early Modern Performance: Invisible Acts* (Houndmills: Palgrave Macmillan, 2009)

Spelman, Henry, *History and Fate of Sacrilege* (London: John Hodges, 1895)

Spiller, Ben, 'Inconstant Identities on the South Bank: *The Duchess of Malfi* and the Homeless Visitor', *Renaissance Journal*, 1.8 (2003), 25–31

Spivack, Charlotte, '*The Duchess of Malfi*: A Fearful Madness', *Journal of Women's Studies in Literature* 2 (1979), 122–32

Starkey, David, ed., *The English Court: From the Wars of the Roses to the Civil War* (London: Longman, 1987)

Steen, Sara Jayne, 'The Crime of Marriage: Arbella Stuart and *The Duchess of Malfi*', *Sixteenth Century Journal*, 22 (1991), 61–76

Stoll, Elmer E., *John Webster: The Periods of His Work as Determined by His Relationship to the Drama of the Day* (Boston: Boston Cooperative Society, 1905)

Storey, John, *Cultural Theory and Popular Culture*, 3rd edn (Harlow: Prentice Hall, 2001)

Sullivan, Garret A., 'Sleep, Conscience and Fame in *The Duchess of Malfi*', in *Memory and Forgetting in English Renaissance Drama: Shakespeare, Marlowe, Webster* (Cambridge: Cambridge University Press, 2005)

Summit, Jennifer, *Lost Property: The Woman Writer and English Literary History 1380–1589* (Chicago: University of Chicago Press, 2000)

Theobald, Lewis, *The Fatal Secret* (London: Printed for J. Watts, 1735), in *Nahum Tate's Injur'd Love, or, The Cruel Husband, and Lewis Theobald's The Fatal Secret*, ed. by James Hogg (Salzburg and Portland, Oregon: University of Salzburg, 1998)

—, *The Fatal Secret. A Tragedy. As it is Acted at the Theatre-Royal, in Covent-Garden* (London, 1735)

Thomas, Keith, *Religion and the Decline of Magic* (New York: Oxford University Press, 1971)

Thomson, Leslie, 'Fortune and Virtue in "The Duchess of Malfi"', *Comparative Drama*, 33 (1999–2000), 474–94

Thomson, Peter, 'Webster and the Actor', in *John Webster*, ed. by Brian Morris (London: Ernest Benn, 1970)

Tiffany, Grace, *Love's Pilgrimage: The Holy Journey in English Renaissance Literature* (Newark: University of Delaware Press, 2006)

Todd, Barbara J., 'The Remarrying Widow: A Stereotype Reconsidered', in *Women in English Society 1500–1800*, ed. by Mary Prior (London: Methuen, 1985)

Trewin, J. C., Rev. of *The Duchess of Malfi*, dir. by Clifford Williams, *Birmingham Post*, 16 July 1971

Tricomi, Albert H., *Anticourt Drama in England, 1603–1642* (Charlottesville: University Press of Virginia, 1989)
—, 'Historicizing the Imagery of the Demonic in *The Duchess of Malfi*', *Journal of Medieval and Early Modern Studies*, 34.2 (2004), 345–72
—'The Severed Hand in Webster's *The Duchess of Malfi*', *Studies in English Literature*, 44 (2004), 347–58
Turner, Kimberly, 'The Complexity of Webster's Duchess', *Ben Jonson Journal*, 7 (2000), 380–400
Twentieth Century Interpretations of The Duchess of Malfi, ed. by Norman Rabkin (Englewood Cliffs, NJ: Prentice Hall, 1968)
Vernon, P. F., 'The Duchess of Malfi's Guilt', *Notes and Queries*, n.s. 10 (1963), 335–38
Vives, Joannes Ludovicus, *A Very Fruteful and Pleasant Boke Called The Instruction of a Christian Woman*, trans. by R. Hyrde (London, 1529)
Wadsworth, F. W., '"Shorn and Abated": British Performances of *The Duchess of Malfi*', *Theatre Survey*, 10.2 (1969), 89–104
—'Some Nineteenth-Century Revivals of *The Duchess of Malfi*', *Theatre Survey*, 8.2 (1967), 67–83
—'"Webster, Horne and Mrs. Stowe": American Performances of *The Duchess of Malfi*', *Theatre Survey*, 11.2 (1970), 151–66
—'Webster's *Duchess of Malfi* in the Light of Some Contemporary Ideas on Marriage and Remarriage', *Philological Quarterly*, 35 (1957), 394–407
Wall, Wendy, 'Just a Spoonful of Sugar: Syrup and Domesticity in Early Modern England', *Modern Philology*, 104, 2 (2006), 149–72
Walter, Melissa, 'Dramatic Bodies and Novellesque Spaces in Jacobean Tragedy and Tragicomedy', in *Transnational and Transcultural Exchange in Early Modern Drama: Theater Crossing Borders*, ed. by Robert Henke and Eric Nichols (Aldershot: Ashgate, 2008), 63–77
—'Drinking from Skulls and the Politics of Incorporation in Early Stuart Drama', in *At the Table: Metaphorical and Material Cultures of Food in Medieval and Early Modern Europe*, ed. by Timothy J. Tomasik and Juliann M. Vitullo (Turnhout: Brepols, 2007), 93–105
—'Shakespeare's News: Autonomy, Authority and the Symbolic Vocabulary of European Novellas in Early Modern England' (unpublished Doctoral Thesis, University of Wisconsin, 2004)
Wardle, Irving, 'Clearing the Vital Hurdle Boldly', *Times*, 17 September 1980
—, 'An Uninhabited Nightmare', *Times*, 19 January 1971
Webster, John, *The Complete Works of John Webster*, ed. by F. L. Lucas, 4 vols (London: Sidgwick & Jackson, 1927)
—*John Webster: The Duchess of Malfi*, ed. by Kathleen McLuskie and Jennifer Uglow (Bristol: Bristol Classical Press, 1989)
—*John Webster: The Duchess of Malfi*, ed. by Clive Hart (Edinburgh: Oliver & Boyd, 1972)
—*The Duchess of Malfi*, ed. by Elizabeth Brennan (London: Ernest Benn, 1964)
—*The Duchess of Malfi*, ed. by Brian Gibbons, New Mermaids (London: A & C Black; New York: W.W. Norton, 2001)

—*The Duchess of Malfi*, ed. by Jackie Moore, Oxford Student Texts (Oxford: Oxford University Press, 2007)

—*The Duchess of Malfi*, ed. by John Russell Brown, Revels Plays (Cambridge, Mass.: Harvard University Press, 1964)

—, *The Duchess of Malfi*, ed. by John Russell Brown, Revels Student Editions (Manchester: Manchester University Press, 1997)

—*The Duchess of Malfi*, ed. by Kathy Casey, Dover Thrift Edition (Mineola, NY: Dover, 1999)

—*The Duchess of Malfi*, ed. by Leah S. Marcus, Arden Early Modern Drama (London: A & C Black, 2009)

—*The Duchess of Malfi*, ed. by Trevor R. Griffiths (London: Hern Books, 1999)

—*The Duchess of Malfi*, ed. by Risa Stephanie Bear, Renascence Editions <http://www.luminarium.org/renascence-editions/webster1.html> [accessed 24 October 2009]

—*The Duchess of Malfi*, in *The Works of John Webster: An Old-Spelling Critical Edition*, ed. by David Gunby, David Carnegie, Antony Hammond and Doreen DelVecchio (Cambridge: Cambridge University Press, 1995), I

—*The Duchess of Malfi: The Complete Text, with Notes and Commentary*, ed. by Larry A. Brown <http://laryavisbrown.homestead.com/files/Malfi/malfi_home.htm> [accessed 24 October 2009]

—*The Duchess of Malfi and Other Plays*, ed. by René Weis, Oxford World's Classics (Oxford: Oxford University Press, 1996)

—*The Selected Plays of John Webster*, ed. by Jonathan Dollimore and Alan Sinfield (Cambridge: Cambridge University Press, 1983)

—*The Tragedy of the Dutchesse of Malfy* (London, 1623)

—*The White Devil*, ed. by Christina Luckyj (London: Methuen, 2008)

Wheatley, H. ed., *Percy's Reliques of Ancient English Poetry* (London: George Allen and Unwin, 1885)

Whigham, Frank, *Seizures of the Will in Early Modern Drama* (Cambridge: Cambridge University Press, 1996)

—, 'Sexual and Social Mobility in *The Duchess of Malfi*', *PMLA*, 100 (1985), 167–86

White, R. S., 'The Moral Design of *The Duchess of Malfi*', in *New Casebooks: 'The Duchess of Malfi'*, ed. by Dympna Callaghan (New York: St. Martin's 2000), 201–16

Whittaker, Herbert, 'Splendid Production of "The Duchess of Malfi"', *Toronto Globe and Mail*, 9 June 1971

Williams, Raymond, *Keywords: A Vocabulary of Culture and Society* (1976; New York: Oxford University Press, 1985)

Wilson, Edmund, 'Notes on London at the End of the War', in *Europe without Baedecker* (New York: Doubleday, 1947)

Wilson, F. P., *Elizabethan and Jacobean* (Oxford: Oxford University Press, 1947)

Wind, Edgar, 'Ruins and Echoes', *Journal of the Warburg Institute*, 1:3 (1938), 259

Winston, Jessica, 'Seneca in Early Elizabethan England', *Renaissance Quarterly*, 59 (2006), 29–58

Wolf, Matt, Rev of *The Duchess of Malfi*, dir. by Phyllida Lloyd, *Variety* 2 February 2003 <http://www.variety.com/review/VE1117919854.html?categoryid=33&cs=1>

Woodbridge, Linda, 'Queen of Apricots: The Duchess of Malfi, Hero of Desire', in *The Female Tragic Hero in English Renaissance Drama*, ed. by Naomi Conn Liebler (New York: Palgrave Macmillan, 2002), 161–84

— *Women and the English Renaissance: Literature and the Nature of Womankind, 1540–1620* (Urbana: University of Illinois Press, 1984)

Woollam, Angela, 'The Stakes of Semantic Significance in *The Duchess of Malfi*', *English Studies in Canada*, 26, 1 (2003), 11–28

Wymer, Rowland, *Webster and Ford* (New York: St. Martin's 1995)

Zimmerman, Susan, 'Invading the Grave: Shadow Lives in *The Revenger's Tragedy* and *The Duchess of Malfi*', in *The Early Modern Corpse and Shakespeare's Theatre* (Edinburgh: Edinburgh University Press, 2005), 128–71

Notes on Contributors

Roberta Barker is Associate Professor and Chair in the Department of Theatre at Dalhousie University in Halifax, Nova Sçotia. She is the author of *Early Modern Tragedy, Gender and Performance, 1984–2000: The Destined Livery* (Palgrave Macmillan, 2007). Her articles have appeared in *Shakespeare Survey, Shakespeare Quarterly, Early Theatre, Modern Drama, Canadian Theatre Review, Literature Compass* and *EMLS*. Among her credits as a director are productions of *The Witch of Edmonton, Fuente Ovejuna, Troilus and Cressida* and *Henry IV, Part One*.

Todd A. Borlik is Assistant Professor of English at Bloomsburg University in Pennsylvania. His articles and reviews have appeared in *The Shakespeare Bulletin, The Shakespeare Newsletter, Early Theatre* and *Literature/Film Quarterly*. His first book, entitled *Ecocriticism and Early Modern English Literature: Green Pastures*, will be published by Routledge in the fall of 2010.

Dympna Callaghan is Dean's Professor in Humanities at Syracuse University. Her books include *Woman and Gender in Renaissance Tragedy* (1989), *Shakespeare Without Women* (2000) *The Sonnets* (2007) as well as *John Webster's 'Duchess of Malfi': Contemporary Critical Essays* (2000), *The Feminist Companion to Shakespeare* (2000) and a Bedford contextual edition of *Romeo and Juliet* (2003), the anthology, *The Impact of Feminism in English Renaissance Studies* (2007) and The Norton Critical edition of *The Taming of the Shrew* (2009).

Christy Desmet is Professor of English at the University of Georgia. She is the author of *Reading Shakespeare's Characters: Rhetoric, Ethics, and Identity* (University of Massachusetts Press 1992). She is the co-editor (with Robert Sawyer) of *Shakespeare and Appropriation* (Routledge,

1999) and of *Harold Bloom's Shakespeare* (Palgrave, 2001). With Anne Williams, she has edited *Shakespearean Gothic*. And with Sujata Iyengar, she is co-founder and co-general editor of *Borrowers and Lenders: The Journal of Shakespeare and Appropriation*.

Frances E. Dolan is Professor of English at the University of California, Davis. She is the author of *Marriage and Violence: The Early Modern Legacy* (University of Pennsylvania Press, 2008), *Whores of Babylon: Gender, Catholicism, and Seventeenth-Century Print Culture* (Cornell, 1999; paperback edition with new preface from University of Notre Dame Press, 2005), and *Dangerous Familiars: Representations of Domestic Crime in England, 1550–1700* (Cornell, 1994). She is also the editor of *The Taming of the Shrew: Texts and Contexts* (Bedford, 1996), and of five plays for the new Pelican Shakespeare.

David Gunby is Emeritus Professor of English Literature at the University of Canterbury, Christchurch, New Zealand, his alma mater, where he taught for more than 30 years following his return from Cambridge, having completed a PhD on the relationship of Anglican theology and Jacobean tragedy under the supervision of Muriel Bradbrook. Though he has published on other dramatists of the period, including Shakespeare, Marston and Tourneur, his overriding passion has been John Webster. He edited *John Webster: Three Plays* in the Penguin English Classics series, and is co-editor of the Cambridge University Press edition of *The Works of John Webster*, the fourth and final volume of which, covering the plays written in collaboration with Dekker, Fletcher, Ford and Massinger, is now in preparation.

Christina Luckyj is Professor of English at Dalhousie University in Halifax, Nova Scotia. She is the author of '*A Moving Rhetoricke:' Gender and Silence in Early Modern England* (Manchester University Press, 2002) and '*A Winter's Snake': Dramatic Form in the Tragedies of John Webster* (University of Georgia Press, 1989) and editor of The New Mermaids edition of *The White Devil* by John Webster (A&C Black 2008). She has published essays in *MLA Approaches to Teaching Renaissance Drama, English Studies in Canada, Enacting Gender on the Renaissance Stage, Renaissance Drama, Studies in English Literature, Performing Maternity in Early Modern England* and *English Literary Renaissance.*

Leah S. Marcus is Edwin Mims Professor of English at Vanderbilt University. She is the author of *Childhood and Cultural Despair* (1978), *The Politics of Mirth* (1986), *Puzzling Shakespeare* (1988) and *Unediting the Renaissance* (1996), and has edited two volumes of the *Writings of Queen Elizabeth I* (2000, 2002, with Janel Mueller and Mary Beth Rose), Norton Critical Editions of *The Merchant of Venice* (2006) and

As You Like It (2011) and an Arden Early Modern Drama edition of *The Duchess of Malfi* (2009).

Curtis Perry is Professor of English at the University of Illinois, Urbana-Champaign. Among his publications are two book-length studies of early modern English literature and political culture: *The Making of Jacobean Culture: James I and the Renegotiation of Elizabethan Literary Practice* (1997) and *Literature and Favoritism in Early Modern England* (2006). He has edited two books – *Material Culture and Cultural Materialisms in the Middle Ages and Renaissance* (2001) and *Eros and Power in English Renaissance Drama: Five Plays by Marlowe, Davenant, Massinger, Ford, and Shakespeare* (2008) – and recently co-edited (with John Watkins) a third, entitled *Shakespeare & the Middle Ages* (2009).

Melissa Walter teaches English and Renaissance literature at the University of the Fraser Valley in Abbotsford, British Columbia. She has published articles on early modern prose, drama, transnational exchange and especially the Italian novella in England.

Index

Acts and Monuments (Foxe) 137
Adams, Thomas 111
Addled Parliament 95
Admirable and Memorable Histories (Goulart) 74
Aebischer, Pascale 60, 166
Agate, James 50
Alexander, Bill 51, 52, 75–6
alienation effect 55–6
  see also distancing techniques
Allison, Alexander 38
Amis, Kingsley 160
anatomy 70–4, 127, 167
Anderson, Thomas 72–3
animal imagery 156
Antonio 6, 9–10, 15–16, 20, 26, 29, 33, 37–8, 52, 57–8, 59–60, 74, 77, 87, 94–100, 106–13, 115, 119–25, 129–33, 139, 144–5, 158, 167, 171–2
Antonio's Revenge (Marston) 78
Antony and Cleopatra (Shakespeare) 156, 171
Aragona, Giovanna d' 88
Archer, William 2, 17, 18–19, 20–1, 22, 48–9
architectural space 89, 93, 96, 98–100, 102
Armstrong, Katherine A. 71
ars moriendi 34, 81, 145–9, 159, 168
Arte and Crafte to Knowe Well to Dye 145
artifice 2, 3
Aston, Margaret 143, 144
The Atheist's Tragedy (Tourneur) 78
Auden, W. H. 53
audience reception 7, 108–9, 116–17
  see also productions
Aughterson, Kate 160, 162, 163–4
Axton, Marie 162

Baker, Susan 158, 166
Baker-Smith, Dominic 33, 137, 143
Bamford, Karen 165
Bandello, Matteo 5, 92, 94, 99
Barber, John 55
Barker, Roberta 2, 10, 74, 75–6, 166
baroque interpretation 53–6
Barranger, Milly S. 166
Bartels, Emily 166
Bartholomew Fair (Jonson) 156
Bear, Risa Stephanie 155
Beaumont, Francis 140
Becon, Thomas 146
Bellany, Alastair 101
Belleforest, Francois de 5
Belsey, Catherine 35–6, 87, 166–7
Belton, Ellen R. 167
Benjamin, Walter 60n.4
Bergeron, David 159, 163, 167
Berry, Kevin 58
Berry, Ralph 150n.15, 151n.19, 164, 165
Best, Michael 166, 167
Black Madonna 78–9
Blackfriars 13n.33, 14, 42, 43, 149
Bliss, Lee 35, 38, 164
Boccaccio 90, 92

see also Senecan-Boccaccian tradition
body imagery 98–9, 100
Bogard, Travis 25, 29, 164
Boguet, Henry 73–4, 173
Boklund, Gunnar 26, 29, 33, 164
Borlik, Todd 9, 11
borrowings 25–6
see also plot: sources for
Bosola 3–5, 7–9, 15, 19–21, 25–32, 35, 51–2, 97, 100, 126, 131–2, 146–8, 156–7, 158
Botelho, Keith 82
Boyer, C. V. 19–20
Bradbrook, M. C. 23–4, 29, 83, 164
Brantley, Ben 57–8
Brecht, Bertolt 53–4, 55, 160, 161, 166
Brennan, Elizabeth 29, 30, 32
Brodwin, Leonora Leet 123
Bronzino 159
Brooke, Rupert 20, 25
Brown, John Russell 9, 29–30, 31, 32, 148, 154
Brown, Larry A. 154, 155
Buckingham, Duke of 102–3, 110
Busino, Horatio (Orazio) 45, 109–10, 136, 141

Calbi, Maurizo 70, 167
Calderwood, James L. 167
Caldwell, Ellen 71
Callaghan, Dympha 10, 67, 119, 158, 164
Capps, Benjamin 160, 162
Caravaggio 142
Cardinal 8, 15, 18, 20, 25, 27, 29–30, 32, 36, 43, 45–7, 49, 51, 99–100, 109–10, 115, 131–2, 136, 139, 141, 144–5
Carey, Elizabeth 156
Cariola 106–8, 120, 131, 139, 148
Carnegie, David 45, 46, 154, 160
Carr, Robert, Earl of Somerset 9, 95
Casey, Kathy 154
Catholicism
corruption and 11, 141
death and 146–7, 148, 172
ecclesiastical courts and 113–14
imagery of 78–9
marriage and, 68, 108–9
in *Measure for Measure* 115
Protestantism and 9, 10, 13n.26, 111–12, 158
satire of 109–10
theatricality and, 142–3
wolves and 111
see also Loreto; pilgrimages; Walsingham
Cave, Richard Allen 32
Cavell, Stanley 70
Cecil, David 27, 29
Cecil, Robert 95
Cecil, William 80
Certaine Very Proper, and Most Profitable Similies (Fletcher) 80
The Changeling (Middleton and Rowley) 71, 89, 156
characterization 20, 23, 47–8
Charles I 10, 102–3, 109–10
Charles II 15
Chaucer, Geoffrey 139
childbirth/pregnancy 96–7, 100, 126–8, 158, 169
children, Duchess's 5, 47, 56, 59, 72, 88, 96, 99, 108, 121, 126–8, 141
Christian framework 27, 30, 32–4
see also Catholicism; Protestantism; religious context
Christie, Agatha 161
cinematic reading 56–60, 160–1
class hierarchy
gender and 7–8, 69
incest and 36
marriage and 4, 75, 122, 123–4
mobility in 4
Clifford, Lady Anne 7
Coddon, Karin S. 155, 159, 165, 167
Cole, David W. 82
Colet, John 146
Collington, Philip D. 73
conventions, realism and 28
corpses *see* death imagery
Correll, Barbara 74, 123, 167–8

corruption, court 9, 95–6, 101
see also tyranny
Council of Trent 108
courtly space *see* architectural space
Cromwell, Thomas 138
The Cruel Brother (Davenant) 89, 101–3
Cynthia's Revels (Jonson) 80

Daileader, Celia R. 128
Davenant, William 89, 93, 101–3
death imagery 72–4, 131–2, 156, 158–9, 171, 173–4
see also ars moriendi
death scene (Duchess) 3, 73, 146–8
Decameron (Boccaccio) 90
DelVecchio, Doreen 154, 160
demonic imagery 79–80
demonic motives 33
Dent, R. W. 25–6, 151n.22
Desens, Marliss 69
Desmet, Christy 4, 11, 68–9, 165, 168
The Devil's Law Case (Webster) 69, 76, 143
Diehl, Huston 121, 136–7, 144
Discipline and Punish (Foucault) 72–3
Discours Exécrable des Sorciers (Boguet) 73–4, 173
distancing techniques 35, 36
see also alienation effect
Doebler, Bettie-Anne 34, 159, 168
Dolan, Frances E. 6, 11, 108, 162–3
Dolce, Lodovico 91
domesticity 87–8, 158
Donne, John 81
Donnellan, Declan 57, 58, 75–6
Dove, Robert 146
Dowd, Michelle 126, 127
Downes, John, 15, 46
Ducassé-Turner, Milagro 81
Duer, Leslie 156, 166, 168
Duffy, Eamon 137
Dyce, Alexander 16

ecclesiastical courts 113–14
The Education of a Christian Prince (Erasmus) 80

Edwards, Gale 58, 59
Edwards, W. A. 22–3
Ekeblad (Ewbank), Inga-Stina 3, 21, 28, 159, 165, 168, 169
Eliot, T. S. 3, 22, 28, 49–50, 55
Elizabeth I
evocation of 100, 135n.34
fountain imagery and 80
Gismond of Salern and 89, 90
marriage and 93
privacy and 88, 95
virginity and 81
Elizabeth Stuart, Princess 9, 10
Ellis-Fermor, Una 24, 29, 31
Elyot, Thomas 80
emblem books 77
Empson, William 112, 136
Enterline, Lynn 126, 168
Erasmus 80, 138, 142–3, 146
Eriksen, Roy 159, 168–9

fables/tales 3, 16, 31
The Fair Maid of the Inn (Fletcher) 21
The Faithful Shepherdess (Fletcher) 71
Farnham, Willard 26–7
The Fatal Secret (Theobald) 15, 46–7, 160, 162
fear, secrecy and 124–5
Feinberg, Anat 169
feminist criticism 38–9, 67
Ferdinand, Duke of Calabria 15, 46, 48, 50–2, 56, 82, 98–9, 102, 108, 110–11, 120–1, 128–9, 132–3, 158
Ferdinand, King of Spain 110–11
Ferdinand II 10
Fielitz, Sonja 70–1
Figgis, Mike 59, 160, 162, 166
film *see* cinematic reading; *individual films*
Filmer, A. E. 49
Finke, Laurie 159, 169
Fitzjeffrey, Henry 1–2
Fletcher, Anthony 80
Fletcher, John 71
Ford, John 12n.4, 14, 93, 156
Forker, Charles R. 36, 83, 164

Foucault, Michel 72–3
fountain imagery 80, 156
The Four PP (Heywood) 138
Foxe, John 137
Franks, Philip 51, 52, 57, 58
Frederick, Prince 9, 10
Fry, Stephen 161

A Game at Chess (Middleton) 110
Garner, Shirley 169
Gascon, Jean 51
gender
  class and 7–8, 69
  critical approach and 157–8
  resources on 171
  sexuality and 67–72
generic complexity 34–5, 158
  see also stylistic hybridity
Gibbons, Brian 82, 83, 154
Gill, Peter 54
Gismond of Salern 10, 89, 95, 96, 100, 102, 103
Globe Theatre 14, 42, 43
Goldberg, Dena 164
Gorboduc (Norton and Sackville) 91
gossip *see* rumours
Goulart, Simon 74
Gowing, Laura 127, 128
Great Contract 9, 95
Green, Reina 69–70
Greenblatt, Stephen 137
Greville, Fulke 94
Grey, Lady Catherine 92–3, 94
Griffiths, Trevor R. 155
Gunby, David C. 10, 33–4, 76–7, 83, 137, 154, 160

H. M. (*Blackwood's Magazine*) 16
Haber, Judith 123, 127, 169
Habermann, Ina 69
Haigh, Christopher 137
Halberstam, Michael 58, 59
Hamlet (Shakespeare) 3, 4, 6, 68, 78, 147–8, 153, 155, 161
Hammond, Antony 154, 160
Harding, George 8
Hart, Clive 31
Haslem, Lori Schroeder 169
Hazlitt, William 14, 16, 20
heart imagery 129–30
Heminges, William 116
Henderson, Andrea 169
Henderson, Katherine Usher 163, 165
Hengist, King of Kent (Middleton) 71
Henry, Prince 95, 100, 152n.38
Henry VIII 138, 144
Heywood, John 138
Heywood, Thomas 156
Hinton, Peter 55
Hirsch, Brett D. 73–4, 169–70
Histoires tragiques (Belleforest) 5
History and Fate of Sacrilege (Spelman) 144
Hooker, Richard 142–3
Hopkins, Lisa 76, 78–9, 150n.5
Horne, Richard Hengist 16–17, 47–8
horror, use of
  in context of World War II 50
  critics on 2, 10, 16–18
  defense of 26, 49
  foregrounding of 54–6
  postmodern 66
  in Shakespeare 21
  Tarantino and 56, 58
Hotel (film) 59–60, 160–1, 162
Howard, Frances 9
  see also Overbury, Thomas
Hunt, Maurice 170
hybridity *see* stylistic hybridity

The Image of Governaunce (Elyot) 80
imagery 156–7
  see also individual types
incest
  in 20th century production 52
  class hierarchy and 36
  focus on 50
  in *Gismond of Salern* 90, 94
  possibility of 21–2, 25, 30, 32
  scepticism of 26
Ingram, Martin 112–13
Instruction of a Christen Woman (Vives) 6

inversion
  Antonio and 123
  revenge plays and 3–4
  of structure 3

Jack, Ian 22–3
Jackson, Ken S. 82, 170
James, P. D. 161
James I
  Arbella Stuart and 113
  corruption and 95
  court of 11
  marriage and 7, 9, 11
  privacy and 88–9
  Protestantism and 10
  ruins and 144
  Spain and 109, 110, 115
James II 46
Jankowski, Theodora 39, 81, 165, 170
Jardine, Lisa 39, 157, 166, 170
Jocasta (Gascoigne and Kinwelmersh) 91
Jones, Emrys 52
Jonson, Ben 80, 143, 156

Keller, Eve 126
Kempe, Margery 138
Kerrigan, John C. 77–8
Kerwin, William 170
Kiefer, Frederick 170
Kill Bill (film) 66
King Henry VI, Part 3 (Shakespeare) 111
King Lear (Shakespeare) 1, 153
King's Men 1, 14, 42, 44, 45, 48
Kingsley, Charles 17
Klapisch-Zuber, Christiane 108
Klein, Joan Larsen 163
Knight of the Burning Pestle (Beaumont) 140
knowledge
  entitlement to 120–1
  uncertainty and 132–3
Kyd, Thomas 3

Lamb, Charles 14, 15–16, 20
Landau, Jack 56–7
Langland, William 139
language
  Brennan on 30–1
  criticism based on 81
  functionality and 27–8
Larque, Thomas 55–6
Latimer, Bishop 138
Leavis, F. R. 22
Leech, Clifford 24–5, 29, 164
Lees-Jeffries, Hester 80, 81
legal context 69–70, 113–14
Leggatt, Alexander 165
Lehmann, Courtney 82
Leinwand, Theodore B. 70, 122, 170–1
Lesser, Zachary 13n.33
Lever, J. W. 96
Levin, Richard 77
Lewes, G. H. 17, 19, 48
Lewis, Cynthia 171
Lindley, Arthur 82–3
Lloyd, Phyllida 58–9, 76
Lopez, Jeremy 77
Lord, Joan M. 171
Loreto 137–8, 139–41
Lucas, F. L. 20–2, 25
Luckyj, Christina 36–8, 157, 160, 165, 171
Lupset, Thomas 146
lusty widow stereotype 5, 6, 123, 171
lycanthropy 30, 74, 81, 100, 111, 114, 158, 168, 169–70, 173
Lycidas (Milton) 111

Macbeth (Shakespeare) 81, 171
Machiavelli 110–11
Madelaine, Richard 73
madness 82, 158, 167, 170
  see also masque of madmen
The Madonna of Loreto (Caravaggio) 142
The Maid's Tragedy (Beaumont and Fletcher) 75
The Malcontent (Marston) 71
Malfi (Horne) 47–8
Mann, J. G. 163
Marcus, Leah S. 7, 11, 83, 136, 154, 155, 160, 161

marketing practices 1–2, 42
Marotti, Arthur 137, 150n.12
Marrapodi, Michele 91
marriage
  Arbella Stuart and 7, 94
  canons on 113–15, 121
  class hierarchy and 4, 75
  freedom and 69
  in *Measure for Measure* 114–16
  as metaphor 9
  rank and 122
  regulation of 9, 11
  remarriage and 68, 122–3, 171
  secrecy and 92–3, 94, 108, 112–13
  validity of 108
  widows and 6
marriage (Duchess's)
  context for 114
  disputing of 121–2
  dramatic comparisons for 3–4
  property and 6
  secrecy of 119–20
  staging of 106–8
  validity of 29, 112–13, 121
  vows of 112
Marston, John 71
Mary, Virgin 131, 137, 139, 141, 142, 149
  see also Loreto; Walsingham
Mary Queen of Scots 73
Mary Tudor, Queen 126–7
masque of madmen 2–3, 28, 35, 49, 98–9, 143, 159, 168, 170
McCarthy, Mary 54
McColl, Colin 58
McLuskie, Kathleen 32, 36, 157, 160, 165, 171
McManus, Barbara 163
McMullan, Gordon 60
McTaggert, James 162
McWhinnie, Donald 51
Measure for Measure (Shakespeare) 11, 114–15, 155–6
medical practice
  resources on 170
  women and 70–2
melodrama 17, 18–19, 20, 22–3, 43, 48–9, 50, 56
Messina, Cedric 160, 161, 162
metatheatrical awareness 8, 74, 77, 87–8, 99
Middle Temple 74, 94, 164
Middleton, Thomas 12n.4, 14, 44–5, 71, 110, 116, 156
Mikesell, Margaret Lael 171
Milton, John 111
misogyny 68–9
Moore, Jackie 154, 155
moral vision 10, 17–18, 19, 23, 24, 29–30
Moralia (Plutarch) 80
Much Ado About Nothing (Shakespeare) 2
Mulryne, J. R. 34
Murray, Peter B. 32–3

Neill, Michael 93, 152n.38, 159, 171
Nightingale, Benedict 57
Noble, Adrian 51
Novelle (Bandello) 92
Novellino (Salernitano) 92

Orlin, Lena Cowen 120, 163
Ormerod, Nick 57
Ornstein, Robert 163
Othello (Shakespeare) 4, 20, 78, 155, 156, 161, 171
Overbury, Thomas 9, 101

Painter, William 5, 6, 26, 29, 92, 94, 99, 106, 154
Palter, Roger 82
Panek, Jennifer 6, 68, 123
Park, Katharine 127
Parmigianino 159
Pearson, Jacqueline 34–5, 159, 165
Pepys, Samuel 15, 46
performance
  criticism based on 75–6
  resources on 160–1
  see also productions
Pericles (Shakespeare) 48
Perkins, William 146, 147
Perry, Curtis 10–11

Peters, Belinda 7
Peterson, Joyce 165
Peterson, Kaara L. 159, 171–2
Phelps, Samuel 16, 47–8
Philips, Jill Ingram 81
Piers Plowman (Langland) 138
A Pilgrimage for Religion's Sake (Erasmus) 138
pilgrimages 137–9, 142
plot
  inconsistencies in 21, 22–3
  sources for 4–5, 26, 73–4
  structure and 36–8
Plutarch 80
Poel, William 18, 19, 49, 51
political context, contemporary 11, 95–6, 109–10
Portrait of a Young Woman (Parmigianino) 159
Portrait of Laura Battiferri (Bronzino) 159
Potter, Lois 52
pregnancy/childbirth 96–7, 100, 126–8, 158, 169
Price, Hereward T. 27–8, 172
privacy
  as consensual act 120
  loss of 97–8
  public life vs. 157–8
  resources on 163
  royal 88–9
  secrecy vs. 87–9
productions
  Alexander's 75–6
  Ashcroft/Gielgud 31
  Donnellan's 75–6
  of Horne's adaptation 16–17, 18, 47
  by Phoenix Society 20
  Poel's 18, 49
  Prowse's 32
  Rylands's 50–1
  see also The Fatal Secret (Theobald)
Protestantism
  Catholicism and 9, 10, 13n.26, 77–8, 110, 111–12, 158
  death and 146–7, 148
  marriage and 11, 68
  in *Measure for Measure* 115
  privacy and 172
proto-Gothic conception of court 89, 93–4, 95, 96, 99, 101, 102–3
Prowse, Philip 32, 55
publication history 9–10, 15, 107

A Question About Hell (film) 160, 162

racial issues, in productions 54
Ram-Alley 68
Ranald, Margaret Loftus 165
Randall, Dale B. J. 172
Randolph, Thomas 116
rank *see* class hierarchy
Ray, Sid 81, 172
realism
  abstraction and 35–6
  conventions and 2–3, 28
  move away from 53–6
  in production 50–2
religious context 77–80, 137
  see also Catholicism; Christian framework; Protestantism
remarriage *see* marriage
Renaissance art 159
Reputation, Love and Death 16
Reservoir Dogs (film) 56
revenge plays 3–4, 20, 66
The Revenger's Tragedy (Middleton) 72, 78, 156
Reynolds, Bryan 82
Rice, Anne 161
Richard III (Shakespeare) 50, 111
Richards, Judith 127
Ricks, Christopher 155
Rist, Thomas 76, 78, 139, 158, 172
Robartes, Foulke 151n.28
Roscius Anglicanus (Downes) 46
Rose, Mary Beth 8, 67, 155, 165, 172
Rowley, William 14, 44–5, 71, 110, 156
ruins 143–5, 149, 159
rumours 96–7, 102, 128–9

see also secrecy
Rylands, George 50–1, 53
Sackler, Howard 160, 162
Salernitano, Masuccio 92
Salingar, L. G. 23
Salmon and the Dogfish 3, 16, 31
A Salue for Sicke man (Perkins) 146
satire 25, 35
Schmitt, Julia 75
Schuman, Samuel, 150n.15, 172
secrecy
church and 130
danger and 124–5
as defining condition 132
marriage and 108
pregnancy and 126–8
privacy vs. 87–9, 119
rumours and 96–7, 128–9
tyranny and 93, 96
Selzer, John L. 166, 173
Seneca 91–2, 96, 146, 148
see also Senecan-Boccaccian tradition
Senecan-Boccaccian tradition 91, 92, 93, 94, 101
sexuality
gender and 67–72
power and 123–4
resources on 173
see also lusty widow stereotype
Seymour, Edward 93, 94
Seymour, William 7, 94, 113
Shakespeare, William
comparisons to 1, 2, 3, 11, 16, 17, 21, 74, 155
sonnet of 143
see also individual works
Shakespeare in Love (film) 1, 161, 166
Shaw, George Bernard 19, 49, 54
Shell, Alison 136
Shelton, Brian 54
Sheppard, Philippa 159, 163
Sheppard, Samuel 14
Shulman, Martin 53
Simkin, Stevie 66, 76
sleep imagery 73
Solga, Kim 55
sovereignty 80–1
space *see* architectural space
The Spanish Tragedy (Kyd) 3, 78
Spelman, Henry 144–5, 149
Spiller, Ben 76
Spivack, Charlotte 38–9
St. Sepulchre's 146–7
Steen, Sara Jayne 7
Stoll, Elmer E. 19, 25
structure 36–8, 76–7, 156
Stuart, Arbella 7, 94, 113
Stubbes, Philip 136
stylistic hybridity 2–3
see also generic complexity
Sullivan, Garrett A. 73
Summit, Jennifer 145
Swinburne, Algernon 17–18, 20
The Syckmans Salue (Becon) 146

Tarantino, Quentin 56, 58
The Taming of the Shrew (Shakespeare) 2
Theobald, Lewis 15, 46–7, 160, 162
Thomson, Leslie 77
Thomson, Peter 2
Thyestes (Seneca) 91
Tiffany, Grace 142
Tillyard, E. M. W. 27
time
gap in 77
theatrical 87–8
see also unity of time
'Tis Pity She's a Whore (Ford) 93, 156
Titus Andronicus (Shakespeare) 1, 78, 80
Todd, Barbara 6
The Tragedie of Tancred and Gismund 93
Tragedy of Mariam (Carey) 156
tragicomedy 34–5, 165
Traub, Valerie 70
Treatise of Dying Well (Lupset) 146
Tricomi, Albert H. 73, 79–80, 173
Tu Quoque (Greene) 68
Tudor, Mary 126–7

Turner, Kimberly A. 68–9
Tussaud, Madame 17
Tussaud laureate 19, 49, 54
Twelfth Night (Shakespeare) 1, 4, 74–5, 153, 155, 167–8
tyranny 93, 96, 98–9, 102
  see also corruption, court

Uglow, Jennifer 32, 36, 160, 165
unities 46–7
unity of time 15, 76–7, 87–8
Utenhove, Charles 80

van Herwij, Stephen 80
Vernon, P. F. 38
villain-hero 19–20
Vives, Joannes Ludovicus 6

Wadsworth, Frank W. 29
Wall, Wendy 71–2, 119, 120, 158, 173
Walsingham 137–8, 140, 142, 143, 145
Walter, Melissa 10–11
Wardle, Irving 54
Warren, Roger 31–2
Webster, John, reputation of 1–2
Webster, Thomas 116
Weis, René 154, 155
Whatham, Claude 162
Whigham, Frank 4, 36, 52, 75, 104n.17, 122, 134n.8, 157, 165, 173
White, R. S. 67, 82
The White Devil (Webster)
  comparisons to 21–2, 156, 164
  critics on 14, 16, 17, 18, 23, 76, 78
  death in 147
  failure of 1
  as female-centred 83
  idolatry in 140
  preface to 3, 11n.3
  Shakespeare and 155
  tragicomedy in 35
widows
  comic 68
  remarriage and 6, 68, 122–3
  see also lusty widow \stereotype
The Widow's Tears (Chapman) 68
Williams, Clifford 51, 53
Wilmot, Robert 93
Wilson, Edmund 50
Wilson, F. P. 27, 29
Wind, Edgar 149
Winifred, Saint 138–9, 140
Winston, Jessica 92
The Winter's Tale (Shakespeare) 4, 73, 141
The Witch of Edmonton (Rowley, Dekker and Ford) 80
wolves *see* lycanthropy
A Woman Killed with Kindness (Heywood) 156
Woodbridge, Linda 67–8, 123, 156, 158, 163, 173
Woollam, Angela 81
Wright, Abraham 14–15
Wymer, Rowland 159, 165

Zimmerman, Susan 72, 159, 173–4